THE STATE MUST PROVIDE

THE STATE MUST PROVIDE

WHY AMERICA'S COLLEGES HAVE ALWAYS BEEN UNEQUAL—AND HOW TO SET THEM RIGHT

ADAM HARRIS

An imprint of HarperCollinsPublishers

HarperCollins books may be purchased for educational, business, or sales promotional use. For information, please email the Special Markets Department at SPsales@harpercollins.com.

Ecco® and HarperCollins® are trademarks of HarperCollins Publishers.

FIRST EDITION

Designed by Paula Russell Szafranski

Library of Congress Cataloging-in-Publication Data has been applied for.

ISBN 978-0-06-297648-2

21 22 23 24 25   LSC   10 9 8 7 6 5 4 3 2 1

To Ada, Alexander, Mennie, and Howard

The State must provide such education for her in conformity with the equal protection clause of the Fourteenth Amendment and provide it as soon as it does for applicants of any other group.

—*Sipuel v. Board of Regents of the University of Oklahoma* (1948)

Contents

Introduction

The subtle crunch of snow under your feet is rare in Alabama, but plush white powder blanketed the ground when I arrived on the campus of Alabama A&M University in Normal, Alabama, for my first semester in January 2010. The packed flakes clung to the buildings like fitted sheets. It made the Hill, as students called the campus, indescribably beautiful. The university is tucked away in the rolling Tennessee Valley of North Alabama. It was the third college founded in the state to educate Black students after the Civil War, and the first with agricultural education in mind. But to me, A&M was simply a place that felt like home.

I was probably always going to end up attending college at A&M. Some of my earliest memories are of the drum majors—high-stepping in maroon capes, sporting felt hats—leading the band with intricately designed maces as if they were going to battle. My mom had gone to A&M in the eighties; my uncle had as well. In fact, he was a drum major himself. Still, it took me six months after high school to realize it was the place for me.

My parents would probably say it was my hard head that landed me instead at Lon Morris junior college in Jacksonville, a quiet East Texas town with a Walmart, a Taco Bell, and not much else. The real reason was basketball. I had been recruited by a handful of Division I programs: Stanford, Cornell, Murray State, Brown, and others, but I suffered an injury my senior year of high school. Lon Morris was my way to show big-time scouts that I still had it. Those coaches never called again, but early in my freshman year, the ones from Alabama A&M did. I jumped at the opportunity. It helped that my sister was already there as a sophomore on the volleyball team. A&M was no longer a home by proxy, where my family was educated; it was my home.

The snow had made the campus's aging infrastructure seem like character, but as the first days of the semester wore on, it melted. I needed a break. I had a habit in high school of getting in the car and driving when I needed a stress reliever. Old habits die hard. Lucky for me, there was a whole city I had yet to explore. Downtown Huntsville was not much to look at, and every time I went to the mall, I ended up buying something I did not need, so roughly two weeks after arriving—after classes had begun, and homework started to pile up—exploring meant visiting the town's other colleges.

There was Oakwood University, another historically Black college, built in 1896. There were the community colleges: Drake State and Calhoun. And then there was the University of Alabama in Huntsville (UAH), founded as a satellite campus of the University of Alabama in 1950, which had grown into an entity all its own. UAH was a straight shot from A&M, and since it was public, I would not have to get by security. As a bonus, its library was open three hours longer than A&M's, so, at the very least, I could attempt to be productive.

Sometime near four o'clock in the afternoon, I loaded up my backpack, locked my door, and headed toward the elevator of Foster Hall, a five-story, red Tetris brick of a building that, having been built in 1993, was the newest men's dormitory at A&M. The elevator was broken; probably overuse during move-in, I thought. I ran down the stairs instead, hopped in my car, navigated my way around the potholes on campus, and headed across town.

Pulling onto UAH's campus felt like lifting a veil. There were newly constructed buildings, the grass was finely manicured, and fountains burst forth from the man-made ponds; the school looked like it had received a face lift within the last few years—or, at the very least, had benefitted from some good maintenance.

Once I settled in at the library, I did a bit of digging. UAH was founded in the 1950s, in part, because segregation was the law. There were two colleges for Black students in the city, Oakwood University, the private Seventh-Day Adventist–affiliated college, and Alabama A&M, which was publicly funded, but which white students could not attend either. The Alabama law that segregated Black and white students was known as Section 256, and though it was not officially implemented until 1901, when the state adopted its constitution, its effects—locking Black people into an unequal educational system, if education was allowed at all—had been an unwritten rule since before the Civil War.

Several states made it a crime to teach an enslaved person to read and write. South Carolina was the first, in 1740. Georgia followed in 1759. In 1833, Alabama instituted a fine of up to $500 as punishment for those caught teaching enslaved people to read. North Carolina banned educating Black people altogether. The bans did not stop Black people, though; they began learning in secret—they risked the lash to learn. When slavery ended, discrimination stayed, but so did the thirst for learning. Southern states threw up every barrier they could to education, and Black people broke them down time and time again. Northern states erected barriers, too, even if not always as overtly.

By the time the 1950s rolled around, it was a foregone conclusion that Alabama would choose to spend more money to create a new school for white students than to integrate. Even more galling to me than the institution's roots was that the differences between UAH and A&M remained so flagrant. I observed several small things that day on the UAH campus. If there had ever been any potholes, they had been filled. The dorms were new, or, if not, they had been renovated; the library had books and journal subscriptions and magazines that I had never even heard of—including the one for which

I now write. And then there were the big things, which I'd learn later: UAH had nearly double the endowment of Alabama A&M, and fewer than 10 percent of its student body was Black, while more than 30 percent of the city of Huntsville was Black. It was a regional institution aimed at serving the city, and yet it did not. Meanwhile, across town, many of the buildings on my campus needed upgrades. The heat was busted in some of the classrooms. The shuttle never seemed to be running when it was the coldest outside.

Some of this might have been chalked up to the grumblings of a melodramatic student—one who had seen the other side and believed the grass was greener. But once I was no longer a student, I learned that my experience was not an anomaly. Then I began covering higher education, and I realized how much it was the norm for Black students across the United States.

America's colleges and universities have a dirty open secret: they have never given Black people an equal chance to succeed. The public institutions that enroll high numbers of Black students have been hamstrung by limited state funding; the ones that have few Black students have been showered with it. The wealth dynamic of private institutions is no different. A college education is the key to the middle class and necessary for most well-paying jobs, yet access to that education has never been evenly provided. America claims to have the finest colleges in the world, but in the last few years their surfaces have begun to show wear, revealing the structural inequalities that lie beneath—and the excavation has just begun. Wealthy and well-connected students, who tend to be white, are able to buy their way into elite colleges after their parents look for "side doors" to get their children in, while Black students can't work hard enough to make up that difference in privilege. An unequal system of primary education has bled over into higher education. It is scandalous, but it is also the natural fruit of a system whose deep roots continue to undermine America's colleges. There are two tracks in higher education: one has money and power and influence, while the other—the one that Black students tend to tread—does not.

This book began as an effort to understand why that was, to un- earth the roots of these two tracks. I wanted to isolate the climacter- ics when higher education could have been made equal, the turning points when centuries of discrimination could have been remedied. Tugging at the fruit led me to 1619—the beginning of chattel slav- ery in America—when Africans were first brought to the shores of Virginia. Closer examination plopped me down in the middle of the eighteenth century with a radical minister with a little land and a big idea: integrated education as part of the solution for building a more perfect union.

History folds over on itself, with new characters cast in the star- ring roles of each episode. The goal of this book is to examine some of those figures, to understand their fights, and to forecast the fight ahead.

Higher education is organized so the institutions with the few- est minority students have the most money, the best services for students, and the highest prestige—not merely private colleges, but public ones as well. That is not by coincidence, but by design. From its inception, the state higher-education system we recognize today was built not on equality, or even an ethos of broad accessibility, but on training a white workforce. Black students were excluded.

Black people have had to fight to get into institutions with white students, so that they might be afforded the same resources as white students. When they tried to enroll, the government fought back as hard as it could in courtrooms and on campuses to prevent them from doing so. The historically Black colleges they attended in the meantime were never adequately funded. The settlements that have been won to support these institutions have not scratched the surface of need or accounted for more than a century of discrimination. As I write, there are still six states that have not proved to the federal gov- ernment that they have desegregated their higher-education systems.

Meanwhile, Black colleges, many of them public, remain woefully underfunded. And even though they account for roughly 3 percent of all four-year institutions, they educate 80 percent of Black judges, 50 percent of Black lawyers and doctors, and 25 percent of Black science, technology, math, and engineering graduates. State governments, and the federal government, have a responsibility to fix this inequity.

Snow has a way of masking old wounds—just as it covered the disrepair on A&M's campus—but it is melting now.

PART I

BUILT

CHAPTER 1

The Roots

The letter began courteously, if not plainly fawning—but for good reason. On April 4, 1844, John Fee found himself writing to a man whom he had never met, though he had admired him from afar. From his perch in Bracken County, Kentucky—a place butting up to the Ohio River, hugging its northern neighbor, that a little more than seven thousand people called home—Fee walked a fine line as he dictated his entreaty. A Presbyterian minister by trade, Fee was looking for Cassius Marcellus Clay, the son of one of Kentucky's wealthiest slaveholders, Green Clay.

Every family member Cassius Clay knew kept human beings in bondage. Growing up, he did not think much of it. He believed slavery was a harsh practice, but it was just the way things were. To him, it was a law of nature; something to turn your nose up at while sticking your hand out to reap its financial rewards. Then, in 1828, Clay's father passed away and left him several enslaved people. Slavery was no longer simply his family's problem—it was his own.

Clay left for college. He first attended Transylvania University in Kentucky, before transferring to Yale University in New Haven, Connecticut. The ivy-strewn institution in the Northeast was three decades away from enrolling its first Black student, but it was fast developing a reputation as a training ground for prominent white abolitionists. It was 1831, and Simeon Jocelyn—a white pastor of the town's Black congregation, and a former Yale student—had introduced plans to build a college for Black people in New Haven. Jocelyn enlisted the aid of William Lloyd Garrison, the fiery orator and founding editor of the abolitionist weekly *The Liberator*, to present the proposal. Jocelyn's plan was shot down by the city council within three days. But Garrison's time in New Haven was not for naught.

That fall, Cassius Clay heard Garrison speak for the first time. Garrison delivered a passionate address on the evils of human bondage and the morality of abolition. "In plain, logical, and sententious language he tread [slavery] so as to burn like a branding-iron into the most callous hide of the slaveholder and his defenders," Clay later recalled. "As water to a thirsty wayfarer," Clay drank Garrison's speech. And then he acted on it. When he finished college and returned home, he emancipated the enslaved people his father had left to him. Those who stayed were paid a wage for their work. He had broken with his family and wore the name his white neighbors in the South thought treason: abolitionist. Some called Clay's return to Kentucky and call for abolition a death wish; John Fee called it brave. And when he addressed Clay, he did so with admiration.

Fee had spent the first three months of 1844 trying to meet Clay in person. "Sir I am a stranger to you in person but I trust not to some of the emotions which move your philanthropic heart," Fee wrote. He wanted to talk about slavery and their shared history. Both men were born to fathers who claimed men, women, and children—and the work of those people—as their own; both were sons of Kentucky; and both had learned to despise slavery in college. To Fee, slavery was a boil infecting the soul of each person who took part in it. Collectively, it left permanent stains on the country's moral conscience. More fundamentally, it was a sin. And as a man of faith, Fee could not abide it. The thoughts he had bottled up for months poured onto the page.

After an extended history lesson on his own family, Fee pressed Clay. "By what mean or means do you suppose the slavery system in our state will be abolished?" he asked. Kentucky was viewed by some as the first domino poised to topple, due, in part, to its proximity to the free states. If Kentucky were to abolish slavery, other southern states might fall in line. Clay, as a former state representative who still held clout in the Whig Party, which had a blossoming antislavery wing, and as one of the wealthiest men in the state, could help urge the state along. Fee, and others in the state with whom he had spoken who were wedded to the cause of abolitionism, were counting on Clay. "They feel that God in his providence has raised you up to take a prominent place in the great work of disenthralling your country of its greatest curse—your fellow man from their greatest calamity," Fee wrote.

As he wound his appeal to a close, Fee knew better than to expect a response. But if Clay felt moved to reply, he wrote, it could be the beginning of a bountiful relationship.

Occasionally a shot in the dark hits its mark, and Fee's letter was the catalyst for a friendship between the two men. It was a friendship built on despising slavery, a friendship that would be tested as the country careened into Civil War. Ultimately, it was a bond that led to the formation of the first integrated, coeducational college in the southern United States—a beacon of educational equality in America.

Fee had been an on-again, off-again resident of Bracken County since he was born there in the fall of 1816. His father, John, was a farmer, one who trafficked in the purchase and sale of human beings. By his son's recollection, John owned as many as thirteen enslaved people. His son was generous to his father in remembering why he participated in the "sinful" institution. "He saw the effects of slavery were bad; that it was a hindrance to social and national prosperity," Fee wrote of his father. The elder Fee did not see an end to slavery in sight, even though he himself had married a Quaker's daughter—the Quakers had petitioned to abolish slavery since 1790—and purchased land for his children in free states.

As a child, Fee was not deeply moved by human bondage. "By false teaching unreflective youth can be led to look upon moral monstrosities as harmless," he remembered. And the false teachings were everywhere. At church, pastors would explain the biblical justifications for slavery. In the community, people would sing its virtues. Even guests at the Fee family's dinner table would pray for slavery's longevity.

Fee's revelation came in 1830. A minister, Joseph Corlis, began teaching at a subscription school—a private school—in the area and stayed with the Fees. He began inviting young John to Presbyterian services with him. Engaging with Corliss, "I was deeply convicted of sin, and gave myself to God," Fee wrote. At least part of that sin, to Fee, was his family's slaveholding. He carried guilt with him to Augusta College, in Bracken County, and then to Miami University, in Ohio, before returning to Augusta to finish his undergraduate schooling. But it was not until he enrolled at Lane Theological Seminary, in Cincinnati, Ohio, in 1842, that his conviction turned into action.

There were fewer than three hundred permanent colleges and universities in the United States in the middle of the nineteenth century. The figure would be dwarfed by the thousands of colleges that came to exist over the next 150 years, but it seemed astronomical in comparison to the time when George Washington, Benjamin Rush, Thomas Jefferson, and other Founding Fathers were imagining what American institutions of higher education could and should be.

In his first address before Congress in January 1790, shortly after North Carolina joined the Union, George Washington told lawmakers that "there is nothing, which can better deserve your patronage, than the promotion of Science and Literature. Knowledge is in every Country the surest basis of happiness." It would now be considered a pedestrian ask for congressional funding if not for its roots. The Founders had been mulling ways to create national character and spread teachings that would bind people in the new nation together. Several of the Founders, Washington, James Madison, and Rush among them, came to the idea that the best way to create good citizens was through higher education. For the most part, this would be limited exclusively to white men, but at least one founder, Rush, allowed that women should be educated as well. Outside of the principles of liberty and government, however, his vision limited women's education to housekeeping and sewing.

As the number of institutions of higher education grew over the next several decades, the question of what it meant to be a good citizen in a democracy became even more important. Did it mean adhering to the nation's custom and abiding by slavery? Or did it mean pushing back against it? The moral bent of professors at some Christian institutions—and at some northern, nonreligious institutions, like Yale—pushed them to oppose slavery. What to do with free Black people was another question, though, and "educate them" was seldom the answer.

In 1835, the trustees of Oberlin College in Ohio, founded one year prior, resolved to admit students "irrespective of color." John Shipherd, an abolitionist and one of the institution's founders, led the push. "Their education seems highly essential if not indispensable to the emancipation of their colored brethren," he told the trustees. "They can nowhere else enjoy needed education unless admitted to our institution." With its resolution, Oberlin became the first college to admit students regardless of their race. Two years later, in February 1837, the African Institute—quickly renamed the Institute for Colored Youth (ICY)—opened its doors in Pennsylvania. Outside of those two institutions, however, options for Black people hoping to get a higher education were close to nonexistent. Millions were still fighting to escape slavery, living under pain of death for being found with a book.

Still, those fledgling white colleges would radically change some of the southern white men who broached the university gates; they would come knowing slavery and leave its opponent. At least, that is what happened for Fee. Two of his classmates, John Milton Campbell, a former schoolmate of his at Miami of Ohio, and James C. White, the former pastor of a Presbyterian church in Cincinnati, urged him to consider his convictions. They knew he was from Kentucky, and that his father was a slaveholder. But they also knew he was driven by his faith. So they turned to the Bible to make their plea for abolition. "Thou shalt love the Lord God with all thy heart, and thy neighbor as thyself," they impressed on him. "Do unto men as ye would they do unto you." Would Fee have another man bond *him* to slavery? He had a religious duty to abhor the practice and came to believe that the prophets of his youth sold a false gospel. If he hoped to preach, he could no longer accept slavery—even if he was not the one keeping people against their will. For his own soul's sake, he needed to become an abolitionist.

As Fee's views on slavery were changing, he wrote letters to his father explaining his transformation. The elder John was none too pleased. "Bundle up your books and come home," he told him. "I have spent the last dollar I mean to spend on you in a free State." The younger Fee had already decided to return home, though. He dogmatically believed his ministry was to convert others away from the sin of slavery; most immediately, that meant his family. The intergenerational difference between Fee and his father was not exactly unique—an untold number of prominent southern white men who became abolitionists, including Clay, would share similar stories—but it was nonetheless cumbersome. Fee's efforts to convert his father only made the elder Fee cling tighter to his proslavery beliefs. It was the way things had been, the way they were supposed to be, and a little northern education was not going to change that.

The elder Fee began hoarding proslavery pamphlets and books. He even offered to pay his son's bills to send him to Princeton Theological Seminary. Despite enrolling and graduating Theodore Sedg-wick Wright, the first known Black student to attend a theological seminary in North America, in 1825, Princeton did not have the same abolitionist reputation that Lane had. His son turned him down. His calling was to stay and preach in Kentucky.

Local churches began reaching out to Fee to preach, but condi-tionally. He had to "let the subject of slavery alone," they would tell him. He could not; he felt he would be abdicating his responsibility as a preacher if he did. When he fell in love with Matilda Hamil-ton, a woman whom he knew from childhood in Bracken County, she coated his resolve with iron. Matilda's adolescent home was one of the final stops along the Underground Railroad; when she was younger, her mother had served a slaveowner tea while an enslaved person hid in the basement. Matilda had seen the horrors of slav-ery and she ardently supported Fee's establishment of antislavery churches. He traveled hundreds of miles on horseback in search of a flock in need of a pastor, to no avail. A church in Louisville seemed promising until its congregation told him to dispense with abolition-ism. The search chugged, slowly, before it produced fruit—Cassius Clay's response to the letter Fee had scribbled to him.

The letters flew back and forth between the men for the next two years—during which time Fee preached to congregations across the state, while also tending to a small congregation in a sixteen-by-sixteen-foot room with a bed and table, near his home in Bracken County—before the budding friendship was nearly quashed. In 1846, opponents of Fee's preaching had grown increasingly hostile. In one instance, two men—one with a club in hand, the other with rocks to throw—stopped Fee and his wife; they escaped only mildly in-jured. Fee was unperturbed by the incidents, and alongside more than twenty-five men, he signed a petition for Clay to speak about emancipation on July 4, 1846. Clay happily accepted the offer—with the qualification that he would have to defer until he returned from the war with Mexico. Local slaveholders were incensed. This was clearly a call for immediate emancipation, they reasoned, after the petition was published in a local abolitionist newspaper.

Upon learning of the opposition, ten men revoked their signatures from the petition to have Clay speak. Clay was spooked. He pulled out of the event himself. But the most intense venom was directed at Fee. A group organized to kill him at his home, but their leader, a landowning slaveholder, was killed before the rendezvous. One man shot at Fee in his house, but his bullet missed. Public spats broke out between Clay and other prominent abolitionists—including William Lloyd Garrison. It would have made sense, then, if Clay did not want to keep close association with Fee after the incidents, but he did not waiver.

Though Fee continued struggling to gain an audience for his antislavery message, his passion had won at least a few admirers. In 1848, *The Examiner,* an antislavery newspaper in Louisville, extolled his virtue, proclaiming, "The day will come when Kentucky will be proud of this honest, single-minded minister of God." Fee wanted his message to extend beyond the state's border, though. So, in 1851, he sat down to draft his manifesto, a pamphlet in which he would decry the evils of the institution. It was a "testimony of God's word against slavery," he wrote. "That verily, 'God hath made of one blood all nations of men.'" It was biblical—Acts 17:26—but it was also bold. And it would become the mantra for the school he would launch less than a decade later: Berea College.

Cassius Clay bragged later in life about his "foresight" on Berea, but at the time, he was just doing a favor for a friend.

In the prelude to the Civil War, southern slaveholders began more aggressively defending the practice, and abolitionists in the state increasingly faced physical attacks. Clay, who had run for governor on an antislavery ticket in 1851 and lost, had been distributing Fee's antislavery pamphlet in Madison County—smack dab in the middle of the state. Several people in the county who had read the treatise were struck by its moral clarity. They wanted to hear Fee's antislavery message firsthand and invited him to speak in the spring of 1853. Fee, who was living and preaching at the time in Lewis County, along the border of Kentucky and Ohio, obliged their invitation.

It was a quick trip for Fee to Madison County and back home. Not long after Fee arrived back in Lewis County, though, members of the church in Madison had written him again. Their pastor was unwell. The church would close if no one helped them. The closure of a congregation that disavowed slavery, "planted as it was in the interior of the state," would be a "calamity," Fee thought. He had reservations, though. Chief among them: the congregation he was building in Lewis County—the smattering of groups he had been preaching to—had started gaining steam. He had a chance to follow his mission—preaching abolition and equality in Kentucky—in the state's heart, but he could not desert the flock he had started on its edges. Luckily, a graduate of the theology department at Oberlin College expressed a desire to replace Fee at his little church home on the border. A suitable replacement, Fee believed. He was free to go to Madison County.

But a church is not itself a parsonage, and Fee was without a house to live in. His friend Clay was well aware of this, and shortly after Fee arrived in Madison County he learned that Clay had purchased roughly six hundred acres, a portion of which would be used to build a church, a "school of education," and a parsonage. Clay did not stipulate that the school be integrated; that "feature," he would later write, "is due to Fee's own leadership, and could not have been foreseen, but has always had my hearty approbation." The bequest did not end with property: Clay offered Fee $200 to help build his home. Conviction does not always pay, but it had finally lined Fee's pockets, and he went back to collect his family—Matilda, by then his wife, and their two children—before returning to their new home in Madison.

Fee decided to name the plot of land Berea. It was apt and prophetic. According to the Bible, the Bereans eagerly heard the word of God and accepted it as the truth, whereas their neighbors, the Thessalonians, expelled Paul from their town when he came preaching the Gospel. The Bereans guarded the preacher when the Thessalonians arrived to heckle and attack him. Berea, Fee believed, would be a place to serve a higher purpose: He would put the truth before himself, even if that meant being met with violence.

The plans to build the school began quickly, and the first building was constructed in what seemed like a blur. While Clay may have intended a primary or parochial school, Fee had bigger goals. He met with his friend George Candee, a fellow minister, to outline the future of the institution. "We talked up the idea of a more extended school—a college—in which to educate not merely in knowledge of the sciences, so called, but also in the principles of love in religion, and liberty and justice in government; and thus permeate the minds of the youth with these sentiments," he later recalled. The institution would rest on the spirit of the verse Fee championed in his pamphlet: Acts 17:26. "[God] hath made of one blood all nations of men." The school would be interracial. It would be an anomaly like Oberlin in Ohio, the rare institution offering interracial education, but Berea would be the only one in the South.

The idea, particularly in a southern state like Kentucky, was radical. Oberlin College had made it clear that interracial education was possible, but what would it look like below the Mason-Dixon?

Fee was unsure that Berea, which, despite its central location, was secluded in the mountains, was the best site for the new college, so, alongside Candee, he began scoping other locations. They first went to Rockcastle County, just south of Madison. Fee had preached there before and thought it might be a suitable place for the school. They petitioned friends to help them build a schoolhouse and a

church in Rockcastle; then they hired Otis B. Waters, a graduate
of Oberlin College, to be the school's sole teacher. It was 1855, two
years after the Supreme Court had decided that the US Constitution
was not meant for Black people in the *Dred Scott v. Sandford* case,
and Fee and Candee had done it—they had established Berea College. But nearly as soon as the school was built, it was burned to the
ground by slaveholders and their supporters. The burning of buildings that would serve as potential meeting places for Black people
was not uncommon. "Mother Emanuel" African Methodist Episcopal
Church in Charleston, South Carolina, for example, was burned to
the ground for the first time in 1822. Meeting places such as churches
and schools represented hope for Black people—hope a slavocracy
could not allow.

The duo tried again. They built another school farther south in
Pulaski County, Kentucky. It was burned as well. Fee and Candee
next eyed Whitley County; there, they were run out of town by a
mob. Meanwhile, Fee kept the school's—and his own church's—
headquarters in the enclave of Berea in Madison County.

By 1856, the Bereans had not been able to formally organize
a school with which to host Black students. Both Fee and Clay attended the nominating convention for the Republican gubernatorial ticket in Kentucky that year. Clay had been one of the founding
members of the party two years prior and delivered introductory
remarks. "The national government has nothing more to do with
slavery than with concubinage in Turkey," he said. Fee was shocked.
Was his friend turning against his antislavery position? Not exactly.
Though Clay had been a proponent of emancipation, he was not a
fan of the federal government's forcing southern slaveholders to free
those they held in bondage—that was the state's right. Clay hoped
only that Kentuckians would see the evil of slavery on their own.

Fee, of course, disagreed. "The national government is responsible for the strength and perpetuity of slavery and this by the enact-
ment of the Fugitive Slave Law," he publicly replied. The law, which

had been passed six years earlier as part of the Compromise of 1850, incentivized officials to arrest people who were alleged to have run-away from slavery.

Several weeks later, the pair jointly planned to host a Fourth of July event in Madison County. Fee spoke first. All men are created equal, he stressed, and the Fugitive Slave Law, implemented by the government, violated that edict. "A law confessedly contrary to the law of God ought not by human courts to be enforced."

Clay demurred. "Mr. Fee's position is revolutionary, insurrectionary, and dangerous," he argued in response. "As long as a law is a statute on the book, it is to be respected and obeyed until repealed by a republican majority." Theirs was a disagreement about the fundamentals of civil rights: Are they natural or do they flow from power? Fee believed they were innate, and people should fight for them—even if that meant a struggle against the government.

Ultimately, Clay confessed that he would not follow the Fugitive Slave Act, and conceded the argument, but his ego was left bruised by the scuffle. He did not visit Fee for more than a year. His pride threatened the livelihood of Berea, at least to Fee's mind. As easily as Clay had provided Fee the land for the church and the institution, he could, ostensibly, take it away. The project of Berea College would have been killed in the cradle. Still, slaveowners regarded Clay, Fee, and all those who dared call themselves abolitionists the same way. When Clay found himself in Indiana in August 1856 stumping for Republican candidates, the *Louisville Daily Courier* sniped that "Cassius M. Clay, of this state, is canvassing in Indiana in [*sic*] behalf of the nigger worshippers." Despite their differences, Clay and Fee were in the same camp and remained friends. Clay, meanwhile, professed that there was never risk for escalation. "He has always been free to criticize my course, but my friendship for him has never abated," he would later write. "Any other man saying what he has at times said of me would have brought on him my greatest indignation. But as I know his sincerity of purpose, and his idiosyncrasies of thought, I have not believed it necessary to defend myself."

Over the next two years, the attacks against Fee intensified; the thought of maintaining a church, much less a college, grew dimmer. On July 19, 1857, an armed mob dragged Fee from the pulpit while he was preaching in Rockcastle, bludgeoned him over the head, and exclaimed that they were going to lynch him and two other ministers before tossing them from the county. "The immediate cause of the outrage was the attempt to establish a school here," the Louisville *Courier-Journal* reported. In February 1858, Fee was kidnapped alongside a friend, Robert Jones, and taken to the swollen banks of the Kentucky river. The water had a chill; and Fee was not a particularly good swimmer. The mob stripped Jones of his coat and his shirt before lashing his back, back and forth, with rods from a sycamore tree. Then they turned to Fee, but before he was struck, a county official stopped the carnage. Fee was spared, though Jones was left savagely beaten.

It would have been hard to tell the violence was aimed at Fee by the editorials in local newspapers. They called him a danger to the peace of society and deemed his preaching "pernicious." Letters to the editor suggested he be hanged. The men of the county passed a resolution to expel Fee and his abolitionist friends. When Fee asked for a delay, a mob showed up at his home to force him from the property.

By 1860, Fee had been driven out of Berea—away from his church, away from his fledgling college. His friends George Candee and Robert Jones were captured by a proslavery mob in January 1860, had their heads shaved, and were covered in tar. The hope for an integrated college in the South seemed dead.

Fee had envisioned Berea as a place where young white people could unlearn and rebuke the sin of slavery, and where the formerly enslaved would be taught. He was still convinced his college could work, and if only people could see Berea in action—the community working together, learning together, eating together—perhaps they could shed their biases. For now, he had to defer the dream, and he moved his family just north of Kentucky to Cincinnati, Ohio.

As Fee was trying to open the doors of education in the South to Black people, a national movement was building to make higher education more accessible to all white men.

Like a band playing the chitlin' circuit before making it big, the idea of college for the masses in the United States hit the smaller markets first. There were schools to educate soldiers, lawyers, clergymen, and doctors, but more than 50 percent of American workers were farmers in 1850. Where were the schools that would teach the farmers to read, write, and comprehend what was on the page? Fewer than sixty thousand students enrolled in American colleges each year, and they were often from well-off families. On November 18, 1851, a group of white farmers met at the Granville Presbyterian Church in Putnam County, Illinois, with eyes on changing that.

The convention had been called by the Buel Institute, an agricultural society and reform group. The organization was led by Ralph Ware, a nonnative Illinoisian who owned a four-hundred-acre tract of land in the state. Even though he was not a native of Illinois, he grew to call it home—and he was desperate to see it improve.

Three weeks earlier, Ware had written to Jonathan Baldwin Turner, a professor at Illinois College in Jacksonville, Illinois, to ask if he could address the meeting. Turner, an advocate for liberal agricultural education, and a significant voice in the common school movement to create elementary and secondary schools for people in the state, was disillusioned with the colleges that existed. The institutions were there to serve a professional class, he believed, not the workers—the farmers and the mechanics. There needed to be something more: liberal agricultural institutions. The colleges would combine a liberal arts curriculum, which would be good for the advancement of agriculture and manufacturing innovation, with a practical agricultural curriculum. He would speak with anyone he could about it. So, naturally, he accepted Ware's invitation.

When the convention began, Oaks Turner, the treasurer of Putnam County and the convention president, admitted that he was only half-aware of why it was being held. Ware took control. He explained to the men that they had been called together to discuss steps to further the development of the agricultural community, but, most important, "to take steps towards the establishment of an Agricultural University."

Three men were appointed by the convention-goers to serve as a committee that would decide how best to make the case. Turner was among them. The trio deliberated as the conference went on, and a handful of speakers delivered short addresses. When the men returned that evening, they had a list of resolutions. Turner delivered a speech to announce them. The dissemination of the speech and the minutes from the meeting, which were published widely, marked a turning point in how the nation viewed its duty to train its citizens.

Turner's remarks were passionate. "Society has become, long since, wise enough to know that its TEACHERS need to be educated; but it has not yet become wise enough to know that its WORKERS need education just as much." Attempts by Old World monarchs and aristocrats to set up such institutions had failed because of their ignoble aims—to make low-caste workers "overseers" for even lower-caste workers. What the country needed was a set of institutions—colleges separate from the West Points and Princetons of the world—that could train and teach the workers. They needed to be colleges, too, not simply common schools—the primary schools where students learned reading, writing, and arithmetic. "The whole history of education, both in Protestant and Catholic countries, shows that we must begin with the higher institutions, or we can never succeed with the lower; for the plain reason, that neither knowledge nor water run up hill," Turner argued. Common schools would not exist without teachers who had learned in colleges.

Turner argued that Illinois's school should be open to all classes of students above a certain age and should be paid for by the students or worked off. But first, the state of Illinois needed to provide the money and the land to create the college. Most of the colleges that existed to that point were private institutions, unaffiliated with and unfunded by state governments. The doors of opportunity could swing open, Turner argued, but only with a nudge from lawmakers. He focused his energy on Illinois, but he wanted an institution like this in every state of the nation.

His was a radical idea, and Turner was clear-eyed about the opposition he would face. "Others may feel a little alarm when, for the first time in the history of the world, they see millions throwing themselves aloof from all political and ecclesiastical control, and attempting to devise a system of liberal education for themselves." This was not higher education coming from on high. This was the people saying they needed to be educated and figuring out how it should be done.

Convention-goers adopted a resolution: they should "earnestly solicit" people to their cause, and ask others to join them in asking the legislature to use state money for the college. The group held two more conventions over the next two years—one in Springfield, the state capital, and one in Chicago. Turner was their star witness and advocate. The first convention, however—the one in the old, wooden Presbyterian church in Granville, Illinois—was the catalyst for a national movement. The idea rooted and grew in state after state, and by the time 1855 rolled around, it was becoming a reality.

The news swept the nation in 1855, the year John Fee was having his college buildings burned down before they could get off the ground, that Michigan was experimenting with a new agricultural college.

Kinsley S. Bingham, the state's governor, had signed a bill that allowed the state of Michigan to purchase a farm—roughly 730 acres—to build a college. The aim of the institution was simple: teach agricultural education free of tuition. The state's economy was built on agriculture and manufacturing, and having a central location to train workers and leaders in the fields would be an economic boon. It was the first of a new kind of college—a *land-grant* college, one for which the state would donate land that could be sold to develop an institution and establish its endowment—and papers across the country raved. "The science of agriculture is the most important of any that has ever engaged the attention of man," the editors of the *Louisville Daily Journal* wrote. They hoped to see "some provision for the advancement of a similar school in every state in the Union." Pennsylvania and Maryland followed suit with establishing agricultural colleges shortly after.

The idea had caught the attention not only of newspapers and state legislatures, though. By 1857, thanks in part to communication from Turner, it had landed on the desk of Lyman Trumbull, a former Illinois State Supreme Court justice who had been elected to the US Senate two years earlier. In October of that year, Trumbull sent a letter to Turner endorsing the professor's plan for a national bill to fund agricultural colleges. The colleges would resemble those Turner had outlined in 1851, but Trumbull was worried. He could not introduce the bill himself. "I think it not unlikely that a grant of lands might be obtained from Congress; but coming from the new States, which have already obtained such large grants for schools and other purposes, it would be likely to meet with less favor," Trumbull wrote. Instead, a lawmaker from one of the old New England states should introduce the bill.

Turner turned to a fresh legislator from Vermont, one of the founders of the Republican Party, to do the deed. On December 14, 1857, Representative Justin Morrill introduced House Bill No. 2, which would allocate land to each state that could be sold to fund an agricultural college. It would be the biggest bet the federal government ever made on higher education.

Justin Morrill was one of the lucky ones. He had been born in 1810 to Nathaniel and Mary Morrill in Strafford, Vermont, a small town girdled by rolling hills that neared the New Hampshire border. Nathaniel Morrill was a blacksmith, and though the family did not have significant means, they had enough, including the two-story white house with green shutters in which Justin Morrill grew up. His education began with the Bible, and he worked his way through the "tedious" though sometimes "attractive" Old Testament books. His home teachings quickly turned into formal schooling in a boxy building that would be replaced by a two-story brick school when he was ten.

After his elementary education, he attended Thetford Academy, a few miles away from his home in Strafford, and Randolph Academy, each for three-month terms. But the schools were bastions of elitism, typically designated for families with money, wealth, and land. Justin's family had some money, but not enough to keep him in the schools. By age fifteen he had dropped out but remained a voracious reader, devouring the Federalist Papers, Thomas Jefferson's *Notes on the State of Virginia*, and novels by the likes of Sir Walter Scott, which he borrowed from Jedidiah H. Harris, a prominent local storekeeper who employed Morrill for a time.

Morrill wanted to go to college, but he was unsure his family could afford it. He resorted to self-education. In 1828, when he was eighteen, instead of leaving Strafford to go away to school he moved to Portland, Maine, where worked as a shop clerk until he could return to take over his own store.

Morrill was a shark. Everything he sold was on credit, everything he bought was in cash. Debtors would be charged 6 percent interest for bills not paid by January 1 of each new year. If they failed to do so, he could collect his debt in property. Morrill also took to investing; he owned stock in banks and railroads and real estate and manufacturing. He now had money, but he was unsatisfied.

On a trip across the country to collect unpaid debts in 1841, he got a taste of what he was missing. The trip, and the journal entries that accompanied it, also reveal that Morrill was agnostic about the social equality of Black people. While riding through Kentucky, he witnessed a ferry toll agent beating an enslaved person. He intervened, telling the toll agent to return the man to his master rather than beat him. "I saved this darkee from a further beating," he wrote. The incident was one Morrill regarded as a moment of compassion, but more than anything, it highlighted his tendency toward the status quo on race; the toll agent was sullying another man's property by beating the enslaved person.

Morrill had earned enough from his businesses that he could retire in 1848, at thirty-eight years old. But he maintained the itch to work. He scratched it with politics and became a fixture of Whig Party circles in the state, advising area leaders on the political leanings of his county. "I was always ready to make a speech or write a political platform resolution, and after a time they began to expect them from me," Morrill later wrote. The Compromise of 1850, which was organized by the Whig senator Henry Clay, a cousin of Cassius's, and Democratic senator Stephen Douglas, defused tensions erupting after the Mexican-American War over what to do with the newly won territory. But it also marked the establishment of the Fugitive Slave Law, and antislavery Whigs saw it as a betrayal of their values. He quickly became disenchanted with the Whigs, as a lot of party members, particularly in the North, did. To the practical Morrill, the compromise fundamentally killed the chances for the party to elect a candidate for statewide or national office, because the party's singular voice had become two. That became clear when, in 1852, Winfield Scott lost the presidential election as the Whig candidate.

The Whigs needed to regroup, but even as they were flailing, Morrill's profile grew. Political operatives in Vermont saw him as a potential Senate candidate, but he knew the party was in too much disarray for a Whig to be elected to such an office. Instead, in 1854, he was nominated for the House of Representatives seat in his district. It would be easier to cobble together a coalition locally than gain support statewide.

The Fugitive Slave Act's resultant discord had caused Morrill to change his tune on returning people who sought freedom to those who would keep them in bondage. He now supported jury trials for enslaved people who were accused of running away. A local paper declared he was a "liberal, honest, and modest," politician. Still, he did not advocate full emancipation, and that meant some Whigs were slow to support him. It did not matter—he was able to squeak his way to victory by roughly 2,500 votes. It was the last election that a Whig candidate would win in the state.

Now, in 1854, with his wife and young son, who had been born a year prior, Justin Morrill had become a US congressman. He had little time to celebrate the victory. The country was becoming more divided over slavery, and it was the first issue the new Congress would take up when Morrill arrived. Then tragedy—the swift and unrelenting devil it is— struck in waves. First his son, Justin Harris Morrill, named for his father and his father's mentor, died at the age of two; then, in December, Jedidiah Harris himself died. Morrill was buried in grief. The man who had done so much to provide Morrill opportunities and help him along in his education was gone. But that he was able to receive an education, a practical education, stuck with him.

By December 1855, Morrill had caught the wave that was sweeping the country; maybe the "greatest good for the greatest number," he reasoned, could be done by creating a practical college curriculum. In February of the following year, he proposed legislation to boost agricultural education. Namely, "one or more national agricultural schools upon the basis of the naval and military academies." One student apiece from each congressional district could be educated at the schools—and the government would pay for it. The measure failed, but it strengthened his interest in championing agricultural schools.

He began talking up the idea of using federal land grants to anyone who would listen. But, as the fracture dividing the country deepened, lawmakers, even in his own party, were skeptical it would pass. "You can try, but of course it is of no use," William Hebard, a congressman from the Second District in Vermont, told him; other lawmakers echoed the sentiment. Quietly, behind the scenes, Lyman Trumbull had been working on Morrill, who had already shown interest in introducing legislation that would establish universities for agricultural education—and Morrill was from an eastern state. It was reasonable that he would be the one to introduce the bill.

In December 1857, Morrill pulled the trigger. He introduced the "Bill Granting Lands for Agricultural Colleges"—House Bill No. 2—and it was referred to the Committee on Public Lands. The bill polled well among the full House, but it faced stiff odds in committee. When it was reported out of the committee on April 15 of the next year, the majority of those on the panel rejected it. One week later, in front of the full House, Morrill took the floor to defend his legislation.

The shopkeeper-turned-congressman delivered a well-reasoned speech not unlike Turner's address to farmers at the Granville Presbyterian Church in 1851. Agricultural productivity in America was on the decline. Between 1840 and 1850, wheat production in New England was down a million bushels and potato production was down sixteen million bushels. The South was hit equally as hard—wheat production in Tennessee, Kentucky, Georgia, and Alabama was down nearly seven million bushels. On the House floor, Morrill asked, "Does not our general system of agriculture foreshadow ultimate decay? If so, is it beyond our constitutional power and duty to provide an incidental remedy?"

The remedy he posited was education; the decline in production was the offspring of an unskilled workforce. A significant investment in training these workers could right the ship. Belgium had done it, he advised Congress. France had as well. Even England, with its detestable caste system, had seven agricultural schools. "We have schools to teach the art of manslaying and make masters of 'deep-throated engines' of war," he argued, "and shall we not have schools to teach men the way to feed, clothe, and enlighten the great brotherhood of man?" Farmers and mechanics needed school, too. It was the government's job to provide it.

Morrill stirred support. The leader of the committee that had recommended killing the bill fussed and filibustered and failed. The House passed the bill 105–100.

As the country inched its way toward war, the bill slowly moved through the Senate, struggling to muster support before the end of the session. Meanwhile, lawmakers fanned out across the country to defend themselves and their parties. Lyman Trumbull, in expressing his motivations for ending slavery, made the Republican position clear: "We, the Republican party, are the white man's party. We are for free white men, and for making white labor honorable and respectable, which it never can be when negro slave labor is brought into competition with it," he said in August 1858 while home in Illinois. "We believe it is better for us that they should not be among us. I believe it will be better for them to go elsewhere." Republicans argued that it would be better if Black people, once freed, should be transferred to "any Central American State" which would help them secure their rights. By removing enslaved labor from the equation, white men would have access to more jobs—and would need to be trained to work fields. There was an agricultural bill working its way through Congress that could provide that training.

In December 1858, when Congress reconvened, Senator Benjamin Wade of Ohio became the bill's lead sponsor in the Senate. Southerners, clinging to every bit of land they could, opposed the legislation. Senator James Murray Mason of Virginia, who helped draft the Fugitive Slave Law, called it "one of the most extraordinary engines of mischief"; another senator referred to it as "one of the most monstrous, iniquitous and dangerous measures which have ever been submitted to Congress." It would seem a college access bill had divided Congress, but during political tumult everything becomes a proxy battle in the partisan war. On February 7, the Senate passed the bill by a razor-thin margin—25 to 22. The House subsequently approved the amended version as well. It was headed to the desk of President James Buchanan. America was on the verge of revolutionizing higher education, even as it was staring down an uprising.

Morrill thought it was as good as certain that Buchanan would sign the measure. He had supported land grants for educational purposes before, so what should change now? But time is a great teacher, and it wore on. A week passed and the bill was unsigned. On February 24, it had become clear what had happened. Southern Democrats had gotten to the president and convinced him that the bill was unconstitutional. It was simply inadvisable. Buchanan vetoed the bill.

The election of 1860 loomed, and it was virtually impossible that the veto would be overturned prior to it. But then Abraham Lincoln was elected president. The bill had new life; meanwhile, the country seemed to be taking its last breaths. On April 12, 1861, when Confederate troops bombarded the Union garrison at Fort Sumter, South Carolina, the friction had turned into a war.

Morrill saw opportunity in the division. With southern legislators expelled from Congress for their treason, he reintroduced his bill on December 16, 1861, with a significant amendment. Not only would the schools teach classical and agricultural education, they would also teach "military tactics." West Point could teach a lot to a few officers; these colleges could teach a little to a lot of soldiers.

Rebel states would be excluded from the land grant. The tweaks were likely motivated by recent Union losses, but they made the bill urgent. But not as urgent as the war. It sat for six months before it was reported out of committee. It passed the House and Senate before arriving on President Lincoln's desk. And on July 2, 1862, the president signed it.

Jonathan Baldwin Turner's dream had been realized; the country was preparing to launch a flood of land-grant colleges—government-supported institutions. But first, it had a war to finish. A war that was fundamentally over slavery and the future of the country.

On September 1, 1864, Kentucky's military-installed government made a proclamation, much to the chagrin of the *Maysville Weekly Bulletin*. "The notorious John G. Fee," the paper read, "has been permitted by the military authorities of Kentucky to return to the State to do more mischief."

CHAPTER 2

A Compromise

Among the wages of war is confusion. John Fee's return from exile in 1864 was quiet, and by the time the *Maysville Weekly Bulletin* caught wind of his arrival back in Kentucky, he had already been there for several months. When his family had been forced out of the state, so had his congregation, so there was little in the way of work for him. The shell of Berea was still there, though. He gathered up the children of the "few sympathizing families" who remained or had come back and taught classes himself, along with his wife, Matilda, and their eldest daughter.

The war was not over yet, even if the Union army's victories in the state had allowed Fee to return to Berea. He realized that until the war was over, neither his home, school, nor church was permanent.

The Union army had started recruiting Black men to Camp Nelson, a Union training camp in Kentucky, in March 1864, and within a few months roughly five thousand Black soldiers were drilling at the post. According to one estimate, 40 percent of Kentucky's Black soldiers passed through the camp at one point, and it became "the principal camp in the state for the enlistment of black troops and the principal refugee camp for contrabands." Fee recognized the unique opportunity in front of him: the chance to establish the foundation for his college. He began trying to figure out the best way to get a position teaching there.

His first thought was to reach out to the American Missionary Association (AMA). The association—a Protestant faith-based group organized around the abolition of slavery, the education of Black people, and the promotion of racial equality—had helped several institutions, churches and schools alike, get off the ground. It had helped Fee in getting Berea started as well. "I have talked with quite a number of colored men," Fee wrote to Simeon Jocelyn, the association's president, who had tried to establish a college for Black students in New Haven in June 1864. Black troops were enlisting rapidly at the camp, and more, Fee said, were "anxious to go if they were asshured [sic] that they will be cared for and that they shall have freedom & pay." It was the second letter Fee had written to Jocelyn about potentially going to one of the camps where formerly enslaved people were enlisting. "Hundreds of these colored men know me & would have confidence in what I would say to them. They need encouragement & instruction." He planned to go and preach to them—"Tell them what are their duties and prospects." To do so, he reasoned, would be good for both the recently emancipated men and the government. If Jocelyn agreed with this thought, Fee implored him to send money along with his blessing.

In a letter dated the same day, Jocelyn responded to Fee. The AMA would be elated for him to go and preach to the camps. They would send money for books and other expenses. "We have decided that you would do well, at once, to take up the enterprise," Jocelyn said. But the mail traveled slow, and Fee did not receive the letter before sending another letter, and another, and still another. "I feel that I ought to go and preach to them," Fee implored. "I desire instructions."

Five weeks had passed, and Fee had still not received the letter from Jocelyn. On July 12, he wrote again: He had already gone to

Camp Nelson. "I have written you almost every week for five weeks past concerning this [*sic*] colored people and no answer," he wrote. "I have felt that I must act." Accompanied by his son, Fee struck out early one July Saturday morning thirty-five miles south to Camp Nelson. There were two regiments of Black troops forming there. On Sunday, he preached to them. That Monday, he sought to secure a position as their regular minister.

The officer in charge recognized him. "I know you, all about you, and have for years," Fee recalled him saying. In 1859, Fee had been on a fundraising trip for Berea in Worcester, Massachusetts, the officer's hometown. The quartermaster told Fee that he would provide everything he needed to preach, "but we want teaching for these colored men as well as preaching. They, especially the non-commissioned officers, need to be taught to write—sign their names to their reports."

Across the South, teachers were being asked to train Black soldiers to read and write, to compensate for what Black people had been banned, often by law, from doing. Though Kentucky did not have explicit antiliteracy laws for Black people, several states did. Alabama, Georgia, Louisiana, North Carolina, Missouri, South Carolina, and Virginia had all passed such slave codes.

The rules were sometimes shirked to allow enslaved people to read the Bible, but after Nat Turner's rebellion in Virginia—in which more than seventy enslaved and free Black people killed dozens of white people over the course of several days—even that became unacceptable in some circles. Following Turner's uprising, Virginia executed him alongside fifty-six other enslaved people accused of being part of the insurrection. More than one hundred additional Black people were killed by the mobs that followed.

Fee readily accepted the job he was being offered. All he needed was a house and desks—he would get the teachers himself. The quartermaster agreed; so too did the camp's leader, General Speed Smith Fry, a native Kentuckian with a graying beard whose eyes had grown weary with the war. The fatigue of fighting had not kept Fry from being excited by the proposition—excited that he would be afforded more literate soldiers.

Of course, some Black troops who joined the Union army were literate; some had even studied at colleges in the North, such as Wilberforce University in Ohio. The numbers, however, were slim. That meant that northern missionaries, and some Black preachers, such as Samuel Lowery, who went to Nashville following the signing of the Emancipation Proclamation to preach and teach the troops in the Ninth US Heavy Artillery, took up the mantle of professor. It was a patchwork, but it was what they had.

As the Black men who enlisted at Camp Nelson came, so did their wives and children. They were initially rejected, sent back to slavery, and back to the threat of death. The white officers suggested the women would spread venereal diseases among the Black soldiers if they were allowed to stay; Fry believed it was not outside the bounds of his authority to keep them out of the camp. The hazard of an uprising among the Black troops, however, forced the leaders of the camp to reconsider. Fee dictated a letter to send to the US secretary of war, Edwin Stanton, who quickly ordered the construction of ninety-two cottages for families, two buildings for hospitals, and even more buildings for schools, dormitories for teachers, and a boarding hall. Fee began teaching as the end of the war no longer seemed unthinkable.

Having been at the camp for less than a month, Fee started to consider the future. "Perhaps Berea is the place where these young colored men now soldiers are to be educated," he wrote as July turned to August. A week later, he wrote to Jocelyn, whom he had finally been in contact with, saying, "I find them manifesting an almost universal desire to learn; and that they do make rapid progress. . . . I feel that it is blessed to labor with such a people." His letters echoed what camp teachers across the South had been quickly figuring out: Black people, given the opportunity, wanted to learn.

War ends in waves. On April 9, 1865, General Robert E. Lee surrendered his troops at Appomattox Court House in Virginia. Two months later, Black people in Texas would be the last to find out that slavery had ended. Sixteen months later, after the remaining Confederate troops had been driven out of leadership, President Andrew Johnson, who had assumed the presidency following the assassination of Abraham Lincoln, signed a proclamation declaring "said insurrection is at an end and that peace, order, tranquility, and civil authority now exist in and throughout the whole United States of America."

By then, Fee had returned to Berea, and reopened his school in January 1866 as Berea Literary Institute. Steadily, Fee recruited his former students from Camp Nelson, as well as some white students, to the institution. The school grew to enroll ninety-six Black students and ninety-one white students that year, to the disdain of the Confederate sympathizers who had been beaten but remained in the area. The *Louisville Daily Courier* took to endorsing candidates by suggesting that their opponents had the support of Fee. "Men are known by the company they keep," the paper's editors would write.

Steadily, over the next several decades, Berea College grew, but there was only so much small, private colleges could do. Educating the masses would be difficult, but it is what Morrill hoped his newly passed bill would accomplish.

Newspapers in Iowa raved about what a "magnificent gift" the Morrill Act would be for the state's young agricultural school. "Our farmer's college, after a heavy, slow, firm, and persevering drag of several years, has now better prospects ahead, and will eventually be one of the most richly endowed institutions in the nation," John Mahin, the editor of the *Muscatine Weekly Journal*, wrote. Just over two months after the bill became law, Iowa became the first state to accept the land grant.

The state allocated $91,000 of its land grant to Iowa Agricultural

College and Model Farm, which had been founded in 1858. The institution had not yet operated on the college level, though—when the Morrill Act was signed, only those three states that had established their agricultural colleges in the middle of the 1850s, Pennsylvania, Maryland, and Michigan, had collegiate-level agricultural schools. Iowa's farmer's school was coeducational from the beginning, but it was far from equal. Slavery had been outlawed in the state since 1839, but Iowa's first constitution required Black people to pay $500 to enter the state; as residents, they could not vote, attend public schools, or serve in the state militia. The discrimination extended to the state's universities, and Iowa Agricultural College and Model Farm was no exception—the school, before or after the Morrill Act, did not enroll any Black students.

Every state legislature, within two years of the act's passing, was required to agree to its terms and establish a college that would receive the funds within five years. If a legislature did those two things, the state would receive thirty thousand acres of public land for each representative and senator it had in Congress. The land could either be sold immediately, as most states decided to do, or the colleges could hold on to it until the prices for the land improved. The funds that resulted from the sale of the land could be used to create an endowment for at least one college to grow from.

In Illinois, where Jonathan Turner was celebrating the bill's passage—though he was likely one of the very few, as the legislation was overshadowed by the war upon becoming law—the battle over where the land grants would go descended into a war of sorts. That is how it was in most states. In Pennsylvania, for example, four colleges fought over the potential funds; in Massachusetts, five towns. But in Illinois, two of the older institutions, Knox College and Shurtleff College, sought to absorb the cash flow. In 1863, during the opening session of the Illinois General Assembly, representatives of the two colleges proposed a bill that would establish two agricultural schools—one in the north of the state, one in the south. The members of the Illinois Industrial League, which Turner had helped establish to advocate the cause of land-grant colleges, were in a stew over the proposal. It was not in the spirit of the Morrill Act to give the money to private, parochial schools. They called a convention in June of that year to discuss how they should contest the measure, and only at the urging of Turner were their concerns addressed. He advocated that any decisions on the matter be postponed, and that the group establish a committee to study the benefits of setting up a single institution. The committee would report its findings to the General Assembly in 1865.

Two years later, in 1867, as the five-year deadline to establish a college that would be the beneficiary of the land-grant funds approached, the assembly formed a committee of its own. They planned to visit cities across the state where the college could be built. Champaign-Urbana was fourth on the list, but the area had good lobbyists and, one by one, it moved up the list. In February 1867, it was named the home of the new agricultural university—to be called Illinois Agricultural and Mechanical College—that would receive the Morrill funds. John Gregory was appointed president of the institution two months later; then its first two faculty members were hired: George W. Atherton, a man land-grant colleges would come to owe their continued existence to, would teach history, and William M. Baker would teach English.

Local versions of the establishment of Illinois's land-grant institution played out across the country with varying degrees of difficulty and ease. When the dust had settled, 17,430,000 acres of land—including more than ten million acres expropriated from nearly 250 Indigenous tribes—was doled out under the act. Legislators, including Justin Morrill, turned their attention elsewhere as the country tried to put itself back together.

After the war, northern philanthropists and religious missionaries flooded the South and created institutions to teach those recently freed from slavery to read and write. They would receive some support from the government, including the Bureau for Refugees, Freedmen, and Abandoned Land—or the Freedmen's Bureau, for short—as well as religious groups such as the American Missionary Association.

The Freedmen's Bureau, established by the War Department after the Civil War, fanned out across the South to provide food, clothing, housing, and health care to recently freed people. Their mission, in part, was to help bring Black people to full citizenship, and education was a vital part of that. In March 1865, as Illinoisians bickered over where the land grant would be established, the bureau was approved to take over the educational functions that missionaries and the army had been performing.

The schools that the bureau would help establish were modeled after two in the North: the Institute for Colored Youth (ICY), and the Ashmun Institute. ICY and Ashmun, both located in Pennsylvania, had been the result of religious philanthropy. A Quaker, Richard Humphreys, established the Institute for Colored Youth in 1837, and the Presbyterian Church chartered Ashmun in 1854. ICY did not host college-level courses, even though it was led by educators who had been trained at some of the nation's integrated colleges (Fanny Jackson Coppin, a black woman who had studied at Oberlin College, led the institute for more than three decades starting in 1869). So, when Ashmun enrolled its first students in 1856, it claimed to be "the first institution anywhere in the world" to provide higher education exclusively to Black men.

The federal government allocated the bureau $500,000 "for buildings for schools and asylums; including construction, rental and repair." Funding from the agency helped establish colleges for Black people such as Fisk University in Tennessee, Atlanta University in Georgia, Saint Augustine's Normal School and Collegiate Institute in North Carolina, and Howard University—where Oliver O. Howard, the head of the Freedmen's Bureau, became the first president in 1867. Prominent Black leaders, such as Frederick Douglass, applauded the efforts the agency made, but they also believed it was being underfunded.

Those Black leaders had a point. The Morrill Act had just doled out millions of acres of land for states to sell so they could build and endow colleges—when all was accounted for, $7,545,405 was generated for their endowments. Leaders of the land grants, however, noted that the colleges were slow to work as intended. There was not enough money for the institutions to be strong, they argued.

In many cases, the allotted space had been sold when the market was heavy with other federal land grants—most prominent among them the Homestead Act of 1862, which granted citizens 160 acres of land, for a small fee, to colonize the western territories, and the Pacific Railroad Act, which gave rail companies land to build a transcontinental railroad. The deluge of federal land hitting the market at once meant that the typical acre was fetching less than a dollar.

Rhode Island sold the 120,000 acres it received under the Morrill Act for roughly 40 cents per acre. Pennsylvania sold its 780,000 acres for less than 60 cents an acre—still, that fetched the state $439,000, an amount nearly equal to the Freedmen's Bureau entire budget for schools and asylums. And as former Confederate states were readmitted to the union, they began to create their own land-grant institutions, ones that explicitly segregated Black and white students.

Tennessee was the first of the former Confederate states to rejoin the union, in July 1866, and when it did so, it became eligible for Morrill funds. The state lacked a public college, so, when it came time for the state to ration out its land grant, it sent the money from the sale to a private, all-white college—East Tennessee University, now named the University of Tennessee—in 1869.

The southern opposition to the public education of Black people, much less higher education, was firm—but it was on the verge of breaking. The University of Mississippi reopened its doors in September 1870, but fewer white students enrolled than had been hoped for. As a state paper, the *Semi-Weekly Clarion*, put it, many families worried about sending their sons—and they were all sons—to school as Reconstruction was taking a firm hold and the possibility that Black students might attend felt real.

But the faculty of the university quickly disabused everyone of that belief. In response to a query in the *Clarion*, the faculty wrote, *"should the applicant belong to the negro race we should, without hesitation, reject him."* They added the italics for emphasis. The university was "designed exclusively for the white race," they wrote, and they would instantly resign if the trustees should require them to receive Black applicants.

But Mississippi was changing. Whereas several southern border states, like Kentucky, experienced short Reconstruction eras, Mississippi's was long. More than two hundred Black people held elected office in the state over the course of eleven years between 1865 and 1876. Among them was Hiram Revels, a Black man from North Carolina with striking eyes and a well-trimmed beard, who had served as a pastor-teacher during the Civil War and taught at Freedmen's schools in Missouri and Vicksburg, Mississippi.

A legislature filling up with Black representation—and Radical Republicans sympathetic to the cause of educating people recently freed from slavery—was primed to launch an institution that would benefit those prospective students. So, in 1871—a year after Congress readmitted Mississippi to the union—the state established Alcorn Agricultural and Mechanical College for Negroes using funds from the Morrill Act. The college, named for the governor, James Alcorn, would sit on the former site of a college that white people had fled to join the Confederate army. John Lynch, a Black man, and the state's Speaker of the House, signed the bill to create the institution. Revels was named its first president.

"As an evidence of the necessity for such an institution it will not be out of place to call attention to the fact that when the writer was first elected to Congress in 1872, there was not one young colored man in the State that could pass the necessary examination for a clerkship in any of the Departments at Washington," Lynch would recall later in life. "Four years later the supply was greater than the demand, nearly all of the applicants being graduates of Alcorn College."

Alcorn was doing the work that the state's flagship college, the University of Mississippi, refused to: educating Black citizens who had been enslaved and kept from learning. It would not last for long.

Clear weather had prevailed in Washington, DC, on February 15, 1872, as leaders from thirty-two states and territories, legislators, and philanthropists descended on the nation's capital for a meeting convened by the new US commissioner of agriculture, Frederick Watts.

Watts had served as the president of the board of trustees at Agricultural College of Pennsylvania—which would become Penn State University—and he was gathering his land-grant colleagues to create some form of cooperation among the institutions and the department. He, perhaps more than anyone in Washington, knew of the struggles the institutions were facing. Proposals ping-ponged around: Perhaps an additional land grant, of not less than a million acres, to states that had received the 1862 funds, was in order. One college president was less strict about the number of acres and argued that a minimum of $500,000 would do the job. But the main takeaway from the convention was clear: the institutions needed more money. The spigots of the government were flowing, and educators wanted lawmakers to top off their jugs.

In attendance on that pristine February day was none other than Justin Morrill, the architect of the 1862 bill. "As a sense of this convention, we deem it of paramount importance to ask of Congress, as we do earnestly for an additional donation of land, or proceeds of land, sufficient to found a professorship of some of the branches of practical science in each of the colleges now wholly or in part sustained by the previous land grant of Congress," Morrill wrote in a resolution he submitted to the conference. He was in agreement that the colleges needed more land and more money in order to be successful.

The wheels were already turning for a separate land grant, one that would benefit the nation's fledgling common schools, forerunners to modern public schools. George F. Hoar, a senator from Massachusetts, had introduced a bill that would essentially be similar to that establishing the land-grant colleges but for primary schools. In 1870, only 1.3 percent of the population between the ages of eighteen and twenty-four were enrolled in higher-education institutions. There needed to be greater emphasis placed on the common schools than on the colleges, the argument went.

Proponents of funding higher education argued, in response, that there still needed to be somewhere to teach the teachers. On February 23, just a week after the convention in Washington, Morrill introduced a new bill: Senate Bill 693, for further endowment of and support for the land-grant colleges. Those colleges had done yeomen's work, and they needed help. The bill, he explained in a statement, was presented to him, "by a committee representing a convention of a body of men of high character and hardly ever surpassed in this country for their intelligence."

He worked to gather the votes for the bill for several months, before, on December 5, he thought he had a majority. He took to the Senate floor to deliver a speech. He made no mention of the paltry, and often barred, enrollment of Black students—or the colleges' uncertain financial futures—but explained that the land-grant colleges were punching above their weight. Were the colleges worth the cost? Of course. "The success which has already attended even the very limited endowments under the original act, to which this is supplementary, gives a most encouraging answer," he said. The original grant was "too restricted" for immediate prosperity to be expected. Still, "in Michigan, Iowa, Kentucky, Illinois, Massachusetts, New York, and Connecticut," the land grants were doing incalculable work in educating students. "Any one of the institutions established in these States will ultimately be worth singly more to our country than the entire cost of the original grant to all of the States," he continued.

A speech, no matter how rousing or laudatory, can do only so much. The bill became chum for attacks by influential legislators who favored the common school legislation and believed that Morrill had torpedoed it. Senator John Sherman, of Ohio, added that he found the legislation to be "a palpable discrimination against existing colleges supported by State and private funds." How was it fair, he reasoned, to give money to fledgling colleges when established ones could provide the same benefit? The bill did not stand a chance.

Morrill and his bill were bloodied. But he had reinforcements in the wings readying to join the fight.

George Atherton had not been in Illinois for more than a year before Rutgers poached him in 1869. The offer to join the faculty of the New Jersey university was unexpected but welcome for the thirty-two-year-old. The endowed position—as the Vorhees Professor of History, Political Economy, and Constitutional Law—was the result of a $25,000 gift from Abraham Vorhees. Atherton's interests extended beyond the campus, though, and his advocacy for the land-grant institutions quickly grew to be a second job. On January 13, 1873, a circular from Rutgers and other agriculturally interested organizations in New Jersey pushed for a bill that would compensate for the inequality of the first Morrill Act. The government had encouraged the development of the land-grant colleges, and therefore that meant that it had a responsibility—an obligation, even—to make sure that they thrived. It was an argument that Atherton would soon thrust into the national spotlight with an address to the National Education Association just a few months later.

Elmira, New York, was "full of strangers" on August 6, 1873; more than 1,500 of them by one estimate. The visitors were in town for the National Education Association's annual convening. It was a veritable who's who of higher-education leaders: There was Charles Eliot, the president of Harvard, and James McCosh, the president of Princeton, who argued that the agricultural colleges created by the Morrill Act were "not accomplishing so great a good" to justify such a large endowment of land. Eliot called Morrill's 1872 bill a "demoralizing" use of public money and stressed that it had gone quite far enough.

Arguing for the Morrill colleges were Joseph White of Massachusetts Agricultural College, which had received part of Massachusetts's land grant, and Daniel Read, the president of the University of Missouri. Further down the list of notables was George Atherton.

Atherton would deliver his address on the next-to-last day of the convention. The speech, titled "The Relation of the General Government to Education," outlined the argument from the New Jersey circular, but with detail so granular it could thread a needle. He had learned the particulars of the original land-grant act in Illinois, spending "many days and nights . . . going over the whole scheme of the classification," and he bought into it. The government's original investment had already been worth its cost, he argued. In less than ten years, 24 of the land-grant institutions had enrolled 2,604 students, and housed 321 faculty members. By comparison, the other 217 institutions in the country that reported to the education commissioner totaled 20,866 undergraduate and graduate students and 3,018 faculty members. The land-grant institutions were, on average, enrolling more students with the same number of faculty members. Some of the schools were already beacons, he said, including the agricultural and mechanical department at Cornell—an institution founded as recently as 1865. The schools were new, but with time (and money), he told those gathered, they would shine. "The nation as a nation must educate," he pressed. "There is no argument to prove the duty of the state governments in this respect which does not apply with at least equal force to the national government."

The speech was a hit. Land-grant leaders extolled it, even if the local paper did not give it top billing the next day. Andrew White, the president of Cornell University, which had received some of New York's initial land grant, wrote to Atherton on August 25 to thank him "most heartily" for the address. "You stood in the breach nobly. . . . We cannot labor too much pain to show the fact that Congress did not intend to endow 'Agricultural Colleges' unevenly or to provide unevenly for Agricultural Departments in Colleges." The government had not intended to do wrong by the colleges, but it had, and the college leaders believed the oversight needed to be addressed with more money.

There were op-eds in *The Nation* and other national publications about the Elmira convention, and, eventually, news of the speech reached Morrill's ears. On December 15, 1873, Morrill introduced a new bill, Senate Bill 167—and once again, the bill would provide more money to the land-grants institutions. The bill was offered by Morrill, but Atherton would later claim that Morrill "accepted as his own a bill which I drafted." It echoed the 1872 bill with slight tweaks; and like that of 1872, it was destined to fail.

This cycle would continue for years. Legislators were unconvinced that more money would solve the institutions' problems. Land-grant legislation was resurrected in Congress after Congress for nearly two decades and shot down time and again.

As a champion for land-grant colleges, Atherton had made a name for himself. His words and advocacy were being heard and felt in the halls of Congress. Other colleges wanted him, and not just to be a professor, but to be a college president. Arkansas's land-grant institution, Arkansas Industrial University, later renamed the University of Arkansas, was one of the first to seek his employ. He declined. Howard University, a Black college in Washington, DC, twice offered him the top job, in 1874 and 1876, and he twice declined. He was even recruited by the Republican Party to run for Congress in the Third District of New Jersey, though he ultimately lost the election.

The same year, 1876, when Atherton was turning down the presidency at Howard for the second time, Alcorn Agricultural and Mechanical College for Negros had fallen into the throes of struggle. Black people accounted for more than half of Mississippi's population and, barred from being able to attend the University of Mississippi, Alcorn was their primary option for public higher education. A group of Democrats known as the Redeemers, however, had launched a "white revolution," and were pushing out the Radical Republicans and Black elected officials who had become staples of the state's political life. The Republican Party in the state effectively ceased operations as the appropriation to Alcorn was slashed. The money that the Republicans had guaranteed Alcorn upon its founding—$50,000 a year for at least a decade—was cut by the so-called Redeemers to $15,000 in 1875. A year later, in 1876, the legislature reduced the appropriation to $5,500 a year.

The state separately tweaked its federal land-grant appropriation to Alcorn as well. Where the university had previously received three-fifths of the state's total land grant—roughly even with its population of Black residents—that amount was reduced to half. The string of overtly racist measures intended to block Black students from receiving a proper education left the university a shell of itself. And that was before the legislature took the additional step of appointing an all-white board of trustees in 1878. Two decades later, that board selected Edward H. Triplett as the university's president; then, after faculty members expressed displeasure with the appointment, the board dismissed nearly all of them. The flowering institution was crushed by white supremacy.

Illiteracy was on Justin Morrill's mind on December 15, 1880, when he stood before Congress. It had become ritualistic for him. Each year, he would advocate the same legislation. Each year, he expected it to be shot down. This time, however, he would speak to a national shame, borrowing an argument from common school supporters.

"It would be vain to hide from ourselves the wide extent of illiteracy among our people," Morrill said. The census painted a clear picture. It showed that there was a school-age population of more than fourteen million, yet only five million of those students were attending school every day. "Think of it!" he exclaimed. "Hardly more than one-third of the millions who should have been in the school-house were there!" The fate of those students, he argued, depended on the passage of Senate Bill 133, which would provide for public education and more money for the land-grant institutions to teach scientific and industrial education. "Every American heart will beat in harmony with an effort to banish illiteracy," he told the legislators gathered. If anyone was born after 1880 and he could not read or write, it should be a phenomenon.

Of course, millions would still be unable to read and write as the decade wore on. There were roughly forty-five Black colleges that had opened since the end of the war, but many of them were not yet operating on a college level. In Kentucky, Berea was doing its part in the effort to educate Black students who had been otherwise barred from education. The school had battled the Ku Klux Klan and local resistance to keep its doors open. It had also contended with unrest within its own walls. Several white students had initially chafed at the idea that they would be in classes with Black students. Some of them fled the campus—only to ultimately return because of the lackluster state of public education in Kentucky. If they wanted to receive an education in Madison County, Berea was their best option.

In 1869, E. Henry Fairchild, a former professor at Oberlin College, became Berea's president; Fee would serve as the chair of the board. In his inaugural address, Fairchild outlined his philosophy— one that fit squarely into Fee's worldview. "How soon will [white] people be prepared to give equal rights and protection to colored people, if from childhood they are taught that colored children are not fit to be near them as equals, but as inferiors," he asked. If white children could not attend school with Black children, how could they ever feel that going to the polls with them or sitting on juries with them was right? Interracial education was necessary to end white hostility toward Black people.

Berea's credo had attracted donors from across the North, from Ohio to the New England states. However, by the 1880s, the anti-slavery fervor that helped grow support for interracial education began to wane. Even places like Oberlin College—the pinnacle of proof that interracial education worked—began to change.

The discord at Oberlin probably did not start in the dining hall, but that is where it became clear. In 1882, the *Oberlin News* noted that there was an incident in Ladies Hall: White students refused to eat at a table with Black students. To accommodate the white students, the matron of the hall set another table for Black students. It sparked immediate criticism. Had Oberlin become a college separate from its founding? Had it fallen victim to what would come to be known as the nadir, the period of lawless discrimination that followed Reconstruction?

A subsequent article in the *News*, in December 1882, stressed that the events were not as "the outside world" had painted them. The table for Black students "had the same waiters and the same food and same everything as their neighbors." Separate, but equal. Another article—this one written by a white student in the student-edited *Oberlin Review*—argued that Oberlin had not changed at all. Sure, it was more class conscious than it had been before, he said, but that was what was giving rise to the semblance of a color line. It was up to the students to make sure the college kept its roots, the student argued. If the students failed, discrimination at the college would get only worse.

A group of Black students writing for the *Review* echoed some of those sentiments, though they disagreed that it was solely on the students to make sure the college retained its identity. The faculty and administration had a central role to play as well. The Black students also took issue with the characterization of the dining hall incident in the *News*. "What other race would be requested to eat at the same table on account of their nationality?" the students asked. "We doubt if under such circumstances Irish or German students would ask to sit together as that disgusting article in the News claimed." There was a fundamental difference, they said. They were forced into segregation because of their skin color. Oberlin's president, James Fairchild, remedied the decision. A segregated table was not allowed. That was far from the end of racial discrimination at the college, though.

In the late 1880s, white students moved off campus to avoid living with Black students and would not stay in boarding homes that housed Black students. White families in the area started refusing to board Black students as well. Black enrollment began to decline at Oberlin. Immediately after the Civil War, the college had comprised roughly 7 percent Black students. By the 1890s, that figured had dwindled to 3 percent—roughly 50 students out of 1,357.

Berea, however, was still holding on. By 1889, its student population was split roughly down the middle. The college enrolled 334 students in total: 177 were Black, 157 were white. In a national environment in which the interest in contributing to racially integrated or all-Black schools was decidedly out of fashion, Berea aimed higher.

George Atherton's role as the leader of the land-grant movement had solidified by 1889. He had become the president of Penn State University, had twice been elected to lead the Association of American Agricultural Colleges, the association most responsible for the direction of the land grants, and was a trusted adviser of Justin Morrill. The latter role is why, in December 1889, Morrill found himself in a familiar position: writing to Atherton in search of advice.

President Benjamin Harrison had made clear that he would not recommend legislation that would help common schools through direct payments from the US Treasury. However, it was apparent that Harrison liked that strategy for funding education more than Morrill's method of enhancing public education through the sale of land grants. Morrill wanted to know if Atherton and his colleagues had devised a strategy that could potentially align with the president's. Impressing urgency, he requested, "please advise me at your earliest convenience."

As suspected, the common schools bill was defeated in March. It appeared that the 1890s would be a repeat of the nearly two decades past. Five days later, Morrill introduced a bill of his own, which tied extra funding for land-grant colleges to common school legislation and which was not markedly different from the recently failed bill. Henry E. Alvord, the president of the Maryland Agricultural College, wrote to Atherton following a meeting with Morrill in April. "The Morrill Bill is dead—beyond resurrection—in its duplex form," Alvord said.

Then, on April 30, Morrill introduced a new bill to fund colleges that was no longer wedded to common school funding but separate from it. The bill, S. 3714, was written to put the colleges on sure financial footing, "on a basis of assured support for all time." The bill requested an annual federal appropriation of $15,000 for each state—and that amount was to be increased each year by $1,000 until 1900. By the time the grant was at full power, each state would receive $25,000 to help endow its colleges. The bill was reported out of committee with a strong recommendation and on June 14 went to the Senate floor for debate.

As he had done time and time again, Morrill addressed Congress on behalf of the land-grant colleges. In a speech of remarkable foresight, Morrill impressed upon his colleagues that "no American will long dwell where there are no village schools, nor be quite contented in a State that does not liberally support collegiate education."

He recalled Washington's Farewell Address and the first president's call to fund education. "Let me urge that the land-grant colleges are American institutions, established by Congress, and, if a small pittance is needed to perfect and complete their organization or to equip them for educational work that is designed to elevate the condition of the greater part of the American people," Morrill said, "I shall confidently hope that it will be granted without reluctance and with the full faith in the national benefits that cannot fail to accrue." What he did not note in his address, however, was a small, though important, section of the act. One week later, when the Senate again stood to discuss the bill, it became a dividing line.

The provision in question regarded separate colleges for Black and white students. The 1862 Morrill Act had not mentioned Black students. States were required only to create a college that taught the agricultural and mechanic arts. Morrill's new bill, however, made a distinction. No state was to receive funds under the bill "for support of a college where a distinction of race and color was made in the admission of students." There was a caveat, though. States could operate separate colleges for Black students. Separate, but equal.

It is difficult to say, exactly, why this provision was added to the new bill. However, there was not a question of whether Black students should receive a portion of the funds. That was a given. The Fourteenth Amendment, passed during Reconstruction, had guaranteed equal protection under the law, even if it had been selectively practiced to that point. Instead, the debate revolved around what exactly an equal institution for Black students looked like. Alabama's senator James Pugh, a former Confederate officer and congressman in the Confederacy, offered an amendment. All institutions that receive state funds to teach Black students the agricultural and mechanical arts should count, he argued, regardless of if they were college level or not. That would cover schools such as the Tuskegee Institute in his home state, which had been founded by Booker T. Washington. Tuskegee was not quite a college at the time, but it performed some of the basic educational functions for which the Morrill Act called.

Northern legislators argued, however, that expanding the pool of institutions eligible to receive the funds would bastardize the bill. If they had wanted a bill that would essentially support common schools, then that is what they would have proposed.

The next day, Morrill rose once again to have the Senate consider his bill. He had added a substitute amendment that he thought would assuage the tensions on both sides of the aisle. It was, essentially, a mirror of Pugh's amendment: it did not matter if it were a college, university, or institute, as long as states funded an institution for Black students in a "just and equitable" division of the new Morrill money. Senator Henry Blair, of New Hampshire, rose as the final vote was being prepared. "I will simply say that I think, and it is an observation to which no one can object, that this whole movement, about which we are so critical and hypercritical and overhypercritical, to take care of the colored people in the distribution of this money, came into the Senate upon the motion of the Senator from Alabama and that no Northern man thought of it."

A handful of senators responded that they would have seen fit for any student to be able to attend the one college they had made available with their Morrill Act funds, but since the state of the South was as it was, this provision was absolutely critical. On June 23, the bill passed the Senate without a recorded vote; the House followed suit on August 17, passing the bill with overwhelming support—135 in favor to 35 against.

On August 20, 1890, President Benjamin Harrison signed the Second Morrill Act into law. It was an act that was designed to appropriate more funds for institutions that sought to educate more white students. And through the course of debate, it ended up creating or endowing a class of institutions that would teach the next generation of Black students.

In 1891, one year after the signing of the Second Morrill Act, Iowa State University, the recipient of both the 1862 and 1890 land grant from Iowa, enrolled its first Black student; the state had decided to admit Black people rather than spend extra money to create a separate institution for them. Theirs was a rare decision, though. While the great compromise of the Morrill Act came to be vitally important to the development of colleges for Black students, it also established a separate-but-unequal system in higher education that would be codified several years later by the Supreme Court in *Plessy v. Ferguson*, and in state laws across the South in the two decades that would follow.

CHAPTER 3

The Fall of Integrated Education

S leeping next to the mice in an unheated shed on the edge of campus at Simpson College, a private college in Indianola, Iowa, George Washington Carver was breaking a barrier. His living quarters were drab; the president of the institution had allowed Carver—the college's first Black student—to live in the abandoned structure after he had arrived on campus in 1890. Carver was low on money, and after paying his tuition and fees, he had little left to his name and could not afford housing. The shed was dirty, but it was rent-free, and it allowed Carver to use his last bit of money on food for the first week of school. He made that food stretch for a month.

Carver had arrived at Simpson College through a mix of fortuitous relationships and determination. He had been born into slavery in Missouri, and, following the end of the Civil War, was adopted by the family that had owned him. Educational options in Missouri, however, were limited for Black people, so he bounced among a handful of towns in his youth in search of a basic education. He went back and forth across state lines until he landed in Minneapolis, Kansas, a town in the state's center that had been named after the city of the same name in Minnesota.

Carver graduated from Minneapolis High School in 1884 and

needed to find work. He moved nearly two hundred miles due east to Kansas City, where he took up a job as a stenographer. The gig did not pay much, but it was enough to get by on. The young George was ambitious, though. He did not want to spend his life copying down the things others had to say. He was excited by the prospect of college. Several brochures he had been reading suggested the nation's colleges would be open to accepting a student such as him—a Black student.

In 1886, he sent an application to Highland College, a Presbyterian school along the Missouri border in northern Kansas. Highland got back to him in short order with good news: he was qualified and had been accepted. The truth of the matter is that it's likely Highland would have accepted nearly anyone who had graduated from high school. The institution, with fewer than one hundred students, was one of several fledgling colleges that popped up all over the country like heat bumps during the fever of higher education after the Civil War. Kansas alone had more than forty degree-granting colleges in 1890, despite having a population just a shade under one and a half million people.

Carver arrived at a well-maintained campus where the shrubbery was pruned and the halls were neatly kept. He made his way to the registrar's office, where he met the principal, who looked his admissions letter up and down. Then, curtly, the school's administrator informed Carver that the school could not accept him and that, in addition to white students, the college accepted only "Indians." While the school's enrollment policy was unusual, it was not unprecedented. Had the principal known that Carver was Black, the institution never would have sent him an acceptance letter. "You didn't tell me you were a Negro," Carver remembered him saying. It was a swift blow of embarrassment and distress to Carver, and four years would pass before he would try again to attend college.

When Carver arrived at Simpson College in 1890, the reception was much different. He was greeted warmly, in comparison with Highland, as the institution's first Black student. "I shudder to think what might have happened if Simpson College had closed its doors," Carver later wrote. "When I came, hungering and thirsting for an opportunity to develop as God gave me light and strength. They made me believe I was a real human being."

Simpson College seemed to have it all, including art, which Carver had originally intended to study. His art teacher, Etta Budd, noticed Carver's artistic talent, but, perhaps paternalistically, she worried that he would not be able to make a career from it. Carver was one of very few men who were specializing in art at the college and, of course, the only Black student in the department. She told Carver that he would best be able to help his people, Black people, through agriculture rather than the arts and that the best place for him to do that was not at Simpson but at Iowa Agricultural College.

Carver dreamed of being an artist, though, and despite his housing—he had, by then, been able to furnish the old shed with some bare-bones furniture purchased by starting his own laundry service and doing odd jobs around Indianola—Simpson had been a welcoming community. Besides, he had already broken the color barrier at one college, and what were the odds that a second college would accept him to do the same? It turned out that he had a powerful ally in his corner. Etta Budd's father, Joseph Budd, was one of the country's top botanists and, coincidentally, a professor at Iowa Agricultural College. Budd offered to accompany Carver to meet her father, and, after deliberation, and coming to the realization that he could, truly, be of greater service to Black people as an agricultural researcher, he accepted.

Carver was accepted to the college with little debate. It probably helped that Iowa Agricultural College, as the state's land-grant college, could not bar students on account of their race because of the newly passed update to the Morrill Act. He would be a rarity in a town where most of the residents had never seen a Black person before, especially one with features as pronounced as his own.

Iowa Agricultural College, as with most Morrill schools, did not require students to pay for tuition and housing, but the aid stopped there. Students had to provide the other accoutrements—linens, bedding, furniture. Biographers would later argue that Carver's lack of these materials was the primary reason college officials chose not to house him in one of the white dormitories. Instead, he lived in an office that one of the professors gave up. It was a step up from the shed at Simpson, but just as isolated. Still in need of money, Carver turned to cutting wood, cleaning stables, and performing janitorial duties in the office building where he lived. Though he could work in the dining hall, administrators barred him from eating there. Instead, he took his meals in the basement with people who worked the fields. Though the institution was nominally integrated, it was functionally segregated; an experience Black *firsts*—the students who broke the color barrier at colleges across the country—would experience for decades to come. Even though Carter performed well in the classroom, he was invisible to his classmates. His experience was broadly reflective of how land-grant colleges outside the South integrated. The institutions accepted Black students because they were legally required to, but they were often functionally segregated.

Carver's social isolation at Iowa's land-grant college mirrored the deterioration of interracial harmony that would soon come to Berea college, which was fighting to maintain funding during a decline in the national interest in supporting programs propping up interracial education.

William Goodell Frost was in Germany when members of the board of trustees at Berea College offered him the top job in 1892. A professor of Greek at Oberlin College, he had taken leave to travel with his three sons and new wife, Eleanor Marsh. He was not as much reluctant to accept the position at Berea as he was exacting; he wanted to be sure that it was the right move for his new family. The decision to choose Frost seemed an easy one for the board at Berea. His mother was the daughter of an abolitionist and his father had graduated from Oberlin in 1848. If there was anyone who could carry on the legacy of Berea following Fairchild's departure in 1889, it would be someone with Frost's pedigree.

Berea presented a "peculiar opportunity," Frost wrote in a letter to the board. The college's work in educating Black people had the "blessing of heaven," but the Kentucky institution could do more. There were now dozens of schools that were providing higher education to Black students, but Berea was one of the truly rare places educating both races. Berea had the opportunity to teach "the races to live and work together, and to afford an object lesson to the whole country, making it possible for advocates of justice everywhere to say, 'There is Berea with hundreds of white and colored students working together in friendly relations on the soil of slavery.'" But in order to be that national beacon, the school needed more students, "and especially," he wrote, "more white students."

The letter did two different types of work: it staved off any potential apprehensions about his ultimate commitment to the education of Black students, and it also outlined what would be his fundraising method for the college—increasing the number of white students, specifically those native to the school's Appalachian region.

Just before Frost arrived at Berea in 1892, the school enrolled 350 students: 184 Black, 166 white; 31 of those students studied in the collegiate department. Frost quickly began traveling the country with a narrative about the "contemporary ancestors"—white ancestors—who lived in the mountains and who were in desperate need of help. Berea was the only school in the region that could serve their educational needs. His effort was successful, and by 1894, he was already pointing to an increase in white student enrollment. There were just under twenty faculty members at the college when Frost arrived in 1892; only one of those faculty members, James Hathaway, a lecturer who was an alumnus of the college, was Black. Within two years of Frost's arrival, Hathaway had been pushed out of Berea, and he departed the school for the State Normal School at

Frankfort in the state's capital. That college, which would become Kentucky State University, was the recipient of some of the state's 1890 Morrill funds.

Black alumni began to sound the alarm about the Frost administration. They argued that the white people running Berea were not practicing the principles espoused by John G. Fee. If God had made of one blood all the people of the earth, it was hard to tell by the prejudice that had been aimed at the Black people who had previously attended the college, who were currently enrolled, and who taught there, they said. Berea had been named for the biblical people who had sheltered Paul when he was heckled and attacked—the Black alumni argued that these new Bereans were no longer guarding the college's original mission.

Frost offered perhaps the best indication of his attitudes on race in private. He had taken a trip to raise funds for the college when the tensions over Hathaway's removal were at their height. His wife was worried; she feared that he would be ambushed upon his return. He shrugged her worry off in his response. "No darkie has nerve enough to be an assassin," he wrote. His presidency was a far cry from the leadership that had established the school as the South's first interracial college, and Fee, who still sat on the college's board, would often be the only board member to vote against the policies that Frost implemented.

The school began to segregate spaces: the dormitories, the dining halls, the sports teams, the band. The students still worked together, though; that was still a fundamental part of the college. But by the mid-1890s, white students had petitioned the administration to boot Black students from the classrooms as well. The effort was quashed. Berea's guiding commitments still carried some weight.

While fundraising, Frost often subdued fears about the supposed consequences of interracial education by pointing to the college's history. "We have tried our simple plan for twenty-nine years," he said, "and the evil consequences have not come and our way is the way of the Christian world at large." The "evil consequences" that Frost alluded to were the racist notions that interracial education would lead to interracial marriage—an unspeakable outcome. "The relations of the races are as wholesome and pure in Berea as in any town in the state," he said.

The white population at Berea began to surge, with nearly one hundred more white students enrolling each year, while the Black population stagnated. A series of factors is likely responsible for this: the skepticism with which Black students viewed the college after the forced resignation of James Hathaway, the rise of Black colleges after the Second Morrill Act, and Frost's intentional push to enroll more white students. The nation was changing as well and moving toward legally cementing segregation into the national landscape. The Supreme Court would soon be hearing a case that would enshrine the separate-but-equal doctrine.

"A Conviction under the Separate Car Act," an unassuming headline in the New Orleans *Daily Picayune* read on February 13, 1891. The case out of Shreveport, Louisiana, was so uneventful to the New Orleans paper that it was relegated to page 8, and it came in behind news that a Black minister had been murdered in Ruston by two white men for allegedly insulting a white boy—the newspaper assured its readers that there was "no sympathy" for the minister— and executive appointments the governor had made in Baton Rouge.

The headline was significant, though. The conviction was the first time the weight of a recently established Louisiana law had been tested. In 1890, the state had passed the Louisiana Railway Accommodations Act, or, as it would come to be called, the Separate Car Act. The law, in keeping with the growing Jim Crow of creating separate and nominally equal facilities for Black and white people, required train cars operating in the state to be segregated by race. R. J. Hood, a train conductor on the Vicksburg, Shreveport, and Pacific line, had allowed Black and white passengers to ride in the same car in January

1891. He was indicted for being in violation of the act and became the first person to be found guilty by a jury since the law's passage.

In the five years between 1887 and 1892, nine states had passed laws segregating rail- and streetcars. The states had been emboldened by the Supreme Court's decisions in the civil rights cases of 1883, when the court ruled that the Civil Rights Act of 1875, a law preventing racial discrimination in public places such as hotels and trains, was unconstitutional. On the first day of August in 1891, the *Arkansas Democrat* ominously noted that "there is a dark cloud rising in Louisiana, caused by the separate car act. The negroes kick and dub the cars 'jim crows.'" Black people in New Orleans had formed a group—the Citizens' Committee to Test the Constitutionality of the Separate Car Law—an easy to understand, if long, name, and began raising money to contest the ruling. The members of the group contended that they were, indeed, citizens, and should be afforded access to the same facilities as white people—real, equal treatment as the equal protection clause of the Fourteenth Amendment had guaranteed them.

The Citizens' Committee hired Albion Tourgée as its lawyer and found a person who might make an ideal test case for its legal argument. The law had not established what it meant by "white" and "coloured"; so, they figured, a mixed-race person might short-circuit the system. Louisiana's racial caste made defined distinctions about how Black a person was. Homer Plessy was an octoroon—one-eighth Black and seven-eighths white—and so he could pass as white. America, however, still closely adhered to the one-drop rule: if a person had one drop of Black blood in his ancestry, he was, for legal and extralegal purposes, Black.

On June 7, 1892, the test case began. With plans to be arrested, Plessy bought a first-class ticket from New Orleans to Covington, Louisiana, got on the train, and sat in one of the cars alongside white passengers. The conductor approached Plessy. "Are you a colored man?" he asked. "Yes," Plessy replied, before the conductor directed him to go to the car that was designated for Black passengers. Plessy refused. A private detective, whom the Citizens' Committee had hired to act as the arresting officer, came forward to detain Plessy and take him to the jail in New Orleans. There, he confessed to having violated the Separate Car Act. The Citizens' Committee had what it needed—a case that would put the Separate Car Act and the flimsy construct of race on trial.

The case snaked its way through the courts for the next four years before, on April 13, 1896, it was argued before the US Supreme Court. Tourgée presented twenty-three "points of contention," though he relied less on precedent than reason. What if a white mother was traveling with her "colored" child? How is anyone able to correctly identify whether another person has a "single drop of African blood"? And if separate cars and facilities were equal, would any white person choose to ride in the Black car? "Probably most white persons, if given a choice [to be Black], would prefer death to life," he argued. There was one legal linchpin he fell back on, though: the Fourteenth Amendment.

Tourgée wanted the justices to think about the first four clauses of the Fourteenth Amendment the most. The first sentence: "All persons born or naturalized in the United States, and subject to the jurisdiction thereof, are citizens of the United States and of the state wherein they reside." Plessy was indeed a citizen of the United States and of Louisiana. The second clause: "No state shall make or enforce any law which shall abridge the privileges or immunities of citizens of the United States." Louisiana had created and enforced a law barring Plessy from a privilege other citizens enjoyed. The third clause: "Nor shall any state deprive any person of life, liberty, or property, without due process of the law." And finally: "Nor deny to any person within its jurisdiction the equal protection of the laws"—equal protection, a clause aimed at preventing recently freed enslaved people from being discriminated against by the government. The Separate Car Act, Tourgée argued, was textbook discrimination, and clearly in violation of the Fourteenth Amendment.

Eight of the court's nine justices adorned their robes and packed into their seats to hear the case that April morning. There was to be little written about the oral arguments that day; instead, the press corps relied on the legal briefs to craft their dispatches. Tourgée, his best arguments in tow, had the opportunity to run through only a few of them. Then came the waiting game. The future of separate and equal was in the justices' hands.

A month and five days passed before the court returned with a mountain of decisions. The court announced its decision would be a 7–1 split; only one justice would dissent: Justice John Marshall Harlan—the only person on the court who had owned a person during slavery.

Justice Henry Billings Brown wrote the court's decision. The majority believed that Tourgée's argument that "enforced separation of the two races stamps the colored race with a badge of inferiority" was a "fallacy." The state was not doing the stamping, he wrote, and if Black people felt that they were being marked inferior by the separate facilities, it was no one's fault but their own. Further, Tourgée's argument "assumes that social prejudices may be overcome by legislation, and that equal rights cannot be secured to the negro except by an enforced commingling of the two races. We cannot accept this proposition," Brown wrote. Social equality would be result of "natural affinities" rather than government interference.

Then Brown did a bit of crystal-balling, reading the minds of those who had crafted the Fourteenth Amendment. "The object of the amendment was undoubtedly to enforce the absolute equality of the two races before the law, but, in the nature of things, it could not have been intended to abolish distinctions based upon color, or to enforce social, as distinguished from political, equality, or a commingling of the two races upon terms unsatisfactory to either." Making distinctions based on race was well within the nature of things, Brown supposed. His opinion would codify the thinking many white people had about the separate-but-equal doctrine: It was legitimate because equal facilities were being provided. It was an easy lie for the court to believe. The court made precedent of a fiction.

But Harlan stood in dissent. While he was not the abolitionist that John Fee, or even Cassius Clay, was, the Kentucky native came from a similar background. His family was among the most prominent slaveholders in Frankfort, Kentucky, and, despite his opposition to the Emancipation Proclamation, he supported the Union cause. His shoddy record on civil rights cases aside—he had agreed that laws barring interracial marriages were constitutional—his condemnation of this court decision was incisive. "The judgment this day rendered, will, in time, prove to be quite as pernicious as the decision made by this tribunal in the *Dred Scott* case," he argued. The law, and its application, should be color-blind, Harlan wrote in his dissent; though the "white race deems itself to be the dominant race in this country," that had no bearing on the Constitution. "In the view of the Constitution, in the eye of the law, there is in this country no superior, dominant, ruling class of citizens." He railed against caste; the founding document, he argued, "neither knows nor tolerates classes among citizens." Where civil rights were concerned, everyone was equal before the law. "The humblest is the peer of the most powerful," he argued, and civil rights were to be guaranteed under the law.

"The destinies of the two races, in this country, are indissolubly linked together, and the interests of both require that the common government of all shall not permit the seeds of race hate to be planted under the sanction of law," Harlan wrote. The government had not only sown the seeds but nurtured them.

The Supreme Court legitimized Jim Crow in *Plessy*. States that preferred to keep their colleges separate and unequal—to discriminate against their Black institutions and the students who attended them—had cover to do so. And as institutions such as Oberlin and Berea contended with white-separatism arguments from within, they would soon face them from outside their gates as well.

At the close of the Civil War, Samuel Lowery, who had been teaching
a battalion of Black troops, moved his family to a town just outside
of Murfreesboro, Tennessee, called Ebenezer. As was often the case
with Black men, Lowery was not certain of when exactly he had
been born, but it would have been in the early 1830s. He studied at
Franklin College, a manual labor college in Indiana, and in December 1866, along with Daniel Wadkins, a fellow alumnus of Franklin,
he founded Tennessee Manual Labor University. The institute aimed
to fulfill many of the Morrill Act's goals. Students would learn agricultural and mechanical arts, but they would also receive a classical
education. "The thousands of colored orphans now uncared for, will
find a home, and there [be] prepared for the duties of life," members
of the board wrote in the *Nashville Union and American* in November 1867. "Educated physically, intellectually and morally, they can
go on the race of life to bless mankind." The college's leaders estimated they'd need $100,000 to successfully operate the college. One
hundred students enrolled when Manual Labor opened its doors in
January 1868.

The late 1860s were difficult for fledgling colleges for Black students. Dozens upon dozens of would-be college leaders had been
asking for money from wealthy northern philanthropists to help establish colleges for freedmen, and the leaders of Manual Labor were
not much different, aside from the color of their skin. White philanthropists often felt more comfortable providing funds to institutions
that were led by other white do-gooders. That meant that the Black
men who were leading Manual Labor University did so without the
same resources as their white counterparts. In 1873, while Reconstruction governments still held power in the South, a Black Tennessee lawmaker introduced a bill that would have provided funds for
Manual Labor, but the legislation failed. Between 1869 and 1905,
the state legislature provided funds for two white private colleges.
The state was not against funding private colleges, but it was not
willing to spend its money on colleges for Black students when it was

not forced to do so. Shortly after its own chance at state funding failed, Manual Labor University ceased operations.

Manual Labor's story was not unique to the time—in fact, it represented what was more often the rule than the exception. It takes a lot to get a college off the ground, and it takes even more when fighting for funding under the suffocating pressure of racial discrimination. Some of those institutions survived, though, and they received a boost from the federal government after 1890.

More than a dozen colleges were created or funded specifically for Black students following the passage of the Second Morrill Act. The Delaware College for Colored Students, for example, was authorized by the state's legislature on May 15, 1891, after years of the state's institutions that served primarily white students blocking meaningful integration. When the college opened, only seven students enrolled, and it would take another six years before it offered full teaching certificates. Prejudice trumped all in the creation of the college. And the school's genesis offered a guide to how other states would view their Morrill schools and the education of Black people in the age of separate but equal. After all, several whites shared the view expressed by James K. Vardaman, who would eventually become the governor of Mississippi. "The Negro isn't permitted to advance and their education only spoils a good field hand and makes a shyster lawyer or a fourth-rate teacher," he wrote in 1899. "It is money thrown away."

How Black people should be educated was a hotly contested question among the burgeoning Black bourgeoisie as well. There was a new Black middle and upper class that had been educated at the Black colleges that had cropped up across the country. T. Thomas Fortune, a graduate of Howard University and a newspaper magnate, argued it was elementary and industrial education southern Black people needed most. "Education is the preparation of the mind for the future of work," he argued. Booker T. Washington, most notable among the Black advocates of trade and industrial training, had attended the Hampton Institute, which educated both Black and

Native American students. He argued in *The Atlantic* in 1896 that "it is through the dairy farm, the truck garden, the trades, and commercial life, largely, that the Negro is to find his way to the enjoyment of all his rights." They would be able to learn those trades at colleges.

But, by the time of Washington's writing, all the Negro's rights had already been jeopardized. The *Plessy v. Ferguson* decision earlier that year had green-lit discrimination in higher education, and states wasted little time in passing laws to make the split permanent. What had often been an unwritten rule before the Civil War began to pop up on the books. States were intentionally creating an unequal system.

Oklahoma was not yet a state when it established its law barring interracial public education in 1897. The Territorial Legislature established Oklahoma Colored Agricultural and Normal University to comply with the requirements of the Morrill Act. (It had funded Oklahoma A&M, which would come to be known as Oklahoma State University, with part of the Morrill funds.)

As segregated spaces became standard operating practice, Berea deepened its commitment to enrolling white students under the presidency of William Goodell Frost. By 1899, the number of Black students attending the college had stagnated to around 150, but the white student population kept increasing, topping 500 by the end of the century. Frost wanted to keep going. The school needed more funding, and it needed to show it was committed to educating the "contemporary ancestors" he had been raving to northern fundraisers about.

John Fee, though by now old, had grown increasingly frustrated with Frost's direction, and tried to keep the barge headed straight. "Let me say that the unique work of Berea College is not 'effacing sectional lines,'" he wrote to *The Republican* newspaper in Springfield, Massachusetts, in 1899. Frost had been misrepresenting the college's vision. The mission of the college was "effacing the barbarous spirit of caste between colored and white at home. Let the friends of Berea College demand faithfulness to the original design of the college." There was more being done to recruit white students than

Black students, he continued, and the Black students felt cast aside because of it.

Then, a southern partner of Berea's in interracial education fell victim to the long arm of the *Plessy* decision. On April 29, 1901, Maryville College in Tennessee acknowledged that it would go along with the state's newly passed law that barred interracial education. The college had for decades not made distinctions between Black and white people in admissions, but the state was forcing it to do so, and its board decided that it would not be worth the $50 daily fine (the equivalent of $1,518 in 2021 dollars) to continue educating students together. The *Nashville American* newspaper gave little space to the decision. "No Contest over the Law Prohibiting Co-Education of Races" the page 3 headline read. Just underneath it, in large text, was a lengthy story: "Origin of the Ku Klux."

Carter G. Woodson arrived at Berea in January 1897, in the middle of the institution's identity crisis. He had likely sought out the college due to the lack of good educational options for Black people where he lived in West Virginia. Neither Storer College, in Harpers Ferry, West Virginia, nor West Virginia Colored Institute, which had opened as the Morrill Act school for Black students, were truly colleges; each offered only secondary education. As much as Berea was changing, it was still a place to which Black students believed they could come and receive a proper education.

Woodson graduated in 1903, and it was opportune timing. If he had been one year later, the man who would come to be known as the "Father of Black History" might never have been able to earn his degree from the college. An executioner was coming for what remained of Berea's way of life.

Carl Day, a large man in his late twenties from Breathitt County, Kentucky, was chosen by the Democrats to run for the state assembly in early 1903. He had a "smooth and intellectual face," and had attended Central University in Richmond, Kentucky—a college that had split from its Presbyterian affiliation at the start of the Civil War due to the institution's allegiance to the South and slavery. After college, Day had become a merchant and lumberjack but also had risen quickly through the Democratic Party's ranks.

Day won his election by a nudge—only ten votes separated him and his Republican opponent—and on November 4, 1903, he became part of the wave of Democrats that flooded into the state's legislature. He wasted no time getting to work.

On January 2, 1904, Louisville's *Courier-Journal* reported that there would be "several important bills" introduced by Day in the next legislative session. At his earliest opportunity, the paper reported, he would introduce "a bill to prohibit white and colored children from attending the same school." The bill would not be unlike similar laws already present in Tennessee, Oklahoma, and other states across the South, but it would differ in one especially important way. Day would impose a "heavy penalty" on anyone who violated the law. The penalties in other states were steep, but Day's would go further than any of them. He needed to make an example. There was only one institution—whether primary, secondary, or collegiate—at which both Black and white students attended school together in Kentucky: Berea College. Less than two months after he was elected, the Breathitt lawmaker planned to tear apart the last remainders of interracial education at Berea.

Nine days later, the paper was able to offer more specifics. The bill would have "considerable backing." Several other lawmakers supported formalizing the bar on interracial education, a social custom that had been adhered to everywhere else in the state outside of Berea. There would no longer be a question about what the state believed its role in education to be: It was to keep the races separate.

The *Courier-Journal* ran the text of the bill in full:

> An act to prohibit white and colored persons from attending the same school.

Be it enacted by the General Assembly of the Common-wealth of Kentucky: That it shall be unlawful for any person, corporation or association of persons to maintain or operate any college, school or institution where persons of the white and negro races are both received as pupils for instruction, and any person or corporation who shall operate or maintain any such college, school or institution shall be fined $1,000; and any person or corporation who may be convicted of violating the provisions of this act shall be fined $100 for each day they may operate said school, college or institution after such conviction.

Second—That any instructor who shall teach in any school, college or institution where members of said two races are received as pupils for instruction shall be guilty of operating and maintaining the same, and fined as provided in the first section hereof.

Third—It shall be unlawful for any white person to attend any school or institution where negroes are received as pupils or receive instruction, and it shall be unlawful for any negro or colored person to attend any school or institution where white persons are received as pupils or receive instruction.

Any person so offending shall be fined $50 for each day he attends such institution or school.

Day introduced the bill, House Bill 25, one day later, and the newspapers minced no words. It was clear that the bill was aimed at Berea College, but it is unknown why, exactly, Day made such short work of bringing forth the legislation. To this day, residents of Berea tell of Day passing through town and seeing two young women hugging on a train platform, one white and one Black. That, to him, was evidence that interracial education would lead to the commingling of the races in other forms—namely, interracial dating and marriage.

Administrators at the college seemed blindsided by the bill, despite inklings that the legislation was coming. During the morning prayer on January 12, 1904, President Frost read a letter to students. He waxed on about the college's history, its commitments, and its principles—despite institutional drift taking hold, in large part, due to his strategic vision. "We have never claimed that it was best to have white and colored children mingled in the public schools of Kentucky," Frost said, according to an account in the local paper, the Berea *Citizen*. "We have never denounced schools which bar out the Negro. But for Berea, under Christian safeguards which exist here, we have seen that it was a good arrangement for both races, and a benefit to the State." Berea was not trying to change the whole state, he was arguing, but just as they left the state alone, they wanted the state to leave them alone. The college president's tepid support for the integrated education in which Berea trafficked was a departure from the past. John Fee had believed it to be a good for society, while Frost saw it as good enough for their bubble.

The students took a vote—first the Black students and then the white students—and, in near unanimous agreement, they chose to keep their college as it was. They elected to maintain an interracial environment.

Quickly, the bill began to move through the state legislature. It was referred to the Committee on Education, and a hearing date was set for February 1. The night before the hearing, Frost once again spoke to the student body. He bucked against critics who said that the passage of the bill was something he wanted to happen. His emphasis on recruiting white students had clearly left an impression. "I am humiliated that any man could misunderstand my own position," he said, defending himself. "Should this bill pass, which it will not, and the Trustees of Berea College consent to wrong the Negro, which they will not, I for one should stand by the colored man, and all the more in his time of need."

But there was little he could do to prevent the bill's passage. On February 2, the *Evening Bulletin*, in Maysville, reported that "it is likely the death knell of Berea college as a mixed school for white and Negro pupils." The education committee had unanimously voted to support Day's bill. Two weeks later, the full House met to discuss the bill, and a handful of amendments were offered. There was the amendment that would exempt penal institutions from the bill; Black and white people could be educated together if they were locked up. Then there was the amendment that barred colleges that were currently integrated—Berea, of course, being the only one—from opening another campus specifically for either race. One college could not operate two campuses, as it would taint the purpose of the law. Several Republicans stood to contest the bill, but all but a handful of Democrats left the room during their remarks; they were committed to Berea segregating.

The amendment to ban one college from operating two campuses was ultimately changed slightly to include a distance limitation. A college could operate two campuses, but they could not be within twenty-five miles of each other. With the amendments added, the bill went to a vote. It was a drubbing any football team would be embarrassed by: 73–5. It went to the Senate.

President Frost tried once more to convince the Senate's education committee to vote against the bill. But it was for naught, and on March 8, the committee moved to advance the bill to the full floor for a vote. One day later, on March 9, it was reported that Day had come down with a case of pneumonia and inflammatory rheumatism. The bill, however, kept moving through the legislature. It passed the full Senate without amendment on March 11 and was signed into law by the governor on March 24, 1904. The coeducation bill, which would come to be known as the Day Law, had achieved what the Ku Klux Klan, the marauders who several times beat John Fee, and the Civil War could not: it barred interracial education at Berea College.

One month after the Senate passed the Day Law, Carl Day died of pneumonia, having achieved legislative victory, and ensuring the separation of races in Kentucky higher education for decades to come.

President Frost challenged the law. While he openly advocated enrolling more white students at Berea, he was still in some ways committed to the original mission of the institution. The case worked its way to the US Supreme Court in 1908, where it would face a bench of roughly the exact makeup that had decided the *Plessy* case. The state could ban the mingling of the races in public spaces, but could it bar private educational institutions from doing as they pleased as well?

The court fell back on its precedent. And once again, Harlan was the only one who dissented. Like John Fee, Harlan was the son of a slaveholder from Kentucky, and he would deliver a forceful dissent in defense of the institution founded with interracial education at the center of its mission.

"Have we become so inoculated with prejudice of race," Harlan wrote in his dissent, "that an American Government, professedly based on the principles of freedom, and charged with the protection of all citizens alike, can make distinctions between citizens in the matter of their voluntary meeting for innocent purposes simply because of their respective races?" The rest of the court clearly believed so. They propped up the idea of separate and equal.

There were very few places where Black people could receive a proper college education when Carter G. Woodson was looking for an institution to attend. Berea had been a beacon, a school, like Oberlin, where the merits and the possibilities of interracial education were laid out for the world to see. It was also one of the first places in the South to embrace the notion that, when given the chance, Black students not only could learn but thirsted for knowledge. Even when the mission was threatened by private interests, Berea held on. It took intentional, malicious legislation by the state to break it apart.

Separate, but equal. The next four decades would be proof of the lie.

PART II

DEFENDED

CHAPTER 4

The Tragedy
of Lloyd Gaines

The trickle of "firsts" in twentieth-century colleges was slow. Black students would break the color barrier at different predominantly white institutions across the North, and each time one graduated, it would be celebrated in the Black press. In 1912, Carter G. Woodson, who had trekked from West Virginia to the hills of Kentucky to attend Berea College, would become the second Black person in the United States to earn a doctorate from Harvard.

Fifty-five years later, his would still be a rare case. In fact, the completion of high school remained all too rare. But when Black students did go to college, they most often attended the separate institutions that had been set up for them across the South, and into the North in places like Ohio, Delaware, and Pennsylvania. The importance of these institutions was underscored by the shuttering of the doors of colleges like Berea to Black students.

A legacy is a difficult thing to shake, though, no matter how hard you may try, and Berea's legacy was teaching Black and white students. The college was barred by the Day Law from educating nonwhite students within twenty-five miles of its home campus, though, the campus on which Black and white students had lived, learned, and worked nearly half a century. So, school administrators began looking at other options for their now-displaced Black students.

At first, the college offered the students scholarships to attend Black colleges. There were a few preferred options: There was the Kentucky Normal and Industrial Institute for Colored Persons, the state college for Black students in Frankfort—a natural option as the only college for Black students remaining in the state after Berea was forced to reject them. And then there were the colleges that were held up as hallmarks for the education of Black people: Fisk University, in Tennessee; Hampton Institute, along the Chesapeake Bay in Virginia, and Tuskegee Institute, the powerhouse led by Booker T. Washington in the heart of the Black Belt in Alabama.

Washington, himself a graduate of Hampton, founded Tuskegee in 1881 and built it into a juggernaut through a mix of will, political calculation, and concession. Though the college was private, his maneuvering had landed it a portion of Alabama's federal land grant. He was particularly adept at wooing white politicians and donors to the idea that his intent with the institution was not to usurp any sort of racial hierarchy but instead to uplift the black race through industrial training. "While in some other affairs race prejudice is strongly marked, in the matter of business, of commercial and industrial development, there are few obstacles in the Negro's way," he wrote. His was a battle against illiteracy and amorality, he would insist, not white supremacy.

Washington's temperament toward matters of race made him agreeable to racist politicians, those who would refuse him "no personal favor" but who would make "bitter attacks" on Black people in front of white audiences. In the Deep South, however, that was exactly the kind of maneuvering that won his school plaudits, funding, and the admiration of those in other states who hoped their institutions might mirror the successes of Tuskegee. When President Frost, alongside the board of trustees and other administrators at Berea, began organizing to help Black students beyond simply sending them away to other colleges, Tuskegee's mission was never far from their minds.

The brain trust of Berea was working on a new project: the Lincoln Institute of Kentucky. The institution would be more than twenty-five miles from their home base, named for the assassinated president, and was intended to be a school not too unlike Berea— though it would be all-Black, in accordance with the Day Law. Still, there were enough differences to raise the hackles of some in the Black community.

During an address on February 7, 1909, Frost laid out his vision for the school. "As the United States managed Cuba until it could go alone, so Berea College is managing the newly-projected Lincoln Institute of Kentucky," he said. Frost rebuffed critics who argued that Berea was doing a disservice to Black students by not planning to create a collegiate department at the new institution. "[It] is not in the greatest need of colored people of our state just now," to have a four-year department at Lincoln, Frost argued. There was already Kentucky Normal and Industrial Institute for Colored Persons, and "when we find a student who has the special capacity and good sense which make it wise for him to receive a longer or different course of training," Frost said, "we shall send him to Fisk." The present goal for the Lincoln Institute, however, would be the training of "an army of teachers" who "can teach cleanliness, promptness and all the other elementary virtues" in Black primary and secondary schools.

Meanwhile, Kentucky was working on its own to create an institution that rivaled Tuskegee. John Grant Crabbe, Kentucky's superintendent of schools, had contracted William T. B. Williams, a professor at Hampton Institute who had taught at Tuskegee, to investigate the conditions of Kentucky Normal and Industrial. Williams pulled no punches in his report. The buildings were unfinished. The girls' dorm lacked fire escapes. The boys' dorm was literally in a mud puddle. There was no power or lighting or machinery in the electrical plant. The teachers were underpaid. The only bright spot was the student body, he wrote, who were "mature and of a high average of ability." It would require "radical departures" from established plans and operations to bring the institution up to speed, Williams argued. The state was willing to pay $40,000 to do it. It was nowhere close to the amount that would be needed.

But the money was something. Over the next several years, if Kentucky took part in federal grant programs, its Black colleges would benefit as well. The funds were often inequitably distributed, though. Years later, a federal report commissioned by President Harry Truman would reveal Kentucky's disparity in funding between its white institutions and Black institutions was among the worst in the nation. The disparity was apparent not only in Kentucky.

Slowly, over the course of the first five decades of the twentieth century, small steps of progress chipped away at this system of inherent inequality in higher education that had been established over the prior century. Each battle laid a step for the next, though the progress was not always linear.

Water Valley, Mississippi, has never been a big town. Its population vacillated between three thousand and four thousand people for more than a century. In 1911, as officials at Berea College were working to set up the Lincoln Institute for Black students in Simpsonville, Kentucky, Lloyd Lionel Gaines was born to Richard and Callie Gaines on a small farm a stone's throw from the city. He was the seventh child of eleven that the Gaineses would have. His father had been a teacher in the rural parts of the state until his growing family meant that he had to turn his attention—as so many Black families did—to sharecropping.

In his first four years of life, Gaines's father and two of his siblings died. A pair of his older brothers were early members of the Great Migration—the mass movement of Black people from the South to the North in search of better job prospects. Before his father's death, the family farm had been productive, but sharecropping was a difficult business. The lives of those who worked the land were at the will of the landowners, who took large shares of the profit, often illegally cheating the farmers out of their due.

In 1926, Callie moved fifteen-year-old Lloyd and the rest of her family to Saint Louis, where her oldest son, George, had been working as a hired hand on the railroads. Though he was old enough to have been in high school, Lloyd began school in Saint Louis in the fifth grade. His one-room schoolhouse in Mississippi—"Too well ventilated by cracks, and poorly heated by a single stove placed in the center of wooden benches"—had underprepared him for the rigors of the classroom.

But with the tools at Waring Elementary School in Saint Louis, and subsequent schools he attended, he was able to progress quickly, and, in 1931, he graduated from Vashon High School. It was the more recently constructed high school of the two that served Black students in the city. Gaines had built up an impressive résumé at Vashon. He earned summa cum laude honors, was the vice president of his senior class, was a member of the debate team, and was in the honor society. He also won a $250 scholarship for an essay on meat inspection.

With that scholarship money, he followed in his father's footsteps and began studying to become a teacher. Stowe Teachers College had been named for Harriet Beecher Stowe, the author of *Uncle Tom's Cabin* and an ardent abolitionist, and was one of the few options for Black students in the state. It was at Stowe that Gaines first joined the junior NAACP, the National Association for the Advancement of Colored People, which had been formed just two years before he was born, to "eliminate racial hatred and racial discrimination." But he did not stay at Stowe long. He had his sights set on more than teaching. With a second scholarship of $50 in hand, Gaines set out one hundred miles east to Jefferson City, Missouri, the home of Lincoln University, the state's land-grant college for Black students.

Lincoln University in Missouri, one of several institutions for Black students named for the late president, was a bootstrap school. It had been established by members of the Sixty-Second US Colored Infantry after the Civil War, and its aims were simple: to educate free Black people in Missouri through some combination of work and study. It became a state institution in 1879 when the state bought the deed to the land. And, fortuitously for both the state, which did not want to educate Black and white students together, and the school, it became a land-grant institution when the Second Morrill Act became law. Lincoln became a proper university when Walthall Moore, the first Black person to serve in the Missouri legislature, introduced a bill in 1921 to make it so; the bill also established a board of curators for the college.

Gaines thrived at Lincoln, from which he would graduate in August 1935. He was an honor student and served as president of the senior class. An undergraduate degree was just the first stop, though—he wanted to be a lawyer. In fact, he would later say that he had wanted to pursue a career as a lawyer "long before finishing high school." There were no law schools in the state of Missouri that accepted Black students; the flagship state college, the University of Missouri, had never accepted a Black student into any of its programs. Instead, Missouri was one of several states that employed a workaround to comply with the doctrine of separate but equal.

Rather than create a law school or a medical school for Black students, southern states would pay to send "qualified" students to another state to study. In his case, Gaines could have taken the money the state was offering and applied to the law schools in Iowa, Nebraska, or Kansas, but he wanted to practice—and to study law—in Missouri as a matter of principle. It was closer to family, and the lack of any substantial savings would have made it difficult for him to attend an out-of-state institution and afford it, despite the money the state would offer. Money had been an issue that dogged Gaines throughout his time at Lincoln. In February of his senior year, he wrote to his brother George of his financial struggles, noting that he had borrowed money for registration, and that he intended to wait until the middle of March to buy the rest of his books. He asked George for five dollars, "if you can spare it."

On top of his practical concerns about going elsewhere for law school, he would later write in an autobiography for the NAACP, "I don't think I would like to practice law in a state that denies me the legal training necessary for that practice." He would be able to better learn the ins and outs of Missouri law at a law school in Missouri. Saint Louis was something of a focal point of civil rights law. It was where Dred Scott, an enslaved Black man, first filed a lawsuit for his freedom and the freedom of his wife and two children. That lawsuit would work its way to the Supreme Court, where Justice Roger B. Taney opined that "neither the class of persons who had been imported as slaves nor their descendants, whether they had become free or not, were then acknowledged as a part of the people" in the Declaration of Independence. The enslaved and their kin had "no rights which the white man was bound to respect," Taney wrote, so they could not have possibly been party to those freedoms. Gaines thought differently. He was a taxpayer and had the right to be educated at a public law school in Missouri. If he were not provided that education, the state would be violating the equal protection clause of the Fourteenth Amendment.

There were glaringly few Black students who received graduate education at the time. In 1934, there were 1,230 Negro lawyers and 159,375 white lawyers in the country. For every 9,667 Black people, there was one Black lawyer, compared with one white lawyer for every 695 white people. The dearth was not for lack of desire but rather for lack of opportunity—and that lack of opportunity meant that Black people were hard-pressed for justice in the courts. Some Black lawyers took the paltry statistics as a challenge. "The great cause of the Negro lawyer in the next generation must be in the South," Charles Hamilton Houston, the NAACP's first litigation director, and the dean of Howard University's law school, would say. "The law schools must send their graduates there and stand squarely behind them as they wage their fight for true equality before the law." But before these would-be lawyers could stand and wage their fight, they needed to get into the law schools.

As Gaines was completing his undergraduate study, Houston had been corresponding back and forth with luminaries in Missouri about the organization's efforts to eradicate educational inequality in the state and across the country. He wrote to the Black press, including Joseph Everett Mitchell, the editor of the *Saint Louis Argus*, one of the city's Black weekly papers. He had hoped to devise a publicity plan to help bolster a case that could challenge the inequities in the state's education system. He also corresponded with Sidney Redmond, an NAACP lawyer in Saint Louis who would ultimately lead the Gaines case. In a letter on July 15, 1935, Houston wrote to Redmond that he did not want him to find a client for the case; that would be the job of the press and other advocates. Instead, he wanted him to investigate "the exclusion of Black students from the University of Missouri" and "disclose the rotten conditions." Redmond would be paid $50 for his investigation.

Though Redmond accepted responsibility for the investigations, he expressed reservations about whether the NAACP would be able to find someone willing to challenge the state and seek to enroll at the University of Missouri. On July 18, 1935, he wrote to Houston with his apprehension. "I believe you will encounter some difficulty in getting a client and that is one matter that should not be delayed too long. Two Negroes have been lynched in Columbia," where the college was located, he wrote. Still, he added, he would keep Houston up to date on his progress.

On August 17, however, a client seemed to be on the horizon. "The president of the State Teachers' Association promised to have a Lincoln student in my office this morning who would file an application at the University of Missouri to enter the Law School," Redmond wrote to Houston. "I am still doing all I can along that line and feel hopeful of something turning up in the very near future." Lloyd Gaines ended up being the something.

Nine days later, on Tuesday, August 26, Gaines stopped by Redmond's office accompanied by one of his professors at Lincoln, Zaid D. Lenoir. Professor Lenoir had given Gaines an application, which he filled out and filed three days later.

President Charles Florence, of Lincoln, was the first public official to respond. Gaines had written to Florence for his transcript— and Florence had previously promised to aid his application however he could—but in his reply, the black college leader reminded Gaines that the state's law forbid school integration, and provided for further education in another state. Soon after, Gaines's application was formally denied. Missouri had in its constitution the "separate education of races," the registrar, Silas W. Canada, told him. According to university officials, it was the first time that a Black person had ever "formally" applied for entrance to the institution. There was precedent, they would posit, and they would not break it. Over the next several weeks, Gaines and the NAACP began building their case.

With the denial in hand, Redmond wrote to Houston: "I feel that we should be able to start action during the week of October 6."

But Houston wanted to be sure. On September 26, 1935, he again wrote to Redmond. "Please keep after Gaines and above all, check his transcript yourself in order to see that he is an A-1 qualified student," he said. "We do not want to back anybody as to whom there could be the slightest personal objection." This case was too important to mess up. Gaines had to be the perfect test.

Missouri was hardly the only state in which the NAACP was trying to find a test case, nor was the NAACP the only group suing for educational equality in state universities. The first lawsuit against segregated state higher education had been filed in North Carolina in 1933 by a pair of lawyers, Conrad O. Pearson and Cecil McCoy, who fought for Thomas Hocutt's admission to the University of North Carolina's college of pharmacy. In Virginia, a young woman was rejected because she was Black and, the state argued, "for other good and sufficient reasons not necessary to be herein enumerated." In Maryland, the NAACP had sued for the admittance of Donald Murray to the University of Maryland's law school; the state subsequently passed its own scholarship act, not too unlike the one in Missouri, to send Black students elsewhere for their graduate education. In Tennessee, a Black student had sued for acceptance into the University of Tennessee's school of pharmacy.

Those cases had not panned out the way that advocates for racial equality had hoped. Houston thought the Missouri case had the potential to succeed where those efforts had been derailed. The NAACP had the necessary documentation, the state's red lines were clearly defined, so there was little room for officials to work around a decision, but they just needed to make sure their plaintiff was perfect. Houston did not want haste to stand in the way of what he saw as the ideal case.

The state of Missouri paid to send thirty-two Black students out of state for graduate or professional education in 1935. It was one of a handful of states that sent its Black students away for school instead of educating them at home. Kentucky, for example, appropriated $5,000 to send Black students out of state for graduate school in 1936; it reduced its annual funds to Kentucky State Industrial College for Colored Persons by the same amount. Gaines abhorred the practice. On top of that, the sums were small: $11 here, $27 there. Not nearly "adequate or sufficient," Gaines's lawyers argued, "to meet the legitimate demands of Negro citizens who have desired and qualified for out-of-state training."

Backed by the NAACP, he filed a petition on January 24, 1936, in the Boone County Circuit Court in Columbia. He asked the court to overturn the university's decision and admit him to the law school. First, Gaines and his lawyers battled Silas W. Canada and the university in legal filings. Then they did so at trial.

The university argued that the Supreme Court of Missouri had been clear: Distance might be an inconvenience for Black students, but "the law does not undertake to establish a school within a given distance of anyone, white or black"; just because this problem systematically harmed Black people, then, was incidental at best. On top of that, Frank M. McDavid, the chair of the board of curators at the University of Missouri, argued during testimony that not only was the board doing what was constitutional by blocking Gaines's admission, but it was also doing a favor to the state's four-year land-grant Black college, Lincoln University, where Gaines had earned his bachelor's degree. "It would be 'most unfortunate' for the education of Negro students and for the future of Lincoln University at Jefferson City," the *Saint Louis Post-Dispatch* reported McDavid saying, "if a Negro were admitted to Missouri University."

Silas W. Canada, the registrar who had been named in the suit, however, testified that this was a double standard. The university accepted a range of different students, "Japanese, Chinese, British Indian, and Mexican," the *Post-Dispatch* reported, "but did not admit Negroes because, as he understood it, it was against the law." Ultimately, the judge in the case, Walter M. Dinwiddie, ruled against Gaines. It would cost $300 to appeal the case to a higher court.

In the meantime, Gaines began school elsewhere, studying economics at the University of Michigan, but he had a difficult time affording the cost of living. He worked as a teaching assistant and made $25 a month, which was enough to cover tuition and board, but, as he wrote to his brother George two months after the district court decision came down, he would need $10 at the beginning of each month. "I'll need that amount in order to stay in school, retain my health, and decency," he wrote.

Gaines did not often let on to the NAACP about how much stress his financial situation caused him. In a letter to Charles Houston in November 1936, Gaines wrote that the money needed for incidentals—which was being sent to him by his brother—was "not of the least concern."

The months wore on before the case arrived at the Supreme Court of Missouri in May 1937. The state was an "island of prejudice," Gaines and the NAACP argued. "On the east, north, and west, Missouri is surrounded by states which admit Negroes to the state universities without social disorder, breach of discipline or other ills," Gaines's counsel wrote in a brief. "The real question is whether Missouri will remain fettered by the past, or whether it will calmly face the future of greater civic participation for her Negro citizenry." Importantly, however, Missouri was not being pressured to accept Black people into higher education by its southern neighbor, Arkansas. So long as the South held its position on barring Black students from its institutions, even as slight of an enrollment of Black students at Missouri's colleges as that of its neighbors was too many.

Gaines's principal argument was simple, though. "No question would be raised if he were in the building as a porter or in any other menial capacity," his legal team's brief read. "The trouble is that as a student he offends the traditions of an age which is dead, and the memories of which should be dead."

As Gaines was finishing his graduate program at the University of Michigan, he learned that his team's legal argument did not sway the court. On December 9, 1937, the Supreme Court of Missouri ruled that there was "no constitutional prohibition against" segregated schools, and, as such, no issue with the University of Missouri's policy if some alternative, equal educational opportunity was provided. If Gaines really wanted to get a legal education, he could go out of state to get one. Gaines's team was beaten but not out of options. They filed for a rehearing days later; there were still "decisive questions" that were outstanding, they argued, including the fact that the university would accept foreign students but not Black students. Their request was denied. On March 1, 1938, they announced their final step: they would take the case to the US Supreme Court.

There was a gentle north wind in Washington, DC, on October 1, 1938, when the Supreme Court met to decide which cases it would be taking on. To the surprise of only those who had not been paying attention, the court agreed to review the opinion of the Missouri high court in Gaines's case. The university pushed back forcefully.

Why wouldn't Gaines just accept the funds to go out of state, the state queried in its brief. His petulance in denying the funds, its lawyers argued, "strongly suggests that his real purpose is to lend his name as litigant to those interested in furthering a movement to bring about social equality between the white and Negro races."

Gaines did not deny that he went to the NAACP after he had been rejected by the university, but in their own filing, his lawyers argued that if Gaines had wanted to accept the "opportunity open to him" for separate-but-equal facilities, he would "have had the right to call upon Lincoln University curators for an education in the law." The NAACP lawyers were pointing out a flaw in the separate-but-equal regime. For the system to work, there at least needed to be a separate offering; and the state needed to provide that offering. The out-of-state law schools could not train Gaines for a Missouri law career the way Missouri's flagship could, by studying the laws specific to the state. Their argument highlighted a legal crack in Jim Crow's edifice.

One month later, they put the theory to the test in court. During oral arguments, Richard L. Stokes, a correspondent for the *Post-Dispatch* who was covering the trial, wrote that Gaines's lawyers, Charles Hamilton Houston and Sidney Redmond, "were permitted to speak almost without interruption." The university's lawyers, however, were "subjected to searching interrogation." The chief justice took the lead in lobbing questions, poking holes in the state's arguments.

If it was "mandatory" that the state set up a law school at Lincoln, why hadn't it? Was the Black college in a financial position to sustain a law school? Did the university not have a chronic deficit? "How can you say that Negroes have equal educational opportunities in Missouri, when they are compelled to leave their own state to find such equality of professional training in other states?" Chief Justice Charles Evans Hughes, a former secretary of state, asked.

The lawyers for the university argued that Black students had the advantage over white students. In fact, they said, Black students received about $150 more a year than white students because of how the out-of-state scholarships worked.

The court was not buying their convoluted argument. "Do you mean to suggest that a pecuniary payment would be adequate compensation for loss of civil rights?" Justice Hugo Black, a former member of the Ku Klux Klan, asked.

The newspapers rightly characterized the defense's argument as disjointed, but they also consistently painted Houston's as emotional. The *Post-Dispatch* noted that though his argument was "dignified and restrained," it had an "undercurrent of emotion." Still, it was airtight. The University of Missouri had the only taxpayer-supported law school in the state. Gaines was a taxpaying citizen and, as a citizen, he was guaranteed equal protection of the law. His rejection at the law school was a denial of those rights. On top of that, Houston argued, "Missouri University has admitted . . . every race save its own Negro citizens. My client has applied for admission under a triple handicap—he belonged to the wrong race, the wrong class, the wrong section."

The court did not need long to deliberate. In December, one month after hearing oral arguments, the court issued its opinion. By a 6–2 vote, the Supreme Court found that by shipping them out of state for graduate and professional school the state was in violation of its duty to protect its citizens. The NAACP had convinced the court. The state was required to provide an equal educational opportunity itself—it could not pass off its responsibility to someone else.

Chief Justice Hughes's opinion, however, did not take issue with the *separate* clause of separate, but equal. "We are of the opinion," he wrote, "that petitioner was entitled to be admitted to the law school of the state university in the absence of any other training in the state." In other words, so long as the state did not have a law school at Lincoln University or anywhere else for the sole education of Black people, it must admit them to the University of Missouri.

Gaines, who had been working in Michigan for the State of Michigan Civil Service Department, left his desk job and returned to Missouri. He planned to enroll at the University of Missouri Law School but suggested that he would prefer a law department to be created at Lincoln University. This configuration would end the fight with a victory sooner and establish a law school in Missouri that allowed him to get on with studying—on with his life. The NAACP had a more systemic plan, though. Simply installing separate programs in each state was not enough. There were 125 students who were receiving tuition from Missouri for graduate study out of state at the time. They were studying medicine and law and journalism and veterinary science, none of which were offered at Lincoln as graduate programs. The university that the state was arguing was equal was not, and there were more than a dozen states across the country similarly situated.

Missouri asked for a rehearing at the US Supreme Court, but it was denied. The Supreme Court added that six other states that had a similar dearth of programs for Black students "will be compelled either to admit Negroes to sit with white boys and girls in their state universities or to build separate Negro universities."

At the beginning of March, the state supreme court placed the Gaines case on its docket for May 1939, where the court was expected to conform with the high court's decision. But before the case could be heard in state court, John D. Taylor, a state representative from Keytesville, Missouri, introduced a bill that would create a spate of graduate classes at Lincoln University. The bill would, ostensibly, offer any courses at Lincoln that were available at the University of Missouri.

Hundreds of Black people protested the measure. They crammed into the Senate committee hearing after the bill passed with overwhelming support in the lower chamber. "It's just an attempt to keep negroes out of the University of Missouri despite the federal court order that they must be admitted," John A. Davis, a Black lawyer from Saint Louis, argued. But the Supreme Court had left the door open to exactly this sort of measure. It did not stipulate that Gaines had to be admitted to the University of Missouri, full stop. Instead, it argued that he must be admitted if there *were no other options in the state*. The court was, knowingly or unknowingly, telling southern states that trafficked in segregation to create the segregated space.

The bill, which was framed in the press as a "bill to raise L.U. standards" passed the Senate by a 25–6 margin. The state would create graduate programs for Black students at Lincoln to "iron out" the differences in the Supreme Court's mandate and keep "with Missouri's traditional policy of separate education," said State Senator William B. Whitlow. The bill would somehow make these programs equal to those at the University of Missouri, which had already spent ninety years developing its courses (funding for the university's programs had been established, in part, through the Morrill Act).

One state senator, Michael Kinney, a Democrat from Saint Louis, argued that such a feat would be impossible "without a staggering financial burden." He acknowledged the elephant: the state had been underserving Lincoln University for so long that it would take significant financial recompense to fix the issues. "It will inevitably be some time before the equality which this bill proposes could possibly be achieved."

Meanwhile, Gaines, who had been fighting his case now for four years, was struggling financially, and was uncertain what, exactly, his future would hold, wrote to his mother, Callie. "I have come to Chicago hoping to find it possible to make my own way," he wrote. "I hope that by this letter I shall make very clear the reasons for such a step."

The company that he had been working for, he said, practiced illegal "tricks of the trade" that he would have become involved in had he stayed. The company was selling shoddy gasoline, and he had to pay for his own coal out of his paltry wages. He worked twelve hours a day, seven days a week, which meant little time for a social life or to commiserate with his business contacts. Unable to find another job, he had left Missouri. He did not want to be a financial burden on his family anymore.

He worried that he himself was the cause of his unemployment. "As for my publicity relative to the university case, I have found my race still likes to applaud, shake hands, pat me on the back and say how great and noble is the idea; how historical and socially important the case," he wrote. "I am just a man—not one who had fought and sacrificed to make the case possible; one who is still fighting and sacrificing—almost the 'supreme sacrifice' to see that it is a complete and lasting success for thirteen million Negroes—NO!—just another man." His letter was solemn, with a sense of regret. "Sometimes I wish I were just a plain, ordinary man whose name no one recognized."

It is easy to forget that the names attached to historic fights bear the brunt of the battles' weight. Gaines had just come from a pair of speeches; one drew a capacity crowd of 1,400 people. During another speech at Sumner High School, in Kansas City, he spoke about "choosing and achieving your purpose in life," even as he had been doubting his own.

"I haven't been able to dig up a single job prospect," he wrote to his mother. "Should I forget to write for a time don't worry about it, I can look after myself ok.

"As ever, Lloyd."

When Houston went back before the Supreme Court of Missouri on May 22 to press the justices to force the University of Missouri to admit Gaines, he assailed the Taylor bill, which had, by then, been signed into law by the governor. It was a "subterfuge in violation of the spirit at least of the Supreme Court ruling," he argued.

The university's lawyer, William Hogsett, disagreed. It was exactly what the Supreme Court had asked them to do, "because it in fact does provide equal educational opportunities for the Negroes." One month later, on June 30, the board of curators at Lincoln University announced that the institution would have its law school—on par with the University of Missouri's—established by the beginning of the fall term, when Gaines was expected to enroll at the University of Missouri's law school. The board estimated that it would take three months to establish a law school equal to one that had been around for sixty-six years—before Lincoln University itself had been founded.

The state supreme court reversed its prior decision in compliance with the US Supreme Court on August 1. Gaines must be admitted to the University of Missouri if the newly created school at Lincoln was of not of equal stature, the court ruled. Justice Caleb A. Leedy, who wrote the court's new opinion, directed the Boone County Circuit Court to examine whether the machinery set up at Lincoln was on par with that at the flagship university. The same judge who had ruled three years earlier, in 1936, that Gaines should have just gone out of state for college would now be deciding whether a hastily established law school was sufficient for him to attend.

The state selected a location, the old Poro College building, for the law school in mid-August, hired a dean, and suggested that classes begin on September 20. The new dean, Louis E. Taylor, had been on the law faculty at Howard University, and took a leave to start the department at Lincoln. The legislature had appropriated $200,000 to establish the law school.

But when classes began, Gaines had disappeared. "An intensive drive has been made to locate Gaines but to no avail," Redmond wrote to Houston on September 30. He had last been seen leaving his apartment in Chicago, which was not unusual, because he had been known to sneak off on his own.

The NAACP needed to take Gaines's deposition before the Boone County court decided whether Lincoln's law school was equal to the University of Missouri's. They asked the national press to try to help locate Gaines. Rumors began swirling. Some thought he had been taken in the night by racists upset with his victory at the Supreme Court, while others suggested he had been spotted in New York City teaching in a schoolhouse.

The most fantastical theory was that he had been bribed to disappear to Mexico City. Someone at the recently established law school claimed he had received a letter from Gaines, postmarked in Mexico, "stating that he was having 'a jolly time on the Two Thousand Dollars he had been given to leave the country.'" The letter was never proved to be from Gaines. His family asked federal agents to investigate his disappearance, but they never did.

On October 11, the *Saint Louis Globe-Democrat* reported that the NAACP had not heard from Gaines for the last four to five months. It was a remarkable admission, because even as the NAACP had been arguing his cause in court, they had not been in contact with him—even as they knew of his financial pressures, and the pressure he himself had felt in continuing with the case. Two days later, Redmond announced that Lucile Bluford, a Black student who had applied to the University of Missouri's journalism program, would sue for admission.

Bluford had submitted her application following Gaines's victory at the Supreme Court. Her application had been accepted, but when she went to register, she was refused because of her race. Bluford had been out of school for more than a year and a half since applying to Missouri, though the state had promised to create a school of journalism at Lincoln University in which she could enroll. Counsel for the NAACP was flummoxed about her case. "I cannot see for the life of me how Lincoln University can establish a school of journalism after September 30 equal to the School of Journalism of the University of Missouri when the University of Missouri is already open," Thurgood Marshall, the NAACP lawyer who represented Donald Murray in the University of Maryland case, argued.

By December, the NAACP began to come to grips with the fact that it might not find Gaines. Charles Hamilton Houston was resigned when he wrote to Sidney Redmond two days after Christmas. "Since we cannot find Gaines we cannot go on," he said. "But I think we should leave on record an exact statement of our position so that in the future people may know exactly why we did not proceed." Gaines was lost to history, but the movement had to continue. To the NAACP, it was a tragedy for educational equality; to Gaines's family, it was quite simply a tragedy. A loved one had disappeared.

In March 1940, a year after the NAACP had last heard from Gaines, it put out another request for information about his whereabouts, to no avail.

The last communication Lloyd Gaines had with his family was the distressed letter he wrote to his mother. "*I am just a man*." The struggle had made the last few years of Lloyd Gaines's life unthinkably difficult. But the fight for educational equality continued with his name attached at every step.

It would be another decade before a victory as significant as his own was again won at the Supreme Court.

CHAPTER 5

A New Guinea Pig

The lawyers at the NAACP were living the same story over and over ever since the disappearance of Lloyd Gaines. They would find a client, argue their case, win a small victory, and then have to do it all over again. After *Gaines v. Canada*, they were waiting for another case that would take them back to the US Supreme Court. Then, in 1945, their quest to erase educational injustice found them in Oklahoma, with a young woman who had a big dream.

Ada Lois Sipuel Fisher was five when Oklahoma had its last documented lynching, but even as a grown woman, six decades later, the memory constantly ran through her mind. The Washita River runs a diagonal path from the Texas panhandle, cutting southwest through Oklahoma and back. On the last day of May 1930, Henry Argo, a nineteen-year-old resident of Chickasha, Oklahoma, was fishing along the river's muddy banks early in the morning. By five o'clock that afternoon, he was in jail.

A white woman, Angie Skinner, claimed that Argo brutally assaulted her and attempted to strangle her nineteen-month-old son. The baby showed no signs of being harmed. Argo insisted he did no such thing. Skinner's neighbors—also white—said they saw no signs of distress or physical harm. But none of the evidence supporting the idea that Argo was innocent mattered at the time. A white woman had accused a Black man of rape. Argo was arrested. Word spread quickly.

Within hours, as many as two thousand men had assembled outside the jail. They took sledgehammers, crowbars, and battering rams to the jail's walls, furiously trying to get their hands on Argo. The National Guard was ordered to the scene around nine o'clock that evening, but they fled when the posse grew out of control. The guard took all the prisoners with them as they left—all the prisoners except for Henry Argo. The crazed mob beat relentlessly at a concrete wall on the side of the jail. They chiseled away until the hole was big enough to see Argo, but the cavity was not quite big enough for a person to fit through, so someone shot into the cell. The bullet struck Argo in the head and drove down into his neck—but the mob was not finished.

George Skinner, the husband of the woman who claimed she was assaulted, was among those who continued to hammer away at the wall until, by morning, it was wide enough for people to climb through. Once inside, Skinner took a knife to Argo's chest. A single blow, right over his heart. Then Skinner went back outside and collapsed, presumably from exhaustion. Argo lay dying; Skinner was taken to the hospital. Argo died three hours later.

Sipuel—Lois, as her friends called her—remembered the lynching of Henry Argo for the rest of her life, even recounting it in her memoir. Those who murdered a man were never charged with a crime, despite the near-universal knowledge of who killed him. It was a pivotal moment for the future lawyer—and the woman who, in 1948, would be the next student to go to the Supreme Court to fight to desegregate classrooms.

Sipuel was born in Chickasha, in southwest Oklahoma, on February 8, 1924, two years before Lloyd Gaines migrated north with his family. Her parents had moved to the segregated town, which was experiencing a population boom, after the Tulsa race riots of 1921, when white mobs tore through one of the most prominent centers for Black business in America, called Black Wall Street, and murdered dozens of Black people. From the beginning, people could tell Sipuel was smart, but they would be hard pressed to get her to admit it— she admired her brother, Lemuel, who she argued was even smarter.

She had moxie—what she would later describe to her son as a "smart mouth"—one that got her into trouble in school and earned her more than one ticket to the office of Robert Goodwin Parrish, the principal of her segregated school. Parrish was a tall, well-groomed man with a glint of gray streaking his hair. "He was a forceful, highly gifted, effective speaker and a superb teacher," Sipuel recalled. When she was sent to his office, he would redirect her frustration. There was never any paddling in the principal's office, as was common then. Instead, the two would talk. They would engage and argue on just about anything. He and other teachers took note of her deftness for debate and helped her channel that "smart mouth" into a place on the debate team.

When Sipuel was in middle school, Dr. W. A. J. Bullock, the family's physician, founded the local chapter of the NAACP. Bullock, a respected businessman who was popular with white civic leaders, was a liaison between the Black and white communities in Chickasha, particularly after the lynching of Henry Argo. He was an activist at heart, though, and in the nascent days of the town's NAACP chapter, he brought a national representative from the organization to speak at a local school about the fight for equality: Thurgood Marshall. The prominent man was the second Black lawyer Sipuel had met (one of her cousins had become a lawyer as well) and was "the most handsome, articulate, brilliant, and charismatic man" she had ever seen. It was a chance encounter, but it was not the last time the two would cross paths.

She graduated high school in 1941 as the valedictorian of her class. She was on the debate team and played the trumpet; she also played basketball and sang in the choir. She had the kind of robust portfolio that parents nowadays carefully craft to get their kids into Harvard. And she owed that to both her parents and her teachers, who made all the students at the school feel special, even though schools were segregated. All her classmates believed they could conquer the world thanks to their teachers, Sipuel later said, despite a "tragically separate" upbringing.

But Harvard was not on her radar—though it likely could have been if she were of another race and gender. The college did not accept women, though its sister campus, Radcliffe, did, in exceedingly small numbers. Harvard itself admitted fewer than twelve Black students each year. The students who were accepted to the university were often assigned rooms with the other Black students.

None of the major colleges in the South were on Sipuel's radar either. Jim Crow was the law of the land, and segregation was his defense attorney. Sipuel instead made her way across state lines to Arkansas, where she attended Arkansas A&M, one of the colleges for Black students established under the Morrill Act. Her tenure there did not last long. After one year, the distance from home became too much. She had started dating Warren Fisher, her brother's friend, with a lanky build, chestnut-brown skin, and striking bone structure. She wanted to be closer to him, too.

Returning home meant limited education options for Sipuel— she could not go to any of the white colleges in the state. The Oklahoma laws were clear: "No coeducational institution for the two races may be operated"; "No instructor shall teach in any such school"; "No white person shall attend such school." It was not unlike Missouri or any of the other states across the South. The only Black college in the state was Langston University, which was built using funds from the Second Morrill Act.

Langston is situated atop a hill in Logan County, a few miles from the county seat of Guthrie. The town was founded as a majority-Black city in 1889 and was named for the Black congressman from

Virginia, John Mercer Langston, who served during Reconstruction. It received a near-instant jolt in 1897 when the territorial legislature devoted a portion of its Morrill Act funds to build a "colored" agricultural and mechanical school there as a separate college for Black people—equal in name only.

Warren Fisher had attended Langston before joining the army; deciding to come home would mean Sipuel would finish her college career at Langston—so, that is what she did.

Sipuel's time at Langston was a mixed bag: she had fantastic, caring professors, but the school's physical facilities were subpar. That was not a coincidence. Much like other historically Black colleges and universities across the country, Langston had been underfunded since its founding: the facilities for students were inferior (and deteriorating); the buildings were in desperate need of renovation; the science equipment required upgrades; the green spaces would flood and just would not drain right. Then there were the things the town lacked, most notably a fire station.

Still, Black colleges of the time were not to be looked at as deficient institutions, as they provided students with opportunities to learn where others did not. As training grounds for doctors, businesspeople, lawyers, and teachers, these institutions were building up the Black middle class. They also provided those students with a *second curriculum*: the knowledge of how to navigate America's racial caste system.

By her junior year, after a fierce rainy season in 1944, Lois and a group of students decided they had reached their wit's end with the soggy state of the campus. They sneaked into the university president's office because they did not have any money to place a phone call, and called Senator Louis H. Ritzhaupt, a physician and state lawmaker whose district included the university, for help. They wanted to set up a meeting with Ritzhaupt at his office, but instead, he told them he would come to the campus himself the next day.

The administration was, understandably, a bit peeved when they found out what the motley crew of students had done, and they summoned them to a meeting with top university officials. The senator was a "friend of the university," the students were told. It would behoove them—and be in the institution's best interest—to be courteous at the meeting with Ritzhaupt. Sipuel worried that if she or any of the other students at the meeting made a misstep, they would be suspended—or even worse, expelled. "I started praying," she recalled. "Dear God, please let it rain tomorrow. We need lots of mud when the good senator arrives."

It did not rain that day. The senator came and the students had a frank and courteous meeting with him. His assessment: yes, there were improvements to be made, but the facilities and funding at the institution were adequate. This was not an uncommon response from legislators during segregation. If only it had rained.

Sipuel and her classmates reached out to Roscoe Dunjee, the editor of the *Black Dispatch*, a Black-owned news outlet, shortly after they were let down by Ritzhaupt. Dunjee, who doubled as an Oklahoma civil rights leader, had been one of the very first students to attend Langston after its founding and understood firsthand the issues that the university faced; he listened to the students' concerns intently. The students left their conversation with him encouraged— excited to be involved in the fight.

Sipuel married Warren in March of her junior year and graduated from Langston a year later, in May 1945. She moved back home to Chickasha, where she started combing through law school catalogs. There was Northwestern University, a predominantly white institution just outside Chicago; each year, northern institutions like Northwestern would enroll a handful of Black students, but never in statistically significant numbers. Then there was Howard University, the historically Black college in Washington, DC, where Charles Hamilton Houston had transformed a last-resort law school into a powerhouse. Perhaps she could become the next Thurgood Marshall there, she thought. She had family members who were lawyers, so it did not seem far-fetched. But she also had an eye toward righting wrongs, recalling the way Henry Argo had been brutally murdered and left without justice.

One morning that fall, Dr. W. A. J. Bullock, the regional director of the NAACP, called Sipuel's mother and asked to speak with the family. He wanted to make sure Lemuel was there as well— Lois's older brother had graduated from Langston a few years before her and was sent to fight in World War II. Dr. Bullock had a project he was working on, and Lemuel, who had returned from the war, seemed like the right person for the job. Sipuel's mother obliged, and Dr. Bullock stopped by that evening. Lois happened to be around, so she sat in on the conversation as well.

Back in September, Dr. Bullock told the family, the Oklahoma state NAACP had heard Thurgood Marshall explain his strategy for challenging segregated schools. The Gaines case had established that states had to provide a separate option for Black students at the very least, even if that option was not equal. If the state was not providing that separate option, then they could not deny a qualified Black citizen's right to attend a "white" institution. Oklahoma had a state-supported law school in Norman, at the University of Oklahoma, but Black students could not go there—they could go only to Langston University, the Black college with no law school.

Lemuel, Bullock told the family, had all the right stuff to apply to the University of Oklahoma to make the challenge anew. He had a 4.0 grade point average, was on the honor roll, and, having served in the war, he was accustomed to taking on a fight. But that war had also taught Lemuel that he was not ready to be pulled away from home, physically or mentally. His education had already been interrupted for three years, and legal battles like the one Bullock and the NAACP were proposing were knock-down, drag-out fights—the Gaines case, and his ultimate disappearance, had made the stakes painfully clear.

Then someone suggested Lois, though she could not quite

remember who. She was smart, her dad noted—and younger than Lemuel, her mom added. Dr. Bullock turned to her to ask whether she'd be interested in carrying the weight of the battle.

"Yes," she quickly replied.

There was still one more hurdle to clear before she could officially become the person who would try to integrate the University of Oklahoma, though. She had to be vetted by Roscoe Dunjee, the president of the state conference of the NAACP branches, whom she had spoken with while at Langston. Other chapters of the NAACP had also been trying to identify students who could successfully carry the lawsuit, and Dunjee had to make sure Sipuel was the right person.

Dunjee had built two cases that had made it to the US Supreme Court in the past. One case, *Hollins v. Oklahoma*, guaranteed Black people the right to a trial by a jury of their peers, and a new trial if Black people had been excluded from the jury simply because of their race. In the other case, *Guinn v. United States*, the court found Oklahoma's grandfather clauses, which restricted Black people's right to vote, and literacy tests, unconstitutional.

Ten days after the meeting with Dr. Bullock at her home, Sipuel carried that same thrill she had experienced meeting Dunjee the first time. Armed with her high school and college transcripts, she and Bullock set off to Oklahoma City. Dunjee's office was on a street "bustling with black business," near a barbershop, cleaner, tailor, and dance hall.

In the meeting, as Dunjee studied Sipuel's academic record, Bullock added that her father was a minister and her husband was in the military. Warren was overseas at the time, Sipuel told him, but he was ready to support her however he needed to. Good, Dunjee told her, as that meant there would be no economic pressure on her to give up the case. Would Sipuel have the "necessary courage and patience" to take this on, he asked?

"Yes. Yes. Oh, yes," she remembered thinking.

Dunjee was sold, but it would be another week before Dr. Bullock would call Lois with the good news: Sipuel would be the person to integrate the University of Oklahoma's law school. There were only roughly one thousand women in American Bar Association–accredited law schools across the country; they planned to make Sipuel one of them. He informed her that the three of them—Lois, Dunjee, and himself—would be traveling to Norman, to the main campus of the University of Oklahoma, in a few weeks.

Weeks turned into months, however, before the time came for Sipuel to apply for admission to the University of Oklahoma College of Law. It was a frigid day in January 1946 when the trio loaded up the car to head south on US 77 to Norman for their meeting with Dr. George L. Cross, the university's president.

"Girlie, are you nervous?" Sipuel recalls Dunjee asking her before they met the president.

"Yes, a little anxious and apprehensive," she said.

"Well, that's natural," Dunjee replied, "but I imagine the students and officials at the university will be more nervous than you when they find out why we're here."

Dr. Cross, a clean-shaven white man with slicked hair and a square jaw, was cordial when he greeted the group. The day before, Dunjee told the president that he would be down that day to discuss "a business matter," but not much else. After introducing Bullock and Lois, Dunjee told the president that they sought admission into the law school for Sipuel. They were not asking for a handout; Lois had impeccable credentials. She was an honor roll student at Langston, the daughter of a prominent minister, and would commute to campus daily from Oklahoma City. Norman was a sundown town, the kind where there was an unwritten rule that Black people could not stay after dark—if they were caught, they risked being lynched.

Cross handed the transcript to his staff assembled around the room. There was no question: Sipuel had the credentials to get in. But there was a key thing she lacked: white skin. And that brought Cross to the decision he said he was required to make by state law.

He dictated her denial, which was typed onto university letterhead:

> Dr. Roy Gittinger, dean of admissions, has examined your transcript from Langston University and finds that you are scholastically qualified for admission to the law school of the University of Oklahoma.
>
> However, I must deny you admission for the following reasons:
>
> 1. Title 70, sections 452 to 464, inclusive, of the Oklahoma Statutes 1941, prohibits colored students from attending the schools of Oklahoma, including the University of Oklahoma, and makes it a misdemeanor for school officials to admit colored students to white schools; to instruct classes composed of mixed races; to attend classes composed of mixed races.
> 2. The Board of Regents has specifically instructed the president of the University of Oklahoma to refuse admissions to Negroes, giving as a basis of their decision, the Statutes of Oklahoma.

That written denial was exactly what they needed. It was proof that she was being denied a legal education solely because of her race—and that there was discriminatory legislation to back up the refusal. They all shook hands and exited the room. Sipuel was surprised by the photographers who had gathered outside the building to capture the moment. Dunjee announced to the gathered press that they would be filing a lawsuit seeking her admission to the school.

Sipuel was a qualified student, and the state had a constitutional obligation to provide her with a legal education.

Then came the waiting. The national branch of the NAACP had been tied up with several other cases and Thurgood Marshall and Robert L. Carter, the lawyers who would be trying the Sipuel case in Oklahoma, were married to those suits. First, Thurgood was supposed to come to Oklahoma to prepare the case filing on February 15, 1946, but he sent Carter instead. Carter, who was number two in command in the NAACP's legal office, was then called back to work on the Irene Morgan case, which opposed racial segregation in public facilities in Virginia.

The waiting game made Dunjee nervous. Sipuel was a "natural," and this could be the perfect case they had been looking for. He knew the potential consequences if this sort of case dragged out for too long. "Delay develops [*sic*] a number of troubles one would not dream about," Dunjee wrote to Marshall on March 13. "I would not like this to be another Lloyd Gaines case before we get in court."

But Marshall was still unable to come to Oklahoma despite Dunjee's pleadings—the war for racial equality was multipronged, and its leaders could not be everywhere at once, often to the disappointment of those waging battles on the ground. The Irene Morgan case was at the US Supreme Court and "the Supreme Court takes no excuse other than sudden death" for delaying. Marshall could not run the risk that he would not be back in time to argue that case.

Dunjee asked Marshall to airmail the petition so that they could file it in court. There had been murmurs that the case was dying, and he did not want those whispers to grow into screams. Carter sent the petition to Dunjee on March 22, 1946. On April 7, backed by the NAACP, Amos T. Hall, a Black civil rights lawyer in Oklahoma who had been working on Sipuel's case, filed the petition, hoping the court would force the University of Oklahoma to accept Lois into its law school. Ben Williams, the Cleveland County district judge who would hear the case, set arguments for April 26, but he postponed the hearing for another month when the state's attorney general, Mac Q. Williamson, and then Fred Hansen, the assistant attorney general, joined the case.

The case was delayed again and again until, finally, in July 1946, Williams heard oral arguments. Thurgood Marshall was ill, and Robert Carter was unable to find a flight into the city. It was up to Amos Hall to argue the case.

"We have appealed through the legislature and the state board of regents year after year to no avail," Hall told the court. Not even a Supreme Court decision in *Gaines* had led the state of Oklahoma to set up a law school for Black students. Instead, Oklahoma was still sending its Black graduate and professional students out of state. The conditions at Langston were "deplorable," he added, and the "measly $15,000" appropriation to send students out of state did not represent educational equity.

The state, which had barred interracial education twelve years before the law school had been founded, in 1909, argued that the court could not force the university to accept Lois, even if it had not been fair to its Black citizens. If the court were to do so, it would place university officials in direct violation of the state's laws. In addition, the state argued, if a Black student wanted a legal education, the state would be willing to provide it. The student would simply have to wait for the infrastructure to be set up. It would have been wasteful, Hansen's logic went, to set up a separate facility for Black students that sat empty.

"They haven't even brought Langston up to an accredited college standard," Hall rebutted. "How do you expect them to set up a law school? The state admits that the regents have no money to establish a law school for Negroes." Besides, the cost of setting up the school was not the Black citizens' problem. "We did not impose upon ourselves this system of dual education," Hall proclaimed. "You placed it on us and if it is expensive it is not our fault."

Judge Williams was not persuaded. He denied the motion to force the university to enroll Sipuel. He agreed with Hansen that university officials should not be directed to break state laws. It was up to the legislature to fix it, the same legislature that had been underfunding its Black college and barring Black students from attending its "white" colleges. This case was as much about forcing Sipuel's enrollment as it was about changing public policy so that her enrollment did not have to be forced. Sipuel and her lawyers appealed to the Supreme Court of Oklahoma.

Over the next two years, Sipuel made several attempts to enroll at the University of Oklahoma College of Law, even as white newspapers questioned the seriousness of her attempt. This had become something of a habit that white newspapermen had taken on. When Black students would seek to enroll in colleges, white journalists would argue that such people were simply lending their names to the cause of social equality and, ultimately, interracial marriage. That argument reared its head time and again from the founding of Berea College on through integration.

Amos Hall traveled to New York City on October 23, 1946, to meet with Robert Carter and Thurgood Marshall to discuss Sipuel's case. The group needed to make sure their arguments were ironclad, and it would be more easily achieved if they conferred in person.

When they filed their brief in early December 1946, they were uncompromising. Equal, segregated education—such as was the law in seventeen states and Washington, DC—was a "legal fiction and judicial myth." They asked the state supreme court to do what the circuit court had failed to: force the university to admit Sipuel into its law school.

The state was equally as forceful in its response. They believed that the failure of Sipuel's legal team to petition the regents to create a law school at Langston was evidence of nefarious intent. "Plaintiff's position here is essentially an attack on the whole policy of segregation," they bemoaned.

When the state's high court heard oral arguments in early March 1947, Hall rebutted the argument that their case was an attack on separate schooling. "The only thing we say is that she is entitled to equal education opportunity," he argued. The state had a legal right under the constitution to separate races, but the races had to be guaranteed equal treatment. Justice Earl Welch then asked Hall whether he believed a law school should have been set up for Black people when one was established for white people. Hall answered affirmatively. "Perhaps it would be expensive to establish a school offering equal opportunities to our people, but separation is a condition established by the state and one for which we did not ask," he said, reiterating his argument from the Cleveland County District Court. Black people were being punished for a prejudice not of their own doing.

The state continued to contend that separation was the law, and that university officials should not be forced to deviate from that law. One month later, the state supreme court agreed, but it implored the state to set up a law school for Black students if one was requested. It also argued, citing the *Gaines* case, that just because the state paid to send Black students out of state for graduate and professional education, it "does not necessarily discharge the state's duty to its Negro citizens," as the opinion read. "Negro students have an equal right to receive their law school training within the state if they prefer it." The court also argued that this case was fundamentally different from the Gaines case. In Gaines's case, the request for a legal education in a separate school could have been furnished. In the Sipuel case, education of Lois at a "white school" could not be done legally. Roscoe Dunjee vowed that the case would be appealed to the US Supreme Court as soon as possible.

On Monday, November 10, 1947, Dunjee and Sipuel's lawyers got what they wanted: the Supreme Court of the United States agreed to take on the case. Sipuel's lawyers argued that it was the "unquestioned duty" of the state to provide equal educational facilities for

Black and white students. It was not doing so, and the Supreme Court needed to address that fact. In the meantime, Roscoe Dunjee was doing everything he could to prevent what could potentially be bad press and urged students at Langston not to hold rallies for the case.

When thirteen white students from the University of Oklahoma were invited to Langston for a discussion about the conditions at the Black college and integration, they arrived to poor weather. The *Daily Oklahoman* reported that after the meeting, the visitors from Norman, "had no trouble understanding Langston's plea for paved streets. A hard rain was falling, and the students bogged down to their ankles in the gumbo mud of the campus." It was not difficult to see the disparity.

Letters began pouring into the offices of the NAACP with advice for how they should argue the case. Milton R. Konvitz, an associate professor at Cornell University, suggested to Thurgood Marshall that he use statistics and statements from the recently released report by the Truman Commission detailing discrimination in higher education. Twenty-four of the twenty-eight members of the commission had agreed that segregation by law should be abolished.

The six-volume report, which had been commissioned by President Harry Truman in 1946, marked the first time in the nation's history that the president ordered the nation's educational infrastructure to be analyzed. What it uncovered was staggering. Black adults over twenty-five years old averaged only 5.7 years of education, while white adults born in the United States averaged 8.8 years. Eighty-two percent of white adults had completed seventh grade; 36 percent of Black adults had. College attainment levels across the board were lackluster, but, again, white adults did significantly better than Black adults, and were four times more likely to have a four-year college degree. In 1947, 75,000 Black students were enrolled in higher education out of more than 2,300,000 students at America's colleges. "Of these, approximately 85 percent were enrolled in 105 segregated institutions," the report said.

The commission also took issue with the differences in spending on Black and white students at both public and private colleges. "The ratio of expenditures of institutions for whites to those of institutions for Negroes ranged from 3 to 1 in the District of Columbia to 42 to 1 in Kentucky," they wrote. "And nowhere in the area, except in the District of Columbia, did there appear a single institution that approximated the undergraduate, graduate, and professional offerings characteristic of a first-class State university." The report was the government admitting the obvious: higher education was failing Black students, and it was a national problem. "Denial of professional education to Negroes affects our already scarce resources for research." The government, however, was slow to act on any of the report's recommendations.

Sipuel's case arrived at the Supreme Court on January 8, 1948, and, as the *Daily Oklahoman* reported, it was a scene to behold. "United States Supreme Court justices Thursday ripped attorneys for the state of Oklahoma with a running fire of hostile questions as they defended refusal of the University of Oklahoma to admit a Negro girl, Ada Lois Sipuel, to its law school," Cullen Johnson, a Washington correspondent for the paper, wrote. The court asked only three questions of Marshall and Hall. "The critical questioning," Johnson wrote, "had seldom been duplicated in the court's austere chambers."

In one exchange, Justice Robert H. Jackson dug into Fred Hansen, the attorney for the state. "There is a way that a negro applicant can get equal facilities—by applying to the board of regents for higher education," Hansen said.

"Can she get them now?" Jackson asked. "If she can, I should think this case would be at an end."

Hansen clarified his remark. "I'm not saying that it could be done tomorrow or the next day, but it would be the duty of the board promptly to open up a law school at the Negro college."

Jackson was not sold. "How can we possibly say that is equal opportunity today?"

"We have the machinery which she can use," Hansen responded. Jackson was baffled. "You argue it, but I don't see it."

Stating the obvious, Justice William O. Douglas added that "she might be an old lady by the time you got the machinery working."

The court's opinion came quickly. The decision was just one page long and clear. The state, the court said, had violated Sipuel's rights under the equal protection clause of the Fourteenth Amendment; Oklahoma was required to provide her a legal education as soon as it did for any other, white students. It was a week before the second semester at the University of Oklahoma was set to begin, and Sipuel had won.

The opinion, not unlike the decision in the Gaines case, did not mention segregation and the state's law prohibiting Black and white students from being educated together. "The Sipuel decision wasn't as definitive as we'd hoped," Sipuel later said. And the state seized on that fact to try to find a workaround quickly. In effect, the decision reinforced what the courts had decided during the Gaines case: It was the state's responsibility to provide an equal alternative in the state. If it did not, it was in violation of the law. However, most people were under the assumption that the decision had come down too close to the new semester for the state to be able to marshal the resources to erect a law school at Langston. "State Told to Provide Equal Facilities Before Next Semester; Time Too Short For Creation of Separate Institution," the *Oklahoman* subheadline read.

"The Monday decision is thrilling," Dunjee wrote to Marshall. "I do not know how to express myself I am so delighted over the results." Still, he was worried that the state would try to set up a makeshift law school at Langston to keep Black students out of the predominantly white institutions. Oklahoma had fought so hard for so many decades to prevent interracial education and was not going to back down easily.

On January 21, 1948, five days before the scheduled beginning of midyear enrollment at the University of Oklahoma College of

Law, the state regents for higher education in Oklahoma moved to do just that: they planned to establish the Langston University School of Law. It would be a law school located in the state capitol and be specifically designed for Black students. The government would turn several of the committee rooms on the fourth floor of the capitol building into classrooms. Then, on January 24, the regents announced the appointment of faculty members: Jerome Hemry, a practicing lawyer with two decades of experience; Randell Cobb, a former state attorney general; and Arthur Ellsworth, a thirty-year-old attorney. They were hired part time for what would be full-time work. Each instructor would continue his private practice, state officials said.

This was an esteemed faculty. Frank Buttram, an Oklahoma City millionaire who served on the board, declared, "We are serious when we say . . . we have set up an equal [school with] . . . even better facilities than the average student at the University of Oklahoma [has]." The school would be operational in two days, he said, and it would compete with the University of Oklahoma College of Law, which had opened its doors in 1909.

Sipuel prepared to head to Norman to enroll at the University of Oklahoma on January 25, but she was told that she was to head to the Langston law school instead at eight a.m., room 426, the following day, when the law school at Langston would open its doors. Sipuel went to Norman to apply at the University of Oklahoma anyway. She was not surprised when, once again, President Cross denied her—but the state may have been surprised that not a single Black student went to enroll at Langston University's law school that day. It was an institution hurried into existence on borrowed property and borrowed time that the state tried to pass off as equal.

Sipuel's case was not definitive, but it was a stepping-stone. It did not spark immediate change in Oklahoma, but in Arkansas the president of the state university system, Lewis W. Jones, announced that the state's all-white public colleges would begin enrolling Black students if co-equal courses were not offered at the state's black college. If there was one thing that was worse than integration, it was bad publicity, and Jones had seen schools across the South taking a beating in the northern press for their commitments to segregation. The University of Arkansas became the first public, all-white institution in the South to admit a Black student when Silas Hunt, a classmate of Sipuel's freshman year at Arkansas A&M, enrolled.

It was not until 1949, after a separate Supreme Court case involving a different plaintiff, George McLaurin, that Sipuel was able to enroll at the University of Oklahoma College of Law. It had been, as Dunjee promised her years prior, a long, drawn-out process. "For two and a half years of intense litigation, I had been the guinea pig, the slender, almost shy 'colored' girl from a small rural community who dared challenge the power and resources of the sovereign state of Oklahoma," Sipuel wrote. Now that she was able to attend the university, though, she realized: "I was still the guinea pig."

CHAPTER 6

"Segregated as Conditions Allow"

T he board of regents at the University of Oklahoma were scrambling after the Sipuel decision. On January 28, 1948, at roughly two o'clock in the afternoon, six Black students, who insisted they were not backed by the NAACP, went to the office of President George Cross at the university to seek admission for enrollment in graduate programs. They had been emboldened by Sipuel's case, and none of the courses they desired were available at Langston.

Cross quickly called Lloyd Noble, the president of the board of regents, who subsequently asked Cross to call an emergency board meeting for the next day. The board needed the emergency session to form a plan of action. The Supreme Court said that the state was required to provide accommodations to Black students as soon as it provided them for white students, and they had none.

Despite two court decisions a decade apart, states across the South had still not begun the process of complying with the idea of separate but equal. They were still not providing the separate option, and when they did, the result was far from equal. Northern schools filled some of the gaps in educating Black students in graduate schools, but these cases were the exception, not the rule. As the Truman Commission report outlined, "It must not be supposed that Negro youth living in States in which segregation is not legalized are given the same opportunities as white youth." Those northern colleges did not maintain data on students by race, though, so it is difficult to know exactly how few Black students there were.

Every University of Oklahoma regent was in attendance the next morning, despite the short notice. Cross laid out the case the students were presenting. Each of them, not unlike Sipuel, was imminently qualified for graduate study. The students were spread across programs: business administration, architectural engineering, school administration, and zoology. Each of them was a citizen of Oklahoma. Four of the students had come from Oklahoma City: George McLaurin, Helen Holmes, Ivor Tatum, and Maurderie Hancock Wilson. The other two came from Langston: Mozeal A. Dillon and James Bond. Oklahoma had been able to rush a law school into place for Sipuel—one she would not attend—but a home and faculty for each of these programs would be a taller task. That did not mean the state would not try.

Oklahoma had three options on the table: it could close the graduate programs the students were applying for (there would be no case if the programs did not exist for anyone), admit the students, or provide equal facilities for the Black students. The state decided to buy itself some time instead.

The board asked Attorney General Mac Q. Williamson for a definitive answer on whether the *Sipuel* decision applied to these students. Williamson argued that it did not and that the six students must not be admitted to the university. Segregation in Oklahoma, as it was across the South, was still the law. On February 2, after a whirlwind few days, Cross notified the Black students that the university would reject their applications.

If the NAACP had not been involved before, it would quickly become involved after the rejections. It was still fighting Sipuel's case, arguing that she should be admitted to the law school at the University of Oklahoma because it was functionally impossible that the school at Langston was close to being an equal offering. But in these six rejections, they had an opportunity to get at least one of the students into the University of Oklahoma quickly and to force the state to admit a Black student into the flagship university. All the potential cases were strong, but the lawyers for the NAACP—Thurgood Marshall, in particular—saw one of them as an ace in the hole.

It is unclear when, exactly, George McLaurin was born. Some reports and correspondence suggest he was born in 1880 and was sixty-eight years old in 1948, and others place his birth in 1894, two years before the Supreme Court declared that segregation itself did not constitute discrimination; his death notice suggests he was eighty-one (and thus born in 1887) when he passed in 1968. Record-keeping for Black births in the United States was shoddy and often nonexistent—a vestige of slavery.

Either way, McLaurin, whose wire-rimmed glasses sat neatly on the dorsum of his nose, had lived a full life by the time he found himself applying for a doctoral degree in school administration at the University of Oklahoma. He had earned a master's degree from the University of Kansas and had worked for years as a professor at Langston University. It was less his experience than his age that Marshall found valuable. McLaurin was married; his wife, Peninah, had been the first Black student to apply to the university for admission in 1923, but she was denied because of her race. Marshall held that as George McLaurin was an older man, segregationists could not reasonably argue that his enrollment at the University of Oklahoma was for the purpose of interracial marriage.

On June 17, McLaurin, Holmes, and Wilson, backed by the NAACP, filed petitions in Cleveland County's court to force the university to enroll them. The headlines quickly noticed how this case differed from Lois's. The state had a law school for Sipuel to attend, even though it had been rushed into existence. But, as the *Daily Oklahoman* noted, the state had "no such weapon in the new cases as there is no graduate school work offered for Negroes in Oklahoma."

President Cross would later write that "it seemed clear that, as fast as a graduate program might be established in one field, application for another would be made." Their injunction was denied.

Amos Hall and Thurgood Marshall kept pushing. The pair filed suit on August 5, 1948, with the US District Court for Western Oklahoma, asking for a permanent injunction that barred the university from applying the state law that banned interracial education at the state's graduate school. Segregation was a wall that needed to be beaten down and this case, Hall and Marshall hoped, could bust a crack into it. The three-judge panel agreed to take up the case.

The hearing came less than three weeks later. On August 24, the panel heard arguments, and the defense stuck to a script similar to that of the *Sipuel* case: The state had not had enough time to prepare appropriate accommodations for the Black students. Judge Alfred P. Murrah, the ranking member on the panel, had a difficult time understanding this argument. What, he asked attorney general Mac Williamson, who was representing the university, is a reasonable amount of time in advance to set up an equal school?

"The matter of time is variable with the individual case," Williamson said. He explained that two years had elapsed between Sipuel's initial application and the Supreme Court decision, following which the state set up a law school in a handful of days. It was an odd way of showing proof that the state could move quickly.

Murrah read the high court's decision in *Sipuel* aloud. "The state must provide it for her . . . and provide it as soon as it does for applicants of any other group." He dug in. "To me that is unmistakably plain," Murrah said. "I can consider that statement in the context of what I consider a living law. They are entitled to [an education] before they are too old to receive it." If the court would have accepted Williamson's criteria, "the state would be entitled to two years on the application of any Negro. I question whether a delay of two years affords the equal protection of the law." Murrah drove his point home. "If that is true the Fourteenth Amendment is a farce."

But at least one of the judges was sympathetic to the argument that the state should have been given more time to provide facilities for Black students, despite Thurgood Marshall's contention that time was not an element. Amos Hall argued in return that the state could have easily known that there was demand for such graduate facilities; if the judges examined the appropriations the state had made to send Black students out of state for their graduate educations, they would know, too. The court said that it would announce its decision in one month, with the idea that McLaurin could enroll in classes late.

While the judges were deliberating, McLaurin again attempted to enroll at the University of Oklahoma. Thirty minutes before the admissions office closed for the day on September 16, McLaurin, alongside his wife, Peninah, and Roscoe Dunjee, spoke with President Cross; the dean of admissions, J. E. Fellows; and Laurence Snyder, the dean of the graduate school. He handed the group his transcript showing his master's degree work. He had all the credits necessary to be accepted, Fellows said, but he could not be admitted.

After the meeting, President Cross issued a statement to the newspapers. "His application is in order," Cross said, "and the only thing that prevents his admission is the state statute." He added that students could be enrolled up to two weeks after the start of the term, meaning that if the court circumvented the state law, McLaurin could be enrolled that semester. For the time being, however, he was denied admission. There was still no doctoral program in school administration set up for Black students at Langston University, and the state was, quite clearly, denying his equal opportunity for an education. The judges had given the state thirty-two days to make arrangements for McLaurin's education, and they had none.

A little under two weeks later, the judges were ready to render their decision. "In so far as the Oklahoma statutes deny or deprive admission of the plaintiff to the university they are unconstitutional and void." It was sharp and declarative. Since Oklahoma's statute blocked equal protection of the law, the court did not believe it needed to grant a separate injunction to force McLaurin's admission.

Oklahoma's governor, Roy J. Turner, wrote a letter to the court saying that he would ask the legislature to amend the state's segregation laws or provide equal facilities for Black people. George McLaurin seemed well on his way to breaking down the barrier Oklahoma had blocked Sipuel from crossing.

Discrimination is a contortionist, bending and twisting until it fits within the confines of the system it is given. The state of Oklahoma was handed a ruling clearly stating that it needed to provide accommodations for George McLaurin's education as soon as it did for any white student. It was an echo of *Sipuel*, an echo of *Gaines*. And the state was busily trying to find the right way to warp their segregation laws to distort what should have been justice.

In accordance with his letter to the court, Governor Turner aimed to figure out if he should call a special session of the legislature or if the ruling meant that there could be a solution until a normal session was held. He held off as long as he could and, despite the ruling's clarity, waited on an interpretation of it from Mac Williamson. It was Turner's preference that lawmakers draft up an entirely new higher-education policy to comport with the federal laws rather than deal with them on a case-by-case basis.

Time was not on the state's side, though. The court had clearly stated that it did not want to issue an injunction, but if McLaurin reapplied for admission and was denied, the court would have no choice but to force the state to accept him. The state was in violation of the constitution.

Days wore on with no action. McLaurin formally submitted his application on Tuesday, October 5, and President Cross informed his staff that they were neither to accept nor reject it; instead, the university was to wait for the advisement of the board of regents, which would meet on Wednesday.

During that meeting, Williamson told the board that there was a way around the issue. It could admit McLaurin and place him in separate, segregated classes. That way, Black students and white students would not be educated together. The setup was not too unlike how George Washington Carver had been treated at Iowa State University, nor how the Black students began to be treated once Oberlin lost its way. Williamson suggested that by doing this, the board would comply with the law of the state and the law of the nation. This would not, however, swing the doors wide open to the other students involved in litigation, most notably Ada Lois Sipuel Fisher. The courts had not yet decided if Langston's law school was equal to the University of Oklahoma's, so the state could sit on making a decision in that case. The *Daily Oklahoman* ran a banner headline: "Williamson Tells OU Admit Negro or Cancel Graduate Education Classes."

The board did neither. Instead, they ordered President Cross to examine the situation and to recommend a course of action one month later. They were all out of what seemed to be workable legal options, aside from Williamson's suggestion, so they turned to the next best thing: delay. They wanted Cross to figure out how to provide McLaurin a graduate education on "a basis of complete segregation."

Several newspapers pointed to what was happening in Arkansas as a prime example of what Oklahoma could do to follow the law. When "faced with a similar problem," one paper wrote, the University of Arkansas admitted a Black student to its law school but gave his classes during different hours than it did its white students. Despite this being an inefficient system for professors who were forced to teach extra classes or the Black student who was left out of classroom discussion, "the arrangement leaves intact Arkansas segregation laws." Yes, Arkansas had admitted Sipuel's former classmate, but it segregated him from everyone else.

Cross, for his part, quickly issued a statement. The enrollment of McLaurin, he said, "would not create a social problem." In fact, he added, "if McLaurin is admitted . . . I will recommend that he be allowed to enroll in courses immediately."

The board's latest delay was one too many for the NAACP. Amos Hall filed another injunction with the district court to force McLaurin's acceptance. In the background, though, McLaurin's lawyers were not simply filing the petition with the district court; they were also going directly to the US Supreme Court asking that the court force the state to accept George McLaurin. For the second time that year, the court was being asked to decide whether Oklahoma would follow the law and provide equal educational opportunities. Associate Justice Wiley B. Rutledge quickly wrote Williamson to inquire what the state was doing about McLaurin's enrollment.

Then, in a surprise Monday announcement, the board of regents decided that McLaurin would be admitted to the University of Oklahoma on Wednesday, October 13. The petition to the Supreme Court—and the embarrassment that may have come along with it—was just enough to light a fire under the board. The admittance was on a contingent basis; McLaurin would be the only Black person admitted to the college that semester, and he would be segregated from other students.

It was a victory. A Black student would attend a formerly all-white college in the South through a mix of litigious might and sheer determination, even though "it was not an unconditional surrender" on the part of the segregationists, as reported by one newspaper.

Still, McLaurin and his lawyers were celebrating. "Equal education has been our primary objective," Amos Hall said. "And we have obtained that." He was not quite right.

George McLaurin was smartly dressed, his hat placed on the desk next to him with his textbook at the ready when two students, George Bassett and Edith Long, approached him. "We want to welcome you here, sir," Bassett said, "and let you know that we hope you will find a warm welcome."

Long added that "we are glad to see you." A photographer for the *Oklahoman* snapped a photo of the two white students smiling as Bassett shook McLaurin's hand.

Upstairs in the education building, another group of students were receiving instructions from their professor, Frank A. Balyeat. The professor told the students that they were relocating to room 104 on the first floor. If Bassett and Long had been welcoming, George McLaurin's other would-be classmates were indifferent as they walked past him into the classroom.

A fifteen-by-eighteen-foot room sat adjacent to classroom 104 in the education building at the university. The anteroom had formerly been a library, but on October 14, 1948, it contained a single desk and chair. On the other side of a wall sat the main classroom, with rows of desks facing toward the front of class, where the professor would lecture. Thirty-one white students sat in the classroom, while one student, George McLaurin, sat in the anteroom, just two feet away. A makeshift partition had originally divided the two rooms, but it had been taken down. The absurdity of the situation was as obvious as the invisible line that segregated McLaurin from his classmates.

The University of Oklahoma's solution to the forced integration of its graduate school was to hold each and every one of McLaurin's graduate classes in this same room on the first floor. They provided separate toilet facilities for McLaurin in the basement of the building; he would eat alone in the student union building; and he had to use a separate table to study in the library.

Still, McLaurin enjoyed his classes. "Everything seems to be natural and usual and I really enjoyed being here," he told reporters. "I am pleased with the way the university officials have received me and their attitude in giving me information." But that pleasure slowly began to wane.

"That is not equal education," Thurgood Marshall told reporters. The now-famous lawyer had flown to Oklahoma to witness
the classes himself, and the conditions were less than satisfactory.
"Why I had pictures taken from five angles in that classroom, and
the whole thing was summed up by one of the men here, he said,
'why, that man is peeking in.'" Instead of giving McLaurin equal education, one with the same dignity as all the other students in his
classes, he was being treated as second class and fundamentally different: unequal. During arguments, Marshall called the university's
arrangement "a strain and humiliating."

The court disagreed with Marshall's argument. To the panel,
it seemed that the University of Oklahoma was doing everything it
could to provide equal education within the confines of the law.
What Marshall was arguing was something different, though. He was
saying that segregation, by its very nature, was the problem.

The court held that it simply could not "obliterate social or racial distinctions which the State has traditionally recognized as a
basis for classification for purposes of education" and other public
gatherings. The Fourteenth Amendment, the court argued, was not
"intended to enforce social equality between classes and races." The
case was backed into a corner by a court that believed in the precedent of social inequality. "God hath made of one blood all people
of the Earth," John Fee would have argued. The court was applying
an age-old addendum: "Unless you are Black."

On December 11, lawyers with the NAACP began preparing
their appeal. The McLaurin case would likely join two other cases—
Sweatt v. Painter, in which a Black student had been barred from
attending the University of Texas because of his race, and Sipuel's
case—at the Supreme Court, where the three would be argued on
the same day.

Few things change the mind faster than a hit to the pocket, and Okla-
homa was on the verge of shelling out a lot of money to begin creat-

ing graduate programs for Black students. The university received three new applications for graduate education in January 1949. Meanwhile, the facilities that the state had provided for Black students to attend law school were going unused, as no Black students had applied to the Langston University law school at the state capitol. Sipuel surely was not going to; after all, NAACP lawyers were still in court for her arguing that there was no conceivable way that the schools were equal.

The University of Oklahoma board argued that it would be "both wise and expedient" to admit qualified Black students to the state's white colleges if they could not receive similar courses at Langston University. "To attempt to maintain segregation of the races in graduate and specialized education would cost so much it would injure our higher education program," the board stated. "If a big percentage of the money available for the higher education must be spent on a few Negroes every other school in the state must suffer."

One by one, the university began admitting Black students on a segregated basis. Opherita Daniels was admitted to work on a master's in social work. Then Maurderie Hancock Wilson was accepted to study sociology. It would have been impossible, though, for them to set up such segregated conditions as they had for George McLaurin. Instead, President Cross announced that the two women would be seated in the back of the classroom and they would be "segregated as conditions allow."

Meanwhile, in Stillwater, Oklahoma, the agricultural and mechanical college, which would come to be known as Oklahoma State University, received its first two applications from Black students. Henry Floyd, a junior at Langston, applied to take political science courses, and Jane Ellison wanted to take courses in home economics. Neither of these subjects was offered at Langston, and the students argued that they should be admitted. Even NAACP leaders were shocked by the development. Roscoe Dunjee was quoted as saying it was "news to me." The NAACP had been laser-focused on graduate programs, but its strategy well could have applied to undergraduate programs, too, and the students recognized that.

On March 3, lawyers for McLaurin filed their petition with the Supreme Court. He requested to be educated at the University of Oklahoma on a nonsegregated basis. At the same time, Mac Williamson began a desperate plea to state legislators to take action. "Ever since the first of last year, I have been the registrar for two state universities," Williamson told reporters after he sent similar letters to leaders of both chambers of the statehouse. "Every time a Negro applies for admission, college authorities ask us for advice." If the legislature did not do anything, Black students would be able to attend white colleges whether the state liked it or not.

And that is exactly what happened. Black students began enrolling at the University of Oklahoma, including Lois. "I will spend the rest of my life trying to prove to Oklahoma that a mistake was made in the attempt to keep me from entering the OU law school," she told reporters. She, along with twenty-five other Black students, would enroll in the university that summer. In response, the administration increased segregation within the classrooms by setting up literal railings to divide the Black and white students. The rails were an "insult," McLaurin said. "I want no segregation at all."

Dunjee played a similar note, saying, "We will prosecute with vigor our fight to end all segregation in state colleges."

But the NAACP did not want to stop at the colleges; it hoped to integrate elementary and secondary schools as well. In late fall, news came that the Supreme Court had agreed to review McLaurin's case. Meanwhile, the antisegregation leaders in the state were organizing a plan to enroll Black students in Oklahoma's all-white high schools. The NAACP was not dropping its fight for equality in higher education, Roscoe Dunjee told reporters, but the main goal for 1950 would be the integration of high schools. Black children would take the same tack that Sipuel, McLaurin, and others had by then taken: they would apply at white high schools that offered courses different from what they could learn at their own schools. "We want courses now available to white students opened to Negroes, too," Dunjee said.

As McLaurin waited for his case to get to the Supreme Court, the lawyers for both sides prepared their arguments for the court. In the state's brief, Oklahoma assistant attorney general Fred Hansen argued that McLaurin's contention that railings constituted segregation would subvert the entire state's system and would "necessarily result in abandoning many of the state's existing educational establishments." More than the logistical problems with McLaurin's battle, though, Hansen argued that if segregation was inherently unequal and the court found for McLaurin, racism might actually become worse. As an Associated Press report noted, "the brief pointed out that since Oklahoma is approximately 90 percent white, that white persons would be elected to school boards who would hire white teachers where classes are predominantly white." Desegregation would make discrimination by individuals more robust and intense. The state, in legally enforcing segregation, was not trying to "humiliate and degrade" McLaurin, Hansen argued; instead, it was doing its Black citizens a favor.

It was standing room only in Washington, DC, as some mix of court observers and those visiting the city for the Easter holiday crowded into the Supreme Court on April 3, 1950. The court planned to hear three cases: *Henderson v. United States*, an NAACP case homing in on segregated railroad dining cars; *Sweatt*; and McLaurin's case. Each case, in its own way, was a challenge to the doctrine of separate but equal.

Just before the four thirty p.m. adjournment, Chief Justice Fred Vinson called Robert L. Carter, the NAACP lawyer, to deliver his opening statement. The next day, the NAACP rehashed the worst of the situation: Yes, McLaurin was able to attend classes, use the library, and eat in the cafeteria, but his movements were restricted. He was forced to sit away from white students. How was it possible that his was an equal experience when he was not living under the same rules and regulations as his white classmates?

The court took two months to deliberate on the case, before, on June 5, Chief Justice Vinson was ready to give the court's decision. In a unanimous opinion, the court announced that the Fourteenth Amendment protected McLaurin from exactly what the state was doing by segregating him in an integrated space. The amendment bans any difference in treatment by the state regarding race. Once a Black student had been admitted to a state-supported school, he must receive "the same treatment at the hands of the state as students of other races." At the same time, the court handed down a ruling in the *Sweatt* case, arguing that the state of Texas did not provide Herman Sweatt an equal education by setting up a separate Black law school for him. Segregation had been bending and twisting itself to fit into a box, but that box kept getting smaller and smaller.

The Supreme Court wanted to be clear on the point they were making, though. It was not as if they were saying separate but equal was wrong. They were simply saying that the state could not treat a Black student differently once he had been admitted. "There is a vast difference—a Constitutional difference—between restrictions imposed by the state which prohibit the intellectual commingling of students, and the refusal of individuals to commingle where the state presents no such bar," Vinson wrote in the opinion. "The removal of the state restrictions will not necessarily abate individual and group predilections, prejudices and choices." But, Vinson added, at the very least, the state should not deprive McLaurin of being able to win the favor of his fellow students on his own.

The *Daily Oklahoman* ran a banner headline: "Supreme Court Knocks Out Graduate Segregation at OU." More than eighty Black students would enroll at the Norman campus the next year; by 1951, four hundred Black students had enrolled at the University of Oklahoma and Oklahoma A&M in Stillwater. But there were little wars continuing everywhere. Just beneath the banner was another head-line: "Campaign Due for Full Equality in All Schools."

Each of the higher-education cases—*Gaines*, *Sipuel*, *McLaurin*, **and** *Sweatt*—were bricks, laying the foundation for a broader challenge. That broader challenge would become known as *Brown v. Board of Education*, in which the court would decide in a more sweeping way than it had in any of the higher-education cases that "separate educational facilities are inherently unequal." It took nearly sixty years to undo *Plessy v. Ferguson*, and it would take even longer to address the harm that the case had caused. A court decision could not, on its own, defeat segregation. After all, discrimination in America is a root, not a branch.

As Black people continued to tug at that root, it only grew deeper, boiling over into the next decade of violence. Integration would ultimately test everything: The court's ability to dictate the behavior of southern populations who did not want to change, and northern colleges' willingness to accept more Black students now that the formal legal barriers had been broken down. And, in places like Berea, whether a purpose lost could be regained.

PART III

FAILED

CHAPTER 7

This Whole Facade

Racist laws that segregated schools fell in a slow-rolling cascade over the three decades following the higher-education cases. Kentucky's Day Law was one of the first, and the law did not die without drama. On the day that the Kentucky House of Representatives voted to repeal the sinister statute, Kash Holbrook, a rugged-looking salesman from the mountains of eastern Kentucky, drew his pistol on the statehouse floor.

On March 7, 1950, the Kentucky Senate had quietly passed a bill that would amend the law that had barred Black students and white students from being educated together. Black students could attend any college in the state, the amendment read, if an institution's board allowed it and if there were no similar courses offered at Kentucky State College for Negroes—the state-supported Black college, which had undergone a host of name changes. The senate could read the writing on the wall—and if not, its members could simply read the rulings that were coming down from the US Supreme Court.

The courts had been ruling that states had to provide the same courses for Black students as soon as they did for white ones in cases like *Sipuel*, *McLaurin*, and *Sweatt*. Kentucky had tried all the familiar strategies to work around the rules. They tried sending Black students out of state and they opened the professional schools to Black students, but with courses held at different times from those attended by white students. When those strategies did not work, they opened classes to Black students at the same time as white students, but in different locations. They stretched and stretched, but the reality of the situation eventually became clear. The law had to be changed, and it seemed an amendment, a 108-word sentence, would be the death knell.

If deliberation over the amendment in the state senate was orderly, the Kentucky House of Representatives' debate was anything but. It was cloudy and cold on March 16, and the House gallery was brimming with spectators as legislators prepared to take up recently passed senate bills. Schoolchildren had packed in shoulder to shoulder. The governor was there, too. Tempers flared when the majority floor leader, James Hanratty, a Democrat from Hopkinsville, brought the bill amending the Day Law for consideration.

"Even if you don't like it, it's the thing that's coming. It's developing right along," Hanratty told his colleagues. The desegregation of schools was starting; it was going to happen. It was better to be ahead of the curve in the South than behind it, he argued. But opponents, such as G. Lee McClain, a Democrat from Bardstown, wanted to table the measure. Others objected more forcefully.

"I don't see how or why we can continue to disregard the Constitution, which I hold to faithfully, if we do our duty," Leonard Preston, a Republican from Glasgow, Kentucky, argued. The Day Law was written into the state's constitution and every modest tweak—every strike at its central purpose—was a violation of the law in its entirety, he argued. The law must either be repealed completely, or the state's Black college must be built up to offer equal educational opportunity. "I have never refused to vote for the amount of money necessary to give Negroes an education second to none," Preston said, contradicting the Truman Commission's findings about the state of higher education for Black people in Kentucky.

But Preston likely knew two things: the legislature would not soon have the support for a full repeal of the Day Law, and that the amount of money necessary to fund an equal education for Black students would never be provided. Years of subpar appropriations for the university had made that clear.

The only Black lawmaker in Kentucky's House of Representatives then spoke up. Jesse H. Lawrence, a Republican from Louisville, asked Preston how long he thought it would take for Kentucky State University to offer equal educational opportunities.

"About thirty years," Preston said. The soonest the college that he voted to make second to none would not be so until at least 1980. Preston had probably not meant to make the argument for integration, nor had he meant to argue for immediate equitable funding for Black colleges, but he unwittingly did both.

When Lawrence spoke again, he drove straight at the most fundamental question: "How does Kentucky's educational policy comply with the United States Constitution, which says that all citizens have certain rights and privileges?"

There were a handful of Democrats who agreed with Lawrence, Hanratty, and the Republicans. Morris Weintraub argued plainly that the issue was "strictly a question of persecution of minorities," and his colleagues who could not see that were blind to bigotry. Could they not abide even so soft an amendment as this? Herbert Tinsley cosigned his declaration. "I think it's time we people in Kentucky approached the subject in a sane and sound way. I think we're doing it in this bill."

The measure went to a vote and passed 50–16. Four decades after the passage of the Day Law, colleges in Kentucky were a governor's signature away from the technical end of segregation in higher education. There were stipulations, of course, but the doors of Kentucky's colleges were being unlocked. Berea would be able to reclaim its legacy. It should have been the biggest news of the day—but the day devolved.

"A fiery display of tempers, fists, and a pistol started a near-riot in Kentucky's House of Representatives today," Hugh Morris, a reporter for the Louisville *Courier-Journal*, wrote. Two Democrats had broken into a fight on the floor of the house: Charles W. Burnley, of Paducah, and Weintraub, who had suggested that some of his party colleagues had succumbed to bigotry. The fight, though, was supposedly over the revival of a string of senate measures—on tobacco, policing, schools, and the like—thought to be killed inappropriately. Burnley wanted to revive the dead measures, Weintraub disagreed, and the two broke into a wrestling match.

"If you don't like it, why don't you resign?" Burnley asked.

As if in the child's game, Weintraub retorted, "Why don't *you* resign?"

The Speaker of the House sent Holbrook, the sergeant at arms, to calm the ruckus. At one point, Holbrook reached into his right coat pocket, half-displaying his pistol and ordering a lawmaker back to his seat. The schoolchildren in the gallery shouted, "He's got a gun!"

No shots were fired in the end, but the Day Law was dead. Four years before *Brown v. Board of Education* began the dismantling of legal segregation, Kentucky had started its own process of complying with the Supreme Court's rulings in higher-education cases. The bill's passage was met with passionate denunciations. "Governor Clement's puppet Senate has dealt another blow to education in Kentucky," one letter to the editor of the *Courier-Journal* newspaper read. "It is silly to hold that equal opportunity cannot be provided without throwing the colored and white children into classrooms and upon campuses together." If this bill were signed into law, it would spell the end of public education in the state, and private schools would spring up across Kentucky to educate students "in an environment harmonious with their background," the author of the letter wrote. "Such citizens will lose interest in appropriations for public school needs and public schools will be starved out of useful existence." The letter-writer did not sign a name, using only an adjective: "Astonished."

Down in Berea, however, the news was met with excitement. The college enrolled its first two Black students in more than forty years the following semester. The identity of the town and of the college was gone, though. It is impossible to flip a switch and expect everything to go back to normal. Many of the Black families who once lived in the mountains near Berea had moved away, and there was little resembling a Black community left. Still, one month after the *Brown* decision came down, Jessie Reasor Zandor graduated from Berea College, the first Black student to do so since the Day Law took effect in 1904.

The tension in the Kentucky statehouse should have been a warning of what was to come across the South as schools sought to integrate after *Brown*. Too many people may have thought like state representative Chick Love, a Democrat from Kuttawa, who in registering his opposition to integration suggested it was a matter of geography: "We're too far South for the two [races] to go together," he said.

James Meredith felt inspired on January 21, 1961, as he sat down in front of his Smith-Corona portable typewriter on Maple Street in Jackson, Mississippi. Meredith, a clean-shaven air force veteran, had seen John F. Kennedy take the oath of office on television the day prior, and one passage played in his mind on a loop.

In jumpy, grainy black-and-white, Kennedy delivered remarks from the eastern portico of the US Capitol in Washington, DC. A little over a minute into his address, Kennedy called on the American spirit. "The same revolutionary beliefs for which our forebears fought are still at issue around the globe—the belief that the rights of man come not from the generosity of the state but from the hand of God," Kennedy said, a light breeze flicking at his neatly combed hair. "We must not forget today that we are the heirs of that first revolution." Meredith did not care much for the flair of Kennedy's speech, but he admired the force. Like Kennedy, Meredith felt like an heir to a revolution.

Meredith's uprising began unassumingly, in the form of a hastily drafted letter to the registrar at the University of Mississippi, in Oxford, Mississippi. The note was undated and brief—just three lines. "Please send me an application for admission to your school," he wrote, before asking for any other materials that might be helpful, such as a course catalog.

When Robert Ellis, the university's registrar, received Meredith's letter, he did not think much of it. Meredith had not mentioned anything disqualifying, so he replied courteously. "We are very pleased to know of your interest in becoming a member of our student body," Ellis wrote back to Meredith on January 26. "If we can be of further help to you in making your enrollment plans, please let us know."

After receiving Ellis's letter, on January 29, Meredith promptly went to go see Medgar Evers, the NAACP's first field officer in Mississippi. Evers had battled for school integration and voting rights, and he had called for a new investigation of the murder of Emmett Till, the fourteen-year-old Black child who was lynched in 1955 for allegedly flirting with a white woman. If anyone knew how to fight the state's racial caste system, it was him. Evers did not hesitate to tell Meredith that he needed to contact Thurgood Marshall, who was by then directing the NAACP Legal Defense Fund. Meredith promptly followed Evers's direction and dashed a letter off to Marshall that evening. It was not a given that he would contact Marshall, though. Despite Meredith's respect for Evers, he feared the NAACP would be in above its head in Mississippi. Down there, racial discrimination was a different beast, Meredith thought.

Two days later, as a warm day morphed into a cold night, Meredith once again found himself at his typewriter. This time he was more formal, if not sarcastic. He had completed the application Ellis had sent to him save for the alumni references, and instead he attached his military service record—a testament to his credibility. As a former member of the Air Force, Meredith was eligible for federally funded educational support through the GI Bill, a government program established after World War II to help troops returning from battle. Though the bill did not explicitly bar Black people from its benefits, they had a difficult time securing them in practice. In education, the bill covered tuition and fees for veterans, and it provided a living stipend during their collegiate studies. It led to a boom in white male college enrollment, but barred from white colleges across the South, Black students found there were few places where they could use it. Meredith was determined to use his benefits at the University of Mississippi.

"I am very pleased with your letter that accompanied the application forms you recently sent to me," he wrote back to Ellis. "I sincerely hope that your attitude toward me as a potential member of your student body reflects the attitude of the school, and that it will not change upon learning that I am not a White applicant." Then came the bombshell: "I am an American-Mississippi-Negro citizen." That is why he would not be able to provide references, he explained. All the university's alumni up to that point had been white, and he knew very few white people. Surely none who had gone to the University of Mississippi, and therefore none who would write him a letter to integrate their alma mater. He licked the envelope and sent the letter off to Ellis.

Before he could get a response from the university, Meredith heard back from Marshall: He wanted more information. The NAACP had not planned any action in Mississippi that dealt with education. The proposition of desegregating Mississippi at the time seemed crazy, Marshall thought, and any Black person willing to fight the racial caste system in that state surely had to be as well. He wanted to speak with Meredith on the phone to make sure that if the organization was going to take on his case, it was to do so with a sane plaintiff.

Meredith went to Evers's house to take the call with Marshall and became upset very quickly with Marshall's disbelief. "The voice on the other end indicated that he might still question the truth of my letter," he later recalled. "And I simply hung up the phone and left the room."

Evers, whose preternatural ability to deal with people had helped him in his civil rights dealings in the state, coaxed both men back to the table. Marshall was simply asking for documentation that would make the case stronger, he argued to Meredith, who ultimately let go of his ego and told Evers where he could get the documents Marshall requested. "I must give sole credit to Medgar Evers," Meredith recalled, "for moving this case forward."

Back in New York, Marshall went to see Candice Baker Motley. At the time, Motley was a young associate counsel with the NAACP Legal Defense Fund. He dropped Meredith's letter on her desk. "This guy's gotta be crazy!" he said. "That's your case." When she asked him why he was giving her the case, he told her that it was less likely that she would be physically attacked in the Deep South than any of the male lawyers they worked with. The racial caste system was stringent, but white men often had Black nannies.

Four days after Meredith sent his application to the university, he received a telegram response from Ellis via Western Union. "FOR YOUR INFORMATION AND GUIDANCE," the telegram read, "IT HAS BEEN FOUND NECESSARY TO DISCONTINUE CONSIDERATION OF ALL APPLICATIONS FOR ADMISSION OR REGISTRATION FOR THE SECOND SEMESTER WHICH WERE RECEIVED AFTER JANUARY 25, 1961." The telegram disregarded the fact that Ellis had sent Meredith application materials just days prior, and after the supposed deadline.

It was a test, and Ellis had failed. A denial was exactly what Meredith wanted. "The objective was to put pressure on John Kennedy and the Kennedy administration to live up to the civil rights plank in the Democratic platform," he said. The University of Mississippi had been ardently against enrolling any Black students. The same edict outlined by professors in 1870—"*Should an applicant belong to the negro race we should, without hesitation, reject him*"—held true nearly a century later, despite the landmark ruling barring segregation in *Brown v. Board of Education*. Meredith knew he would be rejected by the university and, when he was, he needed the federal government to come to his defense.

On February 7, the rumor that Black students had sought to register at the University of Mississippi spread through campus. Plainclothes highway patrol officers and FBI agents, tipped off to a potential disruption, had positioned themselves strategically around the administration building and the gymnasium. But Meredith had already been denied. "All's Calm at Ole Miss," the *Clarion-Ledger* assured its readers the next day. At five o'clock in the afternoon, authorities left the campus, the *Ledger*'s reporter Edmond Noel wrote, "and Mississippi remained the only state in the Union to preserve racial segregation at all levels of its public education system." But the NAACP served notice in the same story.

"As the long lines of white students filed past gun carrying law enforcement officers," Noel wrote, "Roy Wilkins, national executive secretary of the National Association for the Advancement of Colored People, was telling *The Clarion Ledger* via telephone that 'Ole Miss is going to be integrated.'" Meredith had the NAACP on his side now. All he still needed was the federal government.

On March 1, 1961, there was a sign that, perhaps, Kennedy did genuinely care about civil rights. In the East Room of the White House, Kennedy informed reporters that an executive order was on the way. That past September, when Kennedy was running for office instead of occupying it, he suggested that there were a range of civil rights actions he could take without Congress. This first executive order was one of them.

Kennedy's executive order was not supposed to change education; he had his eyes on the workforce. Within a few days, he planned to issue an order that would "strengthen the employment opportunities both in and out of government, for all Americans," he told reporters. Black people were being systematically excluded from any number of federal jobs. How could they expect to be treated fairly in the private sector when the public sector, which professed to take their equality seriously, denied them?

Diversifying the federal government was the low-hanging fruit, and one reporter wanted to ask Kennedy about the nectar a little higher up. In January, the US Commission for Civil Rights had issued a report on public higher education. The report outlined the federal government's role in creating separate and unequal public colleges, the continued underfunding of those institutions, and how federal policy could ameliorate those failures. The commission offered three proposals as remedies. Chief among them: federal money should go only to public institutions that did not discriminate on the basis of race, color, religion, or national origin. What, the reporter asked, did the president think of denying aid to universities that discriminated against minority students?

Kennedy, who had not included any prohibitions on aid for segregated schools in his recent education legislation, dodged the question. It was under study as part of an overall look at "where the federal government might justly place its power and influence to expand civil rights," he said.

Five days later, Kennedy charged on with signing Executive Order 10925. The order required government contractors to "take affirmative action to ensure that applicants are employed, and employees are treated equally during employment, without regard to their race, creed, color, or national origin." It would also establish the President's Commission on Equal Employment Opportunity, the forerunner to the Equal Employment Opportunity Commission. Kennedy appointed his vice president, Lyndon Baines Johnson, to be the chair of the new organization. Kennedy stressed that his order was "both an announcement of our determination to end job discrimination once and for all, and an effective instrument to realize that objective."

The secretary of labor, Arthur Goldberg, was named vice chair. Goldberg, who was white haired and wore thick-rimmed glasses, would be nominated by Kennedy the next year to serve as an associate justice on the US Supreme Court, but, at the time, Kennedy had charged the prominent labor attorney with making this new White House initiative a reality. Goldberg staffed his own department quickly, appointing three Black men to high-ranking positions, including George L. P. Weaver, who had served as the executive secretary of the civil rights committee at the American Federation of Labor and Congress of Industrial Organizations. Goldberg also began aggressively pursuing graduates of historically Black colleges for jobs in the labor department.

When Kennedy signed the order, the words "affirmative action" appeared in federal regulations with regards to discrimination for the first time, though they had been used for years by those who called for the government to be more aggressive in providing rights to all people. Despite today's near-synonymous association of affirmative action with America's universities, Kennedy's order was not about colleges but was a step toward the kind of living up to the civil rights plank of his platform that Meredith had been hoping for from Kennedy, albeit a slow one. Slow steps, though, can lead to catastrophe.

By the fall of 1962, the University of Mississippi was burning.

In war, some battles are better remembered than others; integration at Ole Miss seems like higher education's Gettysburg. Clennon King, a teacher from Alcorn A&M, had tried to integrate the state flagship in 1958 but was whisked off campus and taken to a mental institution. Any Black person who attempted such a thing had to be insane, state officials assumed. Clyde Kennard, who tried to integrate another of the state's white colleges, Mississippi Southern College, was framed for two alleged crimes and sentenced to seven years at the notorious Parchman Farm—a sentence that would prevent him from ever applying to a white college again. He died of colon cancer months after being released from prison in 1963. This was a battle that people did not come back from.

But the NAACP saw something in Meredith. "A Messiah complex," Motley called it.

"I asked myself the question, 'Why should it be someone else?'" Meredith later explained. "If people keep placing the responsibility with someone else nothing will ever be accomplished."

With the national organization's backing, Meredith and Motley resubmitted an application to the university, making copies of all their documents. On May 25, 1961, the university categorically denied him. He did not have what he needed to enroll in the school, they said. He still had no proper letters of recommendation, and, in a new wrinkle added specifically for him, the school now said that it would not accept transfer students from institutions that were not regionally accredited. The historically Black college that Meredith had most recently attended, Jackson State, one of the state's three public colleges for Black students, was one such college. In denying him, the college was admitting his other option was not equal.

Six days later, on May 31, Meredith walked into the courtroom of US District Judge Sidney Mize in Meridian, Mississippi. He was joined by Motley; R. Jess Brown, one of the only Black lawyers in the state who would take on a case such as his; Jack Greenberg, a white lawyer who had helped argue the *Brown* case in front of the Supreme Court; and Medgar Evers. The high court had ruled segregation illegal. They wanted to test the government's commitment to upholding the law.

By the time Meredith was going to court, the NAACP had developed a rhythm for higher-education cases. They knew the files they needed, what courts to go to, and roughly how long making a case would take. The most difficult part would be getting Meredith on campus.

On December 12, 1961, Judge Mize ruled that Meredith had not been denied because of his race; instead, he reasoned, it was due to the missing documents in Meredith's application. The NAACP appealed to the Fifth Circuit Court and won an expedited hearing. The circuit court heard Meredith's case on January 9 and returned with a decision just three days later. The court decided that the missing documents—alumni certificates—discriminated against Black students. "We hold that the University's requirement that each candidate for admission furnish alumni certificates is a denial of the equal protection of the laws, in its application to Negro candidates," the judges wrote in their opinion. But the university knew that, which is why it made efforts to argue that there were other reasons why Meredith was not admitted: "He attended an unaccredited university"; "His application was late." The case was muddied by these details, the court wrote, and they needed more consideration. The judges sent the case back to Mize's courtroom.

And so the case went, up and down, for sixteen months, as the newspapers in the state painted an image of Meredith as a menace. The *Meridian Star* wrote in an editorial that Meredith's enrollment at the university would be akin to the beginning of the end of the white race. "Intermarriage in the South, where we are so evenly divided white and colored, means the end of both races as such, and the emergence of a tribe of mongrels," its editors wrote. "If you value your racial heritage, if you have even the smallest regard for the future of this South of ours—you will be for segregation one hundred percent."

Then there was a breakthrough. On August 31, 1962, the US Department of Justice decided to file an amicus brief—a "friend of the court" brief—in the case. They wanted the Supreme Court to step in, rule for Meredith, and force the doors of Ole Miss open to him.

The semester was starting at the University of Mississippi, and he would have to wait another semester if the court did not act quickly.

The court was not in session, though. It had let out for the summer and had not yet gaveled back in. So, the petition landed on the desk of Hugo Black, the Supreme Court justice in charge of the Fifth Circuit Court. Black, who had served on the bench through all the higher-education cases, consulted his fellow justices. On September 10, he made his decision public: the University of Mississippi could not take any steps to prevent Meredith from being allowed to register at the university, he said. It was a sledgehammer. The nearly two-year legal battle was coming to an end, but the standoff was just beginning.

Three days after Black's ruling, Ross Barnett, the governor of Mississippi, took to the airwaves to make "crystal clear" where he stood. "I have said in every county in Mississippi that no school in our state will be integrated while I am your Governor," Barnett said. "I shall do everything in my power to prevent integration in our school." This was a matter of "principle," Barnett said, and the federal government was intruding on the sovereign rights of the state of Mississippi. "Having long since failed in their efforts to conquer the indomitable spirit of the people of Mississippi and their unshakable will to preserve the sovereignty and majesty of our commonwealth, they now seek to break us physically with the power of force."

Barnett, a lawyer who had been educated at the University of Mississippi, launched his gubernatorial campaign by declaring that "the good Lord was the original segregationist. He put the Black man in Africa—separated him from all the other races." His duty to segregate was biblical, he believed. He was the inverse of John Fee, but he took his holy duty seriously. "You will have a governor who is a vigorous segregationist. I am not a moderate." He had approved of Governor Orval Faubus's tactics in keeping Black students out of Little Rock's Central High School after the Supreme Court forced the Little Rock school district to integrate. He was prepared to use such tactics—the state police, intimidation, sheer force of will—to keep Black students out of his state's flagship university. The scene was set for a showdown. In one corner was Meredith, the mature, landowning Black man trying to get an education at the state's premier university. In the other was Barnett, who embodied the racism that had come to define the South.

Not every white Mississippian with a little power was ready to embrace Barnett's illegal strategy, though. On September 19, members of the board of trustees were trying to find a legal way to defy the court orders. Barnett walked into a secret meeting with the board late that evening at the University Medical Center in Oxford, the home of the University of Mississippi, ready to fight. Unable to come up with a solution, several of the members of the board thought the only option they had was to let Meredith in. Barnett refused; that was not an option. One board member erupted: "We've got to know what's the legal way to keep him out. That's all we want to know, Governor!" If they could not find one, they would be in contempt of court, and they all knew it.

"Forget it, contempt means nothing!" Barnett responded matter-of-factly. "They won't do anything to you. Just don't let the word 'contempt' worry you." He had convinced most of the board with his statement, but Tally Riddell was still on the fence. Riddell's and Barnett's fathers were neighbors growing up, and Barnett made the disagreement personal. "Tally, yo' daddy would turn over in his grave to know you are a nigger-lover and votin' to admit Meredith in this University!"

Barnett next aimed his ire at S. R. "Doc" Evans. But Evans did not take the insults as quietly. "You're fixin' to put me in the penitentiary, because you ain't going to talk to me like that," Evans told Barnett. What was a near scuffle was quickly broken up—Tally Riddell was having a heart attack. He was rushed to the hospital and the meeting disbanded.

—

More than 150 reporters descended on Mississippi to cover the only story that seemed to matter: a governor standing in defiance of the federal government over the integration of colleges. It was a spectacle, and seemed ripe to turn into a bloody one.

James Meredith wore a brown suit and white shirt on September 20, the first day he attempted to enroll at the University of Mississippi. The day before, at twenty-five minutes past midnight, the state legislature had passed the "Meredith Law," which denied admission to any state school to any person convicted of a criminal offense. The same day, September 19, Meredith was accused and convicted of falsifying voter registration forms and sentenced to a year in prison. The Justice Department quickly appealed the decision; the charges were trumped up.

On the twentieth, hundreds of people gathered at the university, and waited hours for Meredith to arrive. At four thirty p.m., his car approached the Continuation Center, where Governor Barnett and school officials were waiting for him. The hundreds had turned to thousands and they were shouting. "Nigger go home!" they exclaimed, but the jeers did not turn into physical violence—not that day. Meredith was whisked into the building to meet with Barnett.

Once inside, face-to-face with the man who believed it his biblical duty to block a Black student's enrollment, Meredith told the governor that he wanted to register at the university. Barnett, known for his antics, unfurled a proclamation sealed in gold. "Using my police powers as the Governor of the Sovereign State of Mississippi, as well as my official academic powers as Registrar of the University of Mississippi, and acting in accordance with the formal legislative decree of Interposition granted me by the Mississippi legislature, I do hereby deny you, James Meredith, admittance to this University," Barnett said, reading from the scroll. If he admitted Meredith, Barnett argued, it would be a breach of peace.

John Doar, the assistant attorney general for civil rights who accompanied Meredith, protested Barnett's decree, but to no avail. The group realized that Barnett would not budge. Twenty minutes after they had arrived, Meredith and his escorts piled back into the car and raced to Memphis, Tennessee, where Meredith was staying in a safe house. They would have to fight the order in court before he attempted to enroll again.

On Tuesday, September 25, 1962, readers of the *New York Times* were greeted by a pair of conflicting headlines. "Court Is Obeyed," one read. To its left: "Barnett Defiant." Both were true. The University of Mississippi's board of trustees had accepted the Fifth Circuit Court's decision to admit Meredith by four p.m. the following day. But Barnett, ever the segregationist, had started to lay down cover for state officials who defied the federal order, and ordered any federal official who sought to arrest or fine defiant University of Mississippi administrators to themselves be arrested. Not even Orval Faubus, the *Times* wrote, "risked the open clash with Federal authority that would result from the seizure of a United States official."

The next day, Barnett stood in front of the board of trustees' office on the tenth floor of the state office building in Jackson. Meredith, flanked by Doar, had flown to the capital city from New Orleans, where the Fifth Circuit had ruled in his favor the day prior. The two met outside room 1007; Barnett blocked the door. "I call on you to permit us to go on in and see Mr. Ellis and get this young man registered," Doar said. Barnett declined. Doar reached for the summons he had brought along with him—Barnett was being charged with "willfully and intentionally" disobeying a restraining order by the Justice Department and would have to appear in court for his defiance. But Barnett refused to accept that as well.

Lawmakers who had packed in behind Barnett began shouting at Doar. "Get going, get going."

Doar calmly confronted Barnett. "Then you refuse to permit us to come in the door?"

"Yes sir," Barnett replied.

Meredith and Doar turned to leave. Segregation won a tense, quiet victory, and the state legislators behind Barnett erupted in celebration. "Three cheers for the Governor!" they shouted. From Birmingham, Alabama, the white supremacist National States' Rights Party announced that it was ready to take up arms to support the principled stand that Barnett was mounting. "We feel patriots from every state in the Union will rally to the defense of Mississippi," Edward R. Fields, the organization's national director, wrote in a letter to Barnett. "Let's show the entire world how far the white man will go to stay white."

Another night passed; another day came. Meredith and Doar traveled to Oxford, accompanied by Chief US Marshal James J. P. McShane, a gruff white man with a stern chin and a pompadour. Their motorcade nearly made it to campus before they were stopped on South Fifth Street and University Avenue. Twenty state troopers, led by Dave Gayden, the state highway patrol chief, stood sentry. They were backed up by more than a dozen sheriffs from surrounding counties. The lieutenant governor, Paul Johnson, maneuvered his way to the front of the human blockade. McShane identified Johnson as the person in charge and explained that the group had come to enroll Meredith. "I'm going to have to refuse Mr. Meredith," Johnson replied. He was acting under Barnett's order and in the governor's place. When Doar tried to serve Johnson the summons he had attempted to serve the governor, Johnson rejected it. This time, the rejection was less peaceful. McShane tried to force his way through the barricade blocking Meredith and the university. But Johnson, alongside the state troopers he brought as muscle, pushed him back, accusing McShane of putting on a show for the television cameras.

Doar, flabbergasted, blurted out. "You people understand that you're in violation of a court order?" He called out the names of state patrolmen, and McShane began taking them down.

"We have told you can't go in and we intend to use whatever force is necessary," Johnson said.

The exchange was brief but, perhaps more than any other, was the perfect encapsulation of how states guarded higher education in the South after the *Gaines* case. States were in violation of the law when they did not provide education to Black students, but they could not have cared less—and they were willing to use every tool they had to keep the status quo. It may have been easier if they had simply used the northern strategy, admitting a few, select Black students, but the southern stand was on principle: the state government would not allow integration.

Johnson won the praise of one of the governor's top advisers: William Simmons, the national coordinator of the Citizens' Councils of America, a network of white supremacist groups primarily in the South. "It's all in a day's work," Simmons said during a conference of highway patrolmen. "Feeling all over the state is just as cocky and confident as it can be." This battle was important to the Citizens' Councils. As Claude Sitton, the Pulitzer Prize–winning chronicler of the civil rights era in the South, wrote in his dispatch for the *New York Times*, if Mississippi, the state where the councils held the most influence, were to fall, it would "undoubtedly weaken their campaign for support elsewhere in the South."

It should have been clear from Barnett's early stance that integrating the University of Mississippi would not be easy. But it was not until September 27 that federal authorities understood what exactly it would take to enroll Meredith at the university in this stronghold of white supremacy. Meredith and an escort of 25 federal marshals left Memphis bound for Oxford but had to turn around before reaching campus. A crowd of 2,500 students, white adults, and 200 policemen carrying clubs while wearing gas masks were waiting at the university for the group. It had all the makings of an insurrection. Even state officials felt the tension. "I plead with you, return, return to the campus," Johnson exhorted over a loudspeaker mounted to a patrol car. "Someone could easily be killed, and it might be an innocent party." But, he added, "if you would like to have this nigger in Ole Miss, just stay where you are."

John F. Kennedy had to do something. He had to match force with force. But even the hint of such a move was met with derision by southern governors—even ones who had supported Kennedy's campaign. John Patterson, the governor of Alabama, told Kennedy in a telegram that if the president were to send troops to Mississippi, "your action would establish the Federal Government as a dictatorship of the foulest sort." Patterson agreed with Barnett: the states should have the right to bar Black students from their institutions if they so chose. "If troops are sent to Mississippi, I ask you if you are prepared to invade Alabama?" Patterson was just months from being out of office. His successor would be George C. Wallace, and on the campaign trail, Wallace had promised to go to prison rather than allow Alabama's colleges to be integrated.

At first, Kennedy tried to go forward without the military. He ordered a 110-man unit of army engineers to Memphis to aide the US Marshals and the Department of Defense with logistical support. They were not going to accompany the group to Oxford, but they could at least provide administrative help; the engineers would also provide food for the marshals. Even before testing the strategy the government knew it would fail. "There was grave doubt in Washington tonight that any force of marshals would be able to deal with the unruly crowds and large numbers of state police prepared to oppose Federal law in Mississippi," the *Times* wrote.

The president was being pushed to take bolder action from all corners. "When the federal government does not support the judiciary in the decisions it makes," Dwight Eisenhower, who reluctantly ordered troops to Little Rock, wrote to Kennedy, "the American people will no longer exist." Kennedy had to act to enforce the court's decisions.

Still, it took a trio of phone calls among the president, his brother and US Attorney General Robert F. Kennedy, and Barnett for the president to act. Kennedy had been trying to talk Barnett back from the cliff; this was rebellion, and the administration could no longer stand for it. If Barnett would not cease, he would have to send in federal troops. Five minutes before the clock struck midnight on the East Coast, the White House press secretary, Andrew T. Hatcher, issued a statement. "The president was unable to receive from Governor Barnett satisfactory assurances that law and order could, or would, be maintained in Oxford, Miss., during the coming weeks." Kennedy readied the troops. He federalized the state's National Guard and ordered US Army personnel to Memphis, Tennessee—an hour's drive from Oxford and the university. Even if the government was not ready to defend Meredith by any means necessary, it had to be prepared to put out an uprising.

On the morning of September 30, Oxford, Mississippi, was on the edge of chaos. By the evening, it had snapped. "There's going to be shooting if they try to enroll that nigger," a farmer told Hoke Norris, a reporter from the *Chicago Sun-Times* at nine a.m. Norris was one of more than three hundred reporters who were in Oxford for the standoff. "Barnett can't back down now."

But, quietly, the governor was already planning to back down—though theatrically. State leaders had grown concerned about the devolution of the situation into all-out war in Oxford. At 12:45 p.m., Barnett spoke with Attorney General Kennedy and outlined his plan for surrender. He wanted a photo to prove that he remained defiant. He would stand in front of a battalion of five hundred unarmed patrolmen, sheriffs, deputies, and others. It would be a stare-down straight out of a classic western. "When Meredith presents himself, I'll do like I did before," Barnett told Kennedy. "I will read a proclamation denying him entrance. I will tell the people of Mississippi now that I want peace and we must have no violence, no bloodshed. When you draw the guns, I will then tell the people. In other words, we will step aside and you can walk in." It would undoubtedly look like an armed conflict and could easily devolve into one. The federal government could not allow it.

Kennedy objected. "I think it is silly going through this whole facade of your standing there, our people drawing guns; your stepping aside; to me it's dangerous and I think this has gone beyond the stage of politics," he told Barnett.

But Barnett could not just walk away without a fight. He had too much invested in this personally, including his reputation among other segregationists. "I have to be confronted by your troops," he said.

Some crises happen seemingly in an instant; others slog along until someone ends up dead. That Sunday was somehow both. In Jackson, the Citizens' Council held a rally in front of the governor's mansion. Three thousand people had come from across the South for the event. A Citizens' Council official screamed through a bullhorn. "It may be that an attempt will be made to seize Governor Ross Barnett from the mansion today," John Wright, the official, said. "We want you to form a human wall around the mansion!" The crowd chanted. "Two, four, six, eight, we don't want to integrate!"

Meanwhile, despite his backroom dealings with Kennedy, Barnett had been appointing deputies to go to Oxford as his representatives that night. George Yarborough, the president pro tem of the state senate and one of the officials Barnett deputized, ordered highway patrol officers to begin taking defensive positions in Oxford. Two hundred of the patrolmen were instructed to report to the home of Ole Miss, alongside seventy of the state's eighty-two sheriffs and their deputies. Hundreds of civilians flooded in from Alabama, Tennessee, Texas, and elsewhere.

When the Cessna plane carrying James Meredith landed in Oxford just after six o'clock in the evening, rows of air force and transport planes had lined up along the runway. Only aircraft approved by the federal government were being allowed to land—that may be the only reason why the grand wizard of the Ku Klux Klan, whose plane was turned away, did not join the throngs gathering near the front of campus. Three hundred federal marshals had circled the white-columned administration building, known as the Lyceum. It was the headquarters of the federal government's operation. Meredith, wearing a suit and with a newspaper and briefcase in tow, was sneaked onto the grounds through a side entrance.

The troops surrounding the Lyceum were hardly a fighting force. Instead, they were deputy marshals, federal prison guards, and border patrolmen. State police were ordered to keep anyone but students, faculty, and university employees off the campus. They were not there to back up the feds but instead were supposed to prevent the situation from becoming a riot. They failed. Around seven thirty p.m., students and protesters began throwing rocks and bottles at the federal officers, who responded with tear gas. The grounds outside the Lyceum began to look like a battlefield through the smoke-cloaked trees. Young white men wildly waved Confederate flags, threw bricks, and cursed at the feds. Word got around that Meredith was already being housed at Baxter Hall, and some of the white men believed it a good idea to burn the building down. They turned their anger on reporters instead. "That guy's a goddamn reporter. Let's kill him," one student screamed at Gordon Yoder, a Dallas cameraman, before a mob swarmed him and tried to take his camera. Paul Guihard, a reporter for Agence France-Presse, was shot and killed—the only reporter known to be killed during the civil rights era.

The state highway patrolmen left campus at 9:10 p.m., and reinforcements for the feds would not arrive for another three hours. Near ten o'clock, President Kennedy called Barnett, urging him to order the highway patrol to return to the campus. One aide to the president warned that if the mob found its way to Meredith, there would be a lynching. "We can't consider moving Meredith as long as the, you know, there's a riot outside, 'cause he wouldn't be safe," Kennedy told Barnett. He needed the governor to restore order. If he would not, the federal troops would have to. As the leaders were speaking, Kennedy received word that a state policeman had been killed in the riot.

"Mr. President, please. Can't you just give an order up there to remove Meredith?" Barnett asked, seizing upon what he viewed as a chance at victory, another chance to put off the integration of the university.

Kennedy became irate. "How can I remove him, Governor, when there's a riot in the street and he may step out of that building and something happen to him?" he shouted. "I can't remove him under those conditions. Let's get order up there, then we can do something about Meredith."

They broke the call off quickly, before conferring again a little while later. The situation was still dire. There was word of snipers in Oxford. Kennedy needed order. As the clock struck ten, Kennedy ordered a military invasion of Oxford. But his troops were ninety miles away. Fifty minutes after his order, students rolled a bulldozer onto campus and directed it straight toward the main door of the Lyceum. In another instance, the mob stole a fire truck and rolled it down the drive in front of campus. Just before midnight, the governor relented, and issued a statement. The battle would not continue in face-to-face standoffs, he said, and instead he would continue to fight it in the courts. "I will never yield a single inch in my determination to win the fight we are all engaged in. I call on all Mississippians to keep the faith and courage. We will never surrender." But he was giving up this skirmish. "My heart still says, 'Never,' but my calm judgment abhors the bloodshed that would follow."

He had waited too long. The riot continued for fifteen hours as federal troops poured onto campus to quell the mob. When the dust settled, three people were dead, and dozens more were wounded. The streetlights were shot out, the gardens were ripped up, and tear gas cannisters and bullet shells littered the campus. Two hundred people were arrested, including students and other agitators.

At eight o'clock on October 1, Meredith, alongside McShane and Doar, was finally able to leave Baxter Hall, surrounded by a guard of marshals and soldiers. They headed toward the Lyceum. Bullet holes dotted the sides of the border patrol car Meredith had been transported in the night before; the windows had been shot out. The deputies put army blankets over the back seat so Meredith and the others could sit down. The marshals were bandaged and bruised. The federal government had fought for integration and won, but there was little celebration. When the press asked Meredith how he felt upon registering for classes, he summed it up plainly: "This is no happy occasion."

Mississippi was integration's bloodiest battle and its most dramatic. Segregation by law would soon fall in other states as well, but never with the cinematics of Mississippi. The federal government came to the aid only when the state lost control. But what would it do when discrimination was no longer written into the law but guided by history? It is easy to activate the National Guard against an uprising; history and tradition are a more difficult enemy.

Even if the most violent scenes rose from the South, discrimination knows no borders. By the mid-sixties, northern and western white colleges had negligible Black enrollments. Kennedy's affirmative action order would become President Johnson's affirmative action order, and colleges began using race in admissions as a tool to diversify their ranks; those with government-sponsored endowments built over generations, and those without. Meanwhile, Black colleges continued to educate the Black masses with might but few resources. The bloodiest fight in the South was over, but higher education across the country was still broken for Black students.

CHAPTER 8

Thirteen Years a Remedy, Thirty Years a Fight, Two Centuries a Struggle

The story of racial discrimination in higher education during the post-desegregation era is a double helix; two strands tied together by a ladder of protests and court battles. By 1966, America's unequal higher-education system, with its well-funded institutions for white students, and its scrappy Black colleges, was slowly changing. Over the next three decades, the major fights for parity at the colleges Black students attended, and equal opportunity at the ones they had been shut out of by hook or crook, would end the same way: in imperfect progress.

The only thing standing between Sargent Shriver and the door on February 22, 1966, was a Black man from Glen Allan, Mississippi.

Jake Ayers had traveled more than a thousand miles to be in Washington, DC, and he could not let his journey end without the money. At forty-six, Ayers was thicker than he once was. There were more gray whiskers in his mustache and more flecks of experience peppering his temples than when he became one of the only Black people in his little plantation town in the Mississippi delta to register to vote in 1958. His hallmark persuasive skills were the same, though, and he would need every one of them if he was going to convince Shriver to help them keep the Black children back home from starving.

In a roundabout way, Ayers had gone to Washington because of a bill signed by President Lyndon Baines Johnson two years prior. It was not the landmark Civil Rights Act of 1964, but a separate piece of legislation: one that addressed poverty. On August 20, 1964, during a midmorning address in the Rose Garden at the White House, Johnson told the American people they had made history. "For so long as man has lived on this earth poverty has been his curse," Johnson said. "Today for the first time in all the history of the human race, a great nation is able to make— and is willing to make—a commitment to eradicate poverty among its people." Johnson was signing the Economic Opportunity Act of 1964, and, as the law's name suggested, its purpose was to "offer opportunity, not opiate," the president said.

The act created the Office of Economic Opportunity (OEO), which would ultimately administer Johnson's long agenda of domestic programs from civil rights to antipoverty programs to education. Shriver, the founding director of the Peace Corps who was married to Eunice Kennedy, the sister of John F. Kennedy, was chosen to launch the office as its first director. Under the office's umbrella, Shriver assembled a team of child-development experts, including Robert Cooke of Johns Hopkins University, and Edward Zigler, the director of the Yale Child Study Center, to develop a program for disadvantaged preschool children—they would eventually call the program Head Start.

Ayers heard about Head Start by happenstance in 1965. He was working at a carpet mill in Greenville, Mississippi—a job he'd held for a decade—and learned that state civil rights leaders were forming an organization: the Child Development Group in Mississippi, or CDGM for short. The Office for Economic Opportunity was giving groups like theirs grants to establish Head Start programs. Ayers began petitioning for Glen Allan to have its own center in town during the summer. It was the kind of thing he did. In 1963, he had convinced the proprietors of a well for white folks to allow Glen Allan's Black residents to run a water pipe to their area. If there were benefits to be had, he wanted them for his community.

His petition for a program worked, and the new operation was set up in a beaten-down, lopsided church in town. Ayers became the chairman of the center, and then a board member for the statewide organization.

As the center was preparing to open its doors, President Johnson was back in Washington delivering another address, this time at the historically Black college in the nation's capital: Howard University. On June 4, 1965, at 6:35 p.m. on the main quadrangle in front of the library on campus, Johnson offered a rangy speech about rights. "You do not wipe away the scars of centuries by saying: Now you are free to go where you want, and do as you desire, and choose the leaders you please," he told the graduating class. "You do not take a person who, for years, has been hobbled by chains and liberate him, bring him up to the starting line of a race and then say, 'You are free to compete with all the others' and still justly believe that you have been completely fair." There was a growing Black middle class, he argued, largely the result of Black colleges like the one he was speaking at; but there was another group of Black Americans for whom there was a much "grimmer story."

When the Head Start center opened in Glen Allan, Ayers confronted just how grim the story of his home was. Many of the children were ill and had never seen a doctor. Several were malnourished; some had never eaten with utensils or at a table with other children. "Deborah entered the center weak and listless," a report about one of the children in the center read. "Too tired to sit up, she would spend the day stretched out on her mat. She rubbed and held her stomach, but would remain still, silent." A handful of the children did not know their own names.

But the longer they were in the program, the more the children improved. Deborah's teacher, Pauline Foster, realized that the child was just hungry. "I took her by the hand and we went into the kitchen and fixed her breakfast before it was time for a snack," Foster said. "She ate all the breakfast then when the time came she ate her snack. At dinner she always eats two servings."

The center was providing necessities for the children, but it was also empowering the Black community in Glen Allan. Teachers and staff were paid $82 a week by the government. For the first time, money was flowing to Black people in the city, and it was not because of white landowners. The center was a success; "the children received medical treatment. They had been fed. They laughed and talked and played together," David Nevin wrote of the program in *Life* magazine. Black residents of Glen Allan started buying things they always wanted, including homes. And it made their white neighbors furious. "Mississippians saw Head Start as a continuation of the hated civil rights movement," Nevin wrote, "and here was the federal government financing it."

The program was intended to last only for the summer, and while Ayers closed it after seven weeks, he had every intention of reopening. Glen Allan's white townies turned to their senator, John C. Stennis, to prevent that from happening. Stennis was a member of the committee that controlled the budget for the Office for Economic Opportunity and a zealous segregationist who voted against every civil rights bill from the Civil Rights Act of 1964 to the establishment of Martin Luther King Jr. Day as a federal holiday in 1983. Stennis started to lean on Shriver, who said he ignored the pressure but, suddenly, began to argue that he was nervous about CDGM for a laundry list of reasons: how it was keeping its books; how it used the cars supplied by the federal government for "civil rights purposes"; the shortage of professional staff; and the fact that, in Mississippi, the centers were made up entirely of Black students. It was reverse segregation, he believed. Ayers did not think that skepticism would translate to a loss of funds for the organization, though. He remained under the impression that the group would receive more money for their work—the money that had been promised to them.

The fall of 1965 was busy in both Washington and Glen Allan. On September 24, President Johnson signed Executive Order 11246, which built on Kennedy's order of four years prior that wrote "affirmative action" into federal guidance. Johnson's order was more forceful in its language than Kennedy's and it ensured "equal opportunity for minorities" in federal contracting. Contractors were expected to take "affirmative action" to make sure that was the case. Order 11246 also shifted civil rights enforcement responsibilities from Vice President Hubert Humphrey and the attorney general to the Community Relations Commission, which was organized under the Department of Labor. Humphrey had been the lead author of the Civil Rights Act of 1964, and, even for its benefits, civil rights advocates saw the move as potentially damaging to the cause. Such commissions were often neglected and held little power. Still, unlike some of the other civil rights measures Johnson signed into law, the order landed as a dud. The *New York Times* did not write about it until three weeks after it was signed, under the headline "Rights Blocs Fear Easing of Enforcement by U.S."

Two months later, on November 8, Johnson signed the Higher Education Act of 1965. The legislation, which had been introduced by two members of Congress from Oregon and was a part of Johnson's Great Society push, strengthened the federal government's role in education. It provided for everything from incentives for low-tuition students and grants for low-income students, to aid for teacher training and graduate education. And for the first time, the act defined what it meant to be a historically Black college or university (HBCU)—a college accredited and established before 1964 whose mission was to educate Black students.

"[This bill] means that a high school senior, anywhere in this great land of ours, can apply to any college or any university in any of the 50 states and not be turned away because his family is poor,"

Johnson said upon signing the bill. "It's a truism that education is no longer a luxury. Education in this day and age is a necessity. And in my judgment, this nation can never make a wiser or more profitable investment anywhere else."

But Black people in places like the Mississippi delta or the Black Belt of Alabama, and in northern cities like New York and Chicago, were not being turned away simply because they were poor. Back in Washington County, home of Glen Allan, the school board had adopted a "freedom-of-choice" plan to come into compliance with federal desegregation laws. On paper, students of any race could attend any school in the district. In reality, the town and its schools remained segregated—save for a few brave families. Ayers enrolled his son, Vernon, in the second grade at the white school. It made sense that he would. The Black school sat thirty to forty students in each class, and while the school was supposed to accommodate one hundred total children, three hundred students were in the building at any given time. Their books were five years old and had been used by the white school first; the spines were mangled, pages were missing, and the backs were torn off. "If we have gained nothing else with school desegregation," Ayers would later say during a congressional hearing, "we have gained one thing. Our children no longer had to use books that did not have all the pages. They did not have to use books without backs."

Twelve other Black children enrolled in Glen Allan's white school as well. The white people in the city were stunned.

Jake's wife, Lillie, was the only person at home the night a six-foot cross was burned in their front yard. Later, seventy-five cars brimming with armed white people drove slowly through the Black part of town. While no one was injured that night, trouble has a way of piling up. Head Start programs had been expanded to constitute year-round centers rather than simply summer projects, but the money for the centers in Mississippi had yet to arrive. Ayers and the CDGM began scraping together funds on the promise that they would be reimbursed by the federal government. Then, Ayers was fired from the mill. He was arrested and jailed for a minor traffic infraction. His life was threatened. And he was running out of money.

By February, he and the CDGM had had enough. That is when he found himself between Shriver and the door. "Mr. Shriver," he said, "the OEO has lied to us and you have lied to us personally and you have made us lie to the community." The office had promised there would be money for the Head Start centers. "I won't go home and tell them any more lies. I won't leave here until you tell us yes or no, that you'll fund us or you'll abandon us and let us die."

By the next day, the CDGM announced that it had been reimbursed for costs. It was Jake Ayers's first big stand for funding for Black people, but it would not be his last. The Head Start centers gave hope to the people in Glen Allan. Historically Black colleges gave hope to Black people dreaming of a higher education across the country. Nearly a decade after his battle with Shriver, Ayers would launch a case that would define what it means for a state to desegregate its colleges.

By 1970, the opportunities for Black students had grown infinitely since Kennedy ran for president. When the bar is on the floor, that is not difficult. The sixties were, in some ways, the end of the era of firsts. The 1969 appointment of a Black man, Clifton R. Wharton Jr., to be the president of Michigan State University—the first African American president of a major university, and a land-grant university, at that—was a capstone to a tumultuous decade.

There was still work to do, though, and it was guided primarily by one regulation: Title VI of the Civil Rights Act of 1964. The outline of the section is simple: "It prohibits discrimination on the basis of race, color, and national origin in programs and activities that receive federal financial assistance." Nearly every college in the country accepted financial-aid funds from the government, so nearly every institution stood to have those funds revoked if it discriminated against Black people or members of any other minority group.

The enforcement of Title VI was weak. Between January 1969 and February 1970, the Office for Civil Rights in the US Department of Health, Education, and Welfare (a forerunner to the Department of Education) conducted a compliance review in nineteen southern and border states. The department concluded that ten states were flagrantly operating segregated systems of higher education. Those states—Arkansas, Florida, Georgia, Louisiana, Maryland, Mississippi, North Carolina, Oklahoma, Pennsylvania, and Virginia—were required to submit desegregation plans within 120 days. Five of the states disregarded the orders of the department; the other five submitted poorly formed plans. But the office only pawed at attempts to force the states to comply or revoke their federal funds—the two things it was tasked with doing.

So, in May 1970, a collection of Black college students, citizens, and taxpayers from the states identified by the department joined together to form a class named for Kenneth Adams, a Black student from Mississippi, and—joined by the NAACP's Legal Defense Fund—filed a lawsuit against Elliot Richardson, the US education secretary. The case, *Adams v. Richardson*, worked its way to a court opinion in two years. The facts were clear cut. The states were flouting their responsibilities, and by not initiating the process to revoke those states' access to the federal purse, the Office for Civil Rights was as well. The department appealed the decision, but it was reaffirmed in 1973. The courts were telling the executive branch it had to do its job and enforce the nation's civil rights statutes. And then came Allan Bakke, using Title VI as a cudgel in the opposite direction.

Allan Bakke was thirty-one years old when he decided he wanted to be a doctor. The white Minneapolis native, son of a white teacher and a mailman, had made several stops before settling in to submit his application to the medical school at the University of California,

Davis. He had moved to Florida, then back to Minnesota to get his undergraduate degree. He joined the Naval Reserve Officers Training Corps to help pay for school and served combat duty as a US Marine in Vietnam. After the war he went to work for NASA in San Francisco and got his master's in mechanical engineering in June 1970.

His life was on track. But seeing what bullets and bombs did to bodies in Vietnam made him want to do more. He took night classes at San Jose State University and Stanford to amass chemistry and biology prerequisites for medical school. "I have an excellent job in engineering and am well-paid," he wrote in his application to the school of medicine at Davis. "I don't wish to change careers for financial gain, but because I truly believe my contribution to society can be much greater as a physician-engineer than in my present field."

By the time Bakke submitted his application, which arrived on the dusty, rural campus on November 26, 1972, he was thirty-two years old. Both Bakke and his friends thought his age would be a knock against him to the admissions committee. "When an applicant is over thirty, his age is a serious factor which must be considered," the committee had told Bakke when he first asked about their policy on age a year prior. "The Committee believes that an older applicant must be unusually highly qualified if he is to be seriously considered." Bakke believed he was exactly that, but age was not the only factor the committee was considering.

In 1968, there were 783 Black students attending medical school in the United States. The paltry statistics were even more jarring considering that nearly 70 percent of those students went to Howard University College of Medicine in Washington, DC, and Meharry Medical College in Nashville, Tennessee, two historically Black colleges. When Davis opened its medical school in 1966, it quickly noticed that it was part of the problem. Its inaugural class of 1968 was all white. The faculty and administration decided they needed to do something more. In 1970, they launched a special admissions program to "enhance diversity in the student body and the profession, eliminate historic barriers for medical careers for disadvantaged racial and ethnic minority groups, and increase aspiration for such careers."

The program was in lockstep with other affirmative action programs that cropped up across the country. Despite their small numbers on predominantly white campuses across the nation, Black students at colleges from the Ivy League to public regional colleges were pushing university administrations for greater representation. The result was often affirmative action programs—both to address historical discrimination and to appease vocal students.

In Davis's first year of its new program, eight out of fifty of the seats were set aside for minority applicants. The school established a regular admissions committee for non-minorities and "non-disadvantaged" minority populations, and there was a special subcommittee for those who marked themselves as being of an "economically and/or educationally disadvantaged minority group." There were separate admissions standards for each group. For the disadvantaged group, there was no minimum GPA requirement for application review. The university decided whether a student was disadvantaged by running through several criteria: Did the student work during his undergraduate studies? Was he in an equal-educational-opportunity program? What did his parents do?

By 1971, sixteen seats out of one hundred were set aside for disadvantaged students. In the first three years of the program, almost no Black or Hispanic students were admitted who did not fall into the "disadvantaged" category. And no white student who applied as disadvantaged was admitted by the special admissions committee.

When Bakke applied in 1973 as a regular applicant, his was one of 2,464 applications that the Davis medical school received. The Vietnam veteran applied to ten medical schools in total, including Minnesota, Stanford, UCLA, the University of San Francisco, Cincinnati, Georgetown, and others. He performed well during his interview at the University of California, Davis, and one reviewer noted that he was "a well-qualified candidate." However, they added, his "main handicap is the unavoidable fact that he is now 33 years of age."

On top of that, his application was late, and the baseline automatic admission score for nondisadvantaged students who applied at such a late date was 470 out of 500 application review points possible. Bakke, at 468 points, was two points shy. He received his form letter of rejection from Davis on May 14, 1973. He was also rejected by every other medical school to which he had applied.

Two weeks later, Bakke drafted a letter to Dr. George Lowrey, the school's head of admissions. "I want to study medicine more than anything else in the world," he said, appealing the committee's decision. Lowrey did not respond, so, from his perch in Sunnyvale, California, Bakke sent another letter one month later, on July 1. This one was more forceful. He had learned about the special admissions program, and he was irate. "I feel compelled to pursue a different course of action," he wrote. He argued for meritocracy. "Applicants chosen to be our doctors should be those presenting the best qualifications, both academic and personal," he wrote. This is how most applicants were selected, he continued, but he was "convinced" unqualified applicants were entering the class. "I am referring to quotas, open or covert, for racial minorities," he wrote. "I realize that the rationale for these quotas is that they attempt to atone for past racial discrimination; but insisting on a new racial bias in favor of minorities is not a just situation." Out of one hundred total seats in the class, there were sixteen that were decided by the special admissions committee, and Bakke believed he deserved a shot at one of them.

Lowrey asked Peter Storandt, one of the young assistants in the admissions office, to handle the correspondence with Bakke. Storandt was thirty years old and a veteran of several admissions offices, as well as the son of an admissions officer at Cornell University. Storandt reviewed Bakke's file and was sympathetic with him; the tone of his response to Bakke signaled as much. In a lengthy letter, Storandt told Bakke that he had done well in the overall rankings for applicants, but there was not enough room for the "remarkably able and well-qualified individuals," who had applied that year. Though Bakke had been concerned about his age, Storandt suggested that it was not the reason he was denied either. "Older applicants have successfully entered and worked in our curriculum." He believed Bakke should reapply for admission and encouraged him to do so by October 1, 1973—the early admissions deadline. That way, he would know sooner whether he had been accepted or not. Then Storandt went beyond what Lowrey had expected of him. If Davis turned Bakke down a second time, he wrote, "pursue your research on quota-oriented minority recruiting." He included a copy of the official description of the special admissions program. "I don't know whether you would consider our program to have the overtones of a quota or not . . . but the fact remains that most applicants to such a program are members of ethnic minority groups." Finally, Storandt suggested that Bakke research a case that had been working its way to the Supreme Court: *DeFunis v. Odegaard.*

Marco DeFunis, a white, Jewish student of Spanish-Portuguese descent, applied to the University of Washington's law school alongside 1,600 others in 1971. DeFunis was denied under the university's admissions policy, which allowed minority students to enter with scores lower than those of white students. He filed a lawsuit claiming that the university was violating the equal protection clause of the Fourteenth Amendment, essentially flipping on its head the clause meant to protect Black people from being discriminated against by the government. A state trial court agreed with DeFunis and ordered that the university admit him. DeFunis began his studies at the law school, but during his second year at the school, the state supreme court reversed the decision of the trial court. The admissions program did not violate the Constitution, they argued, and the policy would help the school attain a racially diverse student body, which would, in turn, launch the careers of more minority lawyers. The Supreme Court would hear the case a few months later.

Storandt's letter piqued Bakke's interest, and several weeks later, the pair met in person over coffee. Bakke peppered Storandt with questions about the policy, and Storandt replied frankly. He told Bakke how many seats were reserved for the special criteria and that no white students had ever been admitted under it. One week after their meeting, Bakke again wrote to Storandt thanking him for the meeting. "I appreciate your interest in the moral and legal propriety of quotas and preferential admissions policies," Bakke wrote. "Even more impressive to me was your real concern about the effect of admissions policies on each individual applicant." They had decided on a plan. Bakke told Storandt that he would apply to the school of medicine again, as well as to other medical schools, and he added that he was willing to raise a legal challenge to racial quotas in admissions—not unlike the DeFunis case. Bakke mailed his second application on August 13.

Two days later, on August 15, Storandt replied. "It seems to me that you have carefully arranged your thinking about this matter and that the eventual result of your next actions will be of significance to many present and future medical students."

The administration was not completely unaware of Bakke's threat of a lawsuit, and it had established a new interview procedure for the entering class of 1974. Applicants would be interviewed by two people: a faculty member and a medical student. A second-year student, Frank Gioia, offered a glowing report on Bakke. His second reviewer, Dr. Lowrey, did not. "The disturbing feature of this man is that he had very definite opinions which were based more on his personal viewpoint than upon a study of the total problem," Lowrey wrote in his review of Bakke. "He was very unsympathetic to the concept of recruiting minority students so that they hopefully would go back to practice in the neglected areas of the county."

Minority communities were being underserved through the lack of trained doctors of different races, and there were systemic reasons for that, dating back to the founding of the republic. Bakke, Lowrey argued, did not understand that. "My own impression of Mr. Bakke is that he is a rather rigidly oriented young man who has a tendency to arrive at conclusions based more upon his personal impressions than upon thoughtful processes using available sources of information," he wrote.

When the regular admissions committee reviewed Bakke's application, he received high marks from Storandt, Gioia, and the others. Dr. Lowrey, however, rated Bakke at 86 of 100. He received 549 of 600 total points on the new scale and was rejected. When the committee members reevaluated his application in the spring of 1974, they denied him for a third time.

Bakke retained the services of Reynold Colvin, an established lawyer in San Francisco, who, on receipt of Bakke's rejection, filed a complaint with the regional civil rights office of the US Department of Health, Education, and Welfare. Bakke was "the victim of racial discrimination in medical school admissions in 1973," the complaint argued. It called Davis's policy a racial quota, and alleged that because there were "set-asides" for minority applicants, Bakke had "missed acceptance by only two-points."

While waiting for a response, the pair decided to go to court. On June 20, 1974, Colvin filed a suit on Bakke's behalf in Yolo County Superior Court. Judge F. Leslie Manker came out of retirement to hear the case in the third-floor courtroom of the rural courthouse in Woodland, California. Donald Reidhaar, the lawyer for the university, argued that this was not a case of Bakke's being turned away because of his race. In fact, there were students *more qualified than he* who had been denied admission as well. The university argued that its program was nothing more than a legal effort to integrate its school and diversify the medical community.

Still, Colvin insisted that Bakke's race was the negative mark that barred him from medical school. He was being denied equal protection of the law under the Fourteenth Amendment.

In late November, Judge Manker agreed with Colvin. In a twenty-three-page ruling, Manker reanimated the words of Chief Justice Earl Warren in his seminal 1954 *Brown v. Board* opinion: "Where the State has undertaken to provide it, [education] is a right which must be made available to all on equal terms." As such, the policy of the university was unconstitutional, and education was not being made available on equal terms. Affirmative action had moved a handful of Black people closer to parity in higher education but, with Manker's decision, its existence suddenly rested on shaky foundation. Manker was not as sure about Bakke himself, though, ruling that the university should not be required to admit him, because even if the special program had not existed, he likely would not have been admitted.

A new year was on the horizon, and it looked bleak for Black students. Between 1965 and 1975, the number of Black students graduating from American medical schools each year jumped dramatically from 200 to 1,200—most still graduating from Howard or Meharry. Then the Bakke challenge froze those numbers in place for a decade, along with the hope for redress for a legacy of discrimination. Colleges across the country were worried about the challenge to the practice of race-conscious admissions—they could be the next to get sued, and these sorts of legal battles were expensive.

Black students, unable to break through to white institutions in statistically significant numbers, went where they could: the nation's historically black colleges. And as the Bakke case worked its way through the courts, Jake Ayers was preparing to challenge the vestiges of slavery and discrimination that were suffocating Black colleges—and the Black people—in Mississippi.

By September 29, 1974, the Board of Trustees for Mississippi's Institutions of Higher Learning—the governing body for the state's colleges—had submitted a proposed plan to the US Department of

Health, Education, and Welfare to come into compliance with federal civil rights laws. The board instructed the presidents of each university in the system to redirect their resources to comply with the plan. The basics of the proposal were to improve educational opportunities for Black students, emphasize equal access, and ensure retention of the students and employees at each of the state's eight public colleges. Several of the predominantly white colleges in the state had only recently hired their first Black faculty members. Mississippi State, which had received land-grant funds from the Morrill Act of 1862 and was less than a decade removed from enrolling its first Black student, in 1967, had only just hired its first Black professor.

The plan would have created attractive programs at the state's historically Black colleges to entice white students to enroll and strengthened the existing programs at those colleges. The plan also put specific projections on the number of students from different races needed at the predominantly white institutions and HBCUs. The federal government rejected the board's proposal due to its failure to address segregation in the state's junior colleges, but that did not matter to the state, which went forward with the plan anyway.

Ayers, whose son, Jake Ayers Jr., would soon be graduating from high school, was frustrated by the state's plan. He saw an opportunity in the federal government's objection to it. On January 28, 1975, Ayers filed a lawsuit on behalf of his son, Jake Jr., and a group that called itself the Black Mississippians Council on Higher Education—a coalition of twenty-one students, parents, and advocates—in federal court. The petition requested the end of racially discriminatory employment practices at the state college board, and the end of discriminatory admission, retention, and treatment practices at the predominantly white colleges—including the use of the Graduate Record Examinations (GRE), the Scholastic Aptitude Test (SAT), and other qualifying examinations that placed Black students at a disadvantage. (Carl Brigham, a Princeton-trained eugenicist who created the SAT in 1926, wrote in his 1923 book *A Study of Ameri-*

can Intelligence that the test would prove the racial superiority of white Americans, and prevent "the continued propagation of defective strains in the present population." That meant the "infiltration of white blood into the Negro.")

The group's chief requests, however, were to make the expenditures, facilities, programs, and funding of the traditionally Black colleges equal to that of the white colleges, and to place the predominantly white university outposts set up in Natchez and Jackson under the control of the corresponding Black schools in the area. An argument had started to permeate the zeitgeist: Now that Black students could attend any institution, was there still a need for historically Black colleges? But the council knew, perhaps better than any, that there was such a need. Nearly all Black students who attended college in Mississippi at the time did so at the state's Black colleges, and the state had mistreated those institutions through debilitating cuts to funding and neglect for more than a century in some cases. "We believe that quality education for Black people can be most effectively achieved by making specific improvements in all public colleges and universities—not by eliminating or downgrading the historically black schools," one council member, Ike Madison, said in a statement. The council counted among its ranks a student who had firsthand experience with the differences at the state's colleges: Bennie G. Thompson.

Thompson was just six years old when the world changed with *Brown v. Board*. But he did not feel its effect immediately. Born in Hinds County, in the city of Bolton, Thompson attended segregated public schools his entire grade-school career. James Meredith had integrated the University of Mississippi two years before Thompson enrolled at Tougaloo College, a small, private, historically Black college that became a hotbed of civil rights activity in the state. He graduated in 1968, the year Martin Luther King Jr. was assassinated in Memphis, Tennessee.

After undergraduate studies, Thompson went to another one of the state's historically Black colleges—Jackson State University—for his master's degree in educational administration. The school enrolled its first white student a year later. Thompson quickly noticed a few things about the institution in the state's capital city. While his professors were caring and attentive, the books in the library were old, as were the science labs and the equipment in them. When he enrolled at the University of Southern Mississippi, a predominantly white college five years removed from integration, to begin a doctoral program in public administration, the deficiencies became more glaringly apparent. "I was made aware of how easy it was as a student to go to the library and find books that you had requirements to research and read," Thompson said. "I found a job on campus, there were counselors available to me at my beck and call, and it was very easy as a student at a predominantly white institution to do well."

This dual perspective—from both the state's Black colleges and its white ones—is why Ayers and the Black Mississippians wanted Thompson to join their cause. He was happy to and became one of the original twenty-one plaintiffs. In March, the US Department of Justice joined the suit against the state of Mississippi. It would be expensive to take the case to court, so the parties decided it would be best to seek a settlement through arbitration. The groups deliberated for the next dozen years. In the meantime, Bakke was fast-tracking his way to the nation's high court.

Neither side of the Bakke case was satisfied with Judge Manker's decision. The university was upset its admissions practices had been deemed unconstitutional; Bakke was mad that, even after all this fighting, he still had not been admitted to the medical school. Both lawyers, Colvin for Bakke, and Donald Reidhaar for the university, appealed to the state supreme court. The court quickly decided to take the case on.

Oral arguments were scheduled for March 1976, and nine

groups filed friend-of-the-court briefs: Six, including the NAACP, supported the university; three, including the American Jewish Congress and the American Federation of Teachers, supported Bakke. Colvin argued that the university, in accordance with the Fourteenth Amendment, and Title VI of the Civil Rights Act, was required to be color-blind and could not discriminate based on race—regardless of the race being discriminated against. It was a perversion of Harlan's dissent in *Plessy*, a caustic perversion at that. But the university held that Bakke would not have been admitted whether there was the policy in place or not.

On September 16, 1976, the state supreme court handed down its forty-eight-page opinion. In a 6–1 ruling, the justices decided that while the goal of the medical school was admirable, it was not an appropriate way to achieve diversity or parity under the law. They examined the case under the "strict scrutiny" standard—the most stringent judicial review—which requires a regulation to have a "compelling state interest," use "the least restrictive means" to achieve that interest, and be narrowly tailored. It was on the last point, *narrowly tailored*, the court argued, that the Davis policy failed. There were other methods to increase diversity in the student body without a special admissions committee with different criteria, though the court did not deign to identify what those means were. As such, the court argued, the policy violated Bakke's rights under the Fourteenth Amendment.

The state supreme court went one step further than Manker did. Bakke, they said, must be admitted to the medical school at the University of California, Davis, unless the school could produce evidence that Bakke would not have been admitted otherwise.

Justice Matthew O. Tobriner was the court's only dissenting voice. Over the course of fifty-seven scathing pages, Tobriner argued that the court had failed to distinguish between races that had been discriminated against and those that had not. The nation was in a period of transition. It had just come out from under hundreds of years of an explicitly racial caste system. It would be illogical to disregard that for some illusion of color-blindness before the law. "Our society cannot be completely color-blind in the short term if we are to have a color-blind society in the long run," he wrote in his dissent. "Wealth, educational resources, employment opportunities—indeed all society's benefits—remain largely the preserve of the white-Anglo majority." The majority's ruling, then, was ironic. "It is anomalous that the Fourteenth Amendment that served as the basis for the requirement that elementary and secondary schools be 'compelled' to integrate should now be turned around to forbid graduate schools from voluntarily seeking that very objective."

His colleagues, however, wrote that it was "abundantly clear" that white people suffered a "grievous disadvantage" by being excluded from those sixteen seats. The university had not met its burden of "demonstrating that the basic goals of the program cannot be substantially achieved by means less detrimental to the rights of the majority."

The case was careering toward the nation's high court. When the Supreme Court made its decision in the *DeFunis* case, five justices agreed that affirmative action in higher education was something they would have to address sooner than later. Justice William Rehnquist issued a stay in *Bakke*, which put a pause on the state supreme court's decision that the university must enroll Bakke.

Appeals began to pour in to officials at the University of California, Davis, to drop the case—not from groups that opposed affirmative action, but from those that supported it. The state supreme court's decision was a narrow one that would not alter dramatically the course of affirmative action, only the program at that particular university. However, if the US Supreme Court ruled in favor of Bakke, it would establish precedent on the limits of the practice—or eliminate diversity as a compelling interest altogether. They wanted a stronger case for the Supreme Court to weigh in on. The university pressed ahead anyway.

On February 22, 1977, the Supreme Court announced that it would hear the *University of California Regents v. Bakke*. The aerospace engineer who dreamed of becoming a doctor was now a Supreme Court decision away from going to medical school and nearing forty years old. This was likely his last shot.

The *Bakke* case became a race toward October as friend-of-the-court briefs came in from all over. There were universities, the NAACP, three lawyers with the American Civil Liberties Union, including Ruth Bader Ginsburg, the American Medical Association, and a host of other prominent student groups and organizations. Harvard University, Howard University, and others argued that the admissions process of each individual university was an independent matter and should not be interfered in by the government. Schools, they argued, should not become tools of the state, and if the state denied an institution's right to use any matter of criteria, including race, in deciding its student body, they would become such a tool. Fifteen briefs were filed on behalf of Bakke, from organizations including the American Federation of Teachers, the Fraternal Order of Police, and the US Chamber of Commerce. The case became a cause célèbre for conservative groups. Martin DeFunis, who had since become a lawyer, wrote the brief for the Young Americans for Freedom.

On October 12, 1977, the court heard oral arguments. "Allan Bakke's position is that he has a right," Colvin argued in front of the court. "And that right is not to be discriminated against because of his race. And that is what brings Allan Bakke to this court."

The case followed the same tenor of the trial and state supreme court arguments until a particularly striking back-and-forth between Colvin and Thurgood Marshall, who had been appointed to the court by President Johnson. Marshall challenged Colvin on the merits of Bakke's case.

"Your client did compete for the eighty-four seats, didn't he?" Marshall asked.

"Yes, he did," Colvin responded.

"And he lost," said Marshall.

"Yes, he did," Colvin repeated.

Marshall pressed Colvin. "Now, would your argument be the same if one instead of sixteen seats were left open?"

"Most respectfully," Colvin responded, "the argument does not turn on numbers." He told Justice Marshall that whether it was one seat or one hundred seats, "if he was kept out by his race," it was wrong. The numbers were not important. "It is the principle of keeping a man out because of his race that is important."

But Marshall was not worried about keeping anyone out of higher education because of his race; he was worried about whether he could get in regardless of his race. That had been the problem he fought against, and the issue he recognized in this case. Racial exclusion from education ended in word with the *Brown v. Board* case, which he had argued in front of the court, but not necessarily in deed. "You're arguing about keeping somebody out and the other side is arguing about getting somebody in?"

Colvin replied, "That's right."

"So, it depends on which way you look at it," Marshall said.

Colvin agreed. "It depends on which way you look at the problem."

"It does?" Marshall responded, cheekily.

"The problem—" Colvin began to say before Marshall cut him off.

"It does?" Marshall said.

Colvin grew frustrated. "If I may finish."

"It does?" Marshall said, again. "You're talking about your client's rights; don't these underprivileged people have rights too?"

It was a jarring moment, and Colvin paused for a moment before responding. "They certainly have rights to compete," he said, stumbling over his words. "They have the right to compete, they have the right to equal competition."

The argument is what the case turned upon. As Archibald Cox, who argued the case for the university, told the court, "There is no perceived rule of color blindness incorporated in the Equal Protection Clause." The law had been interpreted to protect "discrete and insular" minority groups—meaning those for whom the law did not work. Bakke did not fall within that category. The laws of the country were made for men like him. "You have to decide whether we are right in saying that race may be taken into account for proper purposes," Cox said.

The oral arguments ended with a thanks. Two days later, the justices of the Supreme Court held a conference session to discuss the case. Justice William Brennan's initial thought was that Davis's use of race was consistent with the Fourteenth Amendment. Potter Stewart disagreed. "If the Equal Protection clause does nothing else, it forbids discrimination based alone on a person's race. That's precisely what the Davis program does and injurious action based on race is unconstitutional." Stewart believed that race, in any accounting by a state agency, should be forbidden.

Marshall agreed with those who believed the Davis system was fair. "On the quota question," he said, "this is not a quota to keep people out—it's a quote to get someone in."

Lewis Powell, however, thought the quota was unconstitutional. "I can't join Thurgood, Byron, and Bill in thinking that sixteen or eighty-four or any quota was okay," Powell told the conference. "The symbolic effect of the Fourteenth Amendment is completely lost," if he did so, he said. But the Fourteenth Amendment was not symbolic. It was meant to protect marginalized groups. Still, Powell argued, race could be considered, but the "colossal blunder" that Davis made was in picking several seats. "Diversity is a necessary goal to allow a broad spectrum of Americans an opportunity for graduate school," he posited. Applicants should be able to compete for seats, and colleges should be able to take race into account, but institutions should not prescribe a set number of seats. His issue was with quotas, not race. The court was split. Harry Blackmun, who was ill, was unable to participate in the conference. Three justices sided with the university. Four justices sided with Bakke. And Lewis Powell was square in the middle.

The court instructed the lawyers for both Bakke and the university to draft supplemental briefs about the Title VI merits of the case—that an institution that received federal funds should not discriminate based on race for fear of loss of federal funds. Such a remedy would be less severe than changing the meaning of a constitutional amendment. Over the next eight months, justices exchanged memo after memo. They argued about whether they had the votes for certain changes in verbiage, whether any side would have enough support for a decision.

Until the very end, Marshall argued that the case turned on a legacy of discrimination. "I repeat, for the next to last time," Marshall wrote to his colleagues on April 13, 1978. "The decision in this case depends on whether you consider the action of the Regents as *admitting* certain students or as *excluding* certain other students. If you view the program as admitting qualified students who, because of this Nation's sorry history of racial discrimination, have academic records that prevent them from effectively competing for medical school, then this is affirmative action to remove the vestiges of slavery and state imposed segregation by 'root and branch,'" he forcefully argued. "If you view the program as *excluding* students, it is a program of 'quotas' which violates the principle that the 'Constitution is color-blind.'" The high court had never accepted such a principle. "If only the principle of color-blindness had been accepted by the majority in *Plessy* in 1896, we would not be faced with this problem in 1978." The principle, Marshall continued, appeared only in dissent. The nation had been based on the special treatment of race by law for the sixty years between *Plessy* and *Brown*. It would be unconscionable to alter that as soon as Black people began receiving some reparation for the harm of those lost decades.

"This case is here now because of that sordid history," Marshall said. "So despite the lousy record, the poorly reasoned lower court opinion, and the absence as parties of those who will be most affected by the decision (the Negro applicants), we are stuck with this case. We are not yet all equals, in large part because of the refusal of the *Plessy* court to adopt the principle of color-blindness. It would be the cruelest irony for this Court to adopt the dissent in *Plessy* now and hold that the University must use color-blind admissions."

The court was so split in the case that it was destined for the lone voice who fell in the middle to decide it. Lewis Powell had neither the conviction that race should not be used in admissions nor the belief that quotas were an acceptable form of remedying discrimination. "On the assumption that I will announce the judgment in this case, I have tried my hand at a statement," Powell wrote to his colleagues on June 21, 1978. "My primary purpose was to assist the representatives of the media present in understanding 'what in the world' the Court has done!"

When the court met five days later, on June 26, hundreds had gathered outside 1 First Street NE in Washington, DC. This would be the most important civil rights case since *Brown,* the newspapers wrote. There were ultimately six different opinions, a judicial rarity, and the nation's divisions over the case only mirrored how split the court was. Four justices agreed, in some form, with Bakke that the university's affirmative action strategy violated Title VI because it ostensibly capped the number of white students who could be admitted at eighty-four. Four other justices argued that the strategy was permissible under both Title VI and the Fourteenth Amendment.

As Powell expected, with a 4–4 split, the decision fell to him. "Perhaps no case in modern memory has received as much media coverage and scholarly commentary," Powell said, as he prepared to read his opinion. "We also have received advice through the media and the commentaries of countless extrajudicial advocates." But in the end, Powell announced what he believed all along. Race could be used as a factor in admissions, but quotas were unacceptable; race could be used, but not as a remedy for past discrimination. "There is a measure of inequity in forcing innocent persons in [Bakke's] position to bear the burdens of redressing grievances not of their own making," Powell argued. Race was important only so that others may learn from those who were different from them.

Powell cited a brief filed by Harvard University, whose holistic admissions program had been hailed as the right path forward. The program at Harvard argued that race was used only as one criterion among an array of others in making an admissions decision. "Race is considered in a flexible program designed to achieve diversity, but it is only one factor weighed competitively against a number of other factors being relevant," such as grades, extracurricular activities, and athletic prowess, the Harvard brief said. The Harvard program was imprecise. It did not set strict criteria for what put a student over the top in admissions. It made the sauce secret.

But the University of California, Davis, medical school argued that there was a compelling governmental interest in providing redress for "general societal discrimination" against Black people and other minority groups. Powell did not see it that way. Affirmative action could not be about righting historical wrongs, it could be only about diversity. Powell's decision upended the prevailing notion of the equal protection clause—that it was intended to aid discrete and insular minorities—and applied it broadly.

In his dissent, Justice Harry Blackmun prophetically estimated what the result of the decision would be. "I suspect that it would be impossible to arrange an affirmative action program in a racially neutral way and have it successful," he said. "To ask that this be so is to demand the impossible. In order to get beyond racism, we must first take account of race. There is no other way. And in order to treat some persons equally, we must treat them differently."

He was right. Not every college is selective enough to need to use affirmative action, but some of the nation's most deep-pocketed colleges do use the practice. After the *Bakke* case, the percentage of

Black students at the highest-ranked institutions across the country has stagnated, remaining at roughly 6 percent of first-years at the nation's most illustrious colleges, despite comprising 15 percent of college-age Americans.

Affirmative action, or perhaps more appropriately, race-conscious admissions, has been upheld in case after case in the forty years that followed the *Bakke* decision. There were the University of Michigan cases in 2003, *Grutter v. Bollinger*, which alleged that the institution's law school admissions policy was discriminatory, and *Gratz v. Bollinger*, which said the same was true of its undergraduate policy. And then there were the *Fisher v. University of Texas* cases in 2013 and 2016, which argued that that institution's policy discriminated as well. Each time the constitutionality of race-conscious admissions policies has been challenged, it has prevailed, but that is because its strength is in its weakness, in its feeble ability to correct for historical discrimination.

Several states—California, Washington, Michigan, Nebraska, Arizona, and Oklahoma—have banned affirmative action through voter referenda. Jeb Bush, the former governor of Florida, banned it through executive order. The state legislature of New Hampshire banned the practice. In each state, Black enrollment at flagship colleges has fallen. And even though the doors of higher education are open, Black students still tend to end up at colleges with the least amount of funding.

With hopes for aggressive affirmative action programs blunted after *Bakke*, the work of educating the masses of Black students fell where it always had: to Black colleges—but the institutions were in a fight for their lives.

Every offer Mississippi made to the Black Mississippians seemed like a trap. In 1982, Mississippi Institutions of Higher Learning, the state's higher education coordinating body, designated Jackson State University, the Black college in the state's capital, an "urban university," and charged school officials with limiting the number of students it accepted on the margins. The move, Black college advocates argued, would interfere with the mission of the university, which had always been accepting the students other colleges would not. In 1986, Mississippi recommended closing one of the state's Black colleges, Mississippi Valley State University, so that the funds from it could go to other institutions serving Black students. The recommendation was never fulfilled, but the plaintiffs were furious. If not for the Black colleges willing to accept and nurture them, where else would those marginal Black students go, the Black Mississippians asked. Certainly not to any of the predominantly white universities.

After the *Bakke* case, enrollments of Black students at predominantly white institutions remained unchanged in the South. Between 1976 and 1982, Black students consistently made up 9 percent of full-time undergraduates in the South's white colleges. However, nearly half of those Black students attended junior colleges, not four-year white colleges.

By 1987, twelve years after the 1975 petition was filed, the Black Mississippians decided they had had enough. Jake Ayers Sr. died of a heart attack in 1986; other plaintiffs began to die as well. The case needed energy, and it needed a resolution. The Black students in Mississippi who began first grade when the trial started could very well be enrolling at the state's Black colleges in the fall. They had to reason with themselves: How long is too long to keep fighting?

They took the state to court, landing in the Jackson courtroom of Neal B. Biggers Jr., who had been nominated to the seat by President Reagan in 1984. The temperature flirted with 90 degrees as the sweltering Mississippi sun burned in a cloudless sky on April 27, 1987, when oral arguments began. "This is the case all America is looking at," Alvin O. Chambliss, the fiery attorney for the Black college group, told the Jackson *Clarion-Ledger* ahead of the trial. "Mississippi never equalized the educational opportunities among the universities after state-imposed segregation was declared illegal by the federal courts." And each year, he said, "the gap between historically black universities and historically white universities grows wider."

Inside the courtroom, Chambliss ran down a list of complaints: Mississippi had made standardized-test scores the sole factor for automatic admission at all state colleges, but the thresholds were higher at the white colleges. The plaintiffs argued that the system shut out many Black students who had good grades but did not perform well on the tests. Meanwhile, many of Mississippi's white colleges offered the same academic programs as its Black colleges, making it hard for Black colleges to compete for white students. Added to that was the fact that the state had, for decades, spent less money per student on its Black colleges, which created the differences that were obvious to Bennie Thompson the moment he arrived at the University of Southern Mississippi.

The lawyer for the state, William F. Goodman, whose molasses drawl slugged with every statement, argued that theirs was a case without a plausible resolution. "The thrust of this case is racial without suggesting a remedy," he said. "It seeks a vague finding of unconstitutionality." Black students had freedom of choice, Goodman said, and they were choosing to go to the Black colleges.

When Jake Ayers Jr. was interviewed by the *Clarion-Ledger* in May 1987, he had a different take on why Black students attended the state's HBCUs. The younger Ayers had not taken much interest in his dad's civil rights activity when he was growing up. After high school, he attended a two-year historically Black college, Mary Holmes College, before joining the air force. He moved to Oklahoma and took a job with a roofing company, and he had not thought about the suit in years when Jerry Mitchell, the reporter for the *Ledger*, reached him. Black students in Mississippi "never really gave it a thought," to attend white colleges, Ayers told Mitchell. "The thing to do was to go to the black colleges. Those are the colleges where I had cousins attend. You never really thought about going to Ole Miss or Mississippi State." Those institutions, he argued, seemed unattainable to Black students.

Still, Judge Biggers agreed with the state. It was easy after sifting through all the evidence to become unnerved by the "inefficiencies" of the state's higher-education system, he argued in an opinion he issued on December 10, 1987. There were likely too many universities doing too many similar things. Perhaps some of the institutions should be closed, he suggested, echoing the state's proposal to close one or more of the Black colleges. However, that was not what was at issue. Instead, the issue was whether any practices of the state were "racially motivated to bring about results which deprive black citizens of benefits provided to white citizens." Biggers believed that there were none. "Mississippi's current actions demonstrate conclusively that the State is fulfilling its affirmative duty to disestablish the former *de jure* segregated system," Biggers said. Since the state did not have overtly racist laws written into its books, it was in the clear. Chambliss was not surprised by the ruling, and he quickly announced that the plaintiffs would be appealing the case to the Fifth Circuit Court of Appeals.

Another three years passed before the appellate court took up the case. It ended with another victory for the state. But the decision was not without dissent. The state argued that its obligation to end de jure segregation ended the day it adopted an open admissions policy, the dissenting judges wrote, but that was an "erroneous" view. "A state violates its duty to undo its wrong when it makes decisions that directly reinforce the historical traces of separate post-secondary educational paths for blacks and whites," the judges, led by Patrick Higginbotham, wrote. When Black students challenge a state policy as discriminatory, it is no longer their responsibility to prove they are being discriminated against. Instead, it is the state's responsibility to prove that it is not discriminating and to identify legitimate reasons for its actions.

But dissents do not win cases, and the Black Mississippians were growing old. Lillie Ayers, Jake's wife, took over as chief plaintiff, at age sixty-three, as the case headed for the US Supreme Court.

On November 13, 1991, sixteen years after the case began, the

high court heard oral arguments. Chambliss opened his arguments
with a history lesson in a pastor's cadence. He restated the case: Mississippi had violated Title VI of the Civil Rights Act, which protects
people from discrimination based on race, color, or national origin
in programs that receive federal financial assistance.

Justice Antonin Scalia, the pugilist conservative stalwart, wanted
to know what remedies Chambliss was proposing. The worst thing to
do "would be to establish a black university that has the full curriculum and is fully good as what is now the predominantly white university," Scalia said. White students would go to the white colleges, Black
students to black colleges. Segregation would get worse, not better.

That is not what Chambliss wanted. "You will always see some
level of racial identifiability on those campuses," he said. But the
goal was real desegregation, not a new doctrine of separate-and-
equal. It was not the Black colleges' fault that white students went to
predominantly white institutions; instead, it was the state's fault for
allowing white colleges to unnecessarily duplicate courses that were
already available at the Black schools.

Kenneth Starr, the U.S. solicitor general, picked up the argument
from there. He pointed to Mississippi Valley State University and
Delta State University, the neighboring institutions that showed the
yawning gulf between Black colleges and white colleges. Why, he
asked, would a white student who could attend either school pick
the one "that has continued to suffer deprivations of funding and
facilities?"

But if the Black colleges are underfunded, said Scalia, why don't
more Black students go to the white colleges? If Mississippi's colleges
were still segregated, perhaps, he continued, it was because of the
sum of thousands of individual choices that both Black and white
students were making. The state was not choosing for them. Further,
it was not just the Black colleges that were underfunded, argued
Goodman, the lawyer for the state of Mississippi, picking up on Scalia's skepticism. It was all the state colleges.

Justice Clarence Thomas, fresh off a marathon confirmation hearing, and who later developed a reputation of rarely speaking from the bench, pressed Goodman. Thomas pointed out that the Black universities had been discriminated against. Did that create a difference between the Black colleges and white colleges? And did that mean the state owed them? No, Goodman replied. "In today's world," he said, "we have absolute genuine freedom of choice."

And that was the fundamental disagreement between the state and the Black citizens, the disagreement between the justices who sided with Bakke and those who sided with Thurgood Marshall, and the disagreement that still plagues higher education today. Mississippi did not believe it had a problem. Things were bad in the past, but that was over now. The problems ended the day nominally race-neutral programs were introduced. The plaintiffs, however, thought there was no way you could look at the system and not see the lingering racial issues that needed to be addressed.

On June 26, 1992, fourteen years to the day since the *Bakke* decision was announced, the Supreme Court, in an 8–1 decision, agreed with the Black Mississippians. Even if Mississippi's policies are "race neutral on their face," wrote the majority, they can still perpetuate segregation. The majority of justices did not, however, want to send the wrong message. "If we understand private petitioners to press us to order the upgrading of Jackson State, Alcorn State, and Mississippi Valley State *solely* that they may be publicly financed, exclusively black enclaves by private choice, we reject that request," Justice Sandra Day O'Connor wrote in the court's opinion. But that was not what the plaintiffs were arguing for at all. They wanted parity, not purity.

If the state were to take the assumption that this meant they were not required to increase appropriations to the Black colleges, Justice Thomas hoped to disabuse them of the notion. "It would be ironic, to say the least, if the institutions that sustained Blacks during segregation were themselves destroyed in an effort to combat its vestiges." For the first time in nearly two decades, the Black citizens had a win—a big win.

The ruling set a new standard for how far a state needed to go to redress the lasting wounds of segregation in higher education. "What other kind of sledgehammer do you need?" Thompson, who by then had become the Hinds County supervisor, told the *Clarion-Ledger.*

Chambliss was equally elated. "This decision is a great thing. It's the most important thing since *Brown v. Board of Education,*" he told the *Chronicle of Higher Education.* "Everything is on the table now."

The plaintiffs and Mississippi went back into arbitration. But after a few more years, the weight of three decades of litigation became heavy on the plaintiffs. They had staved off another plan to close Mississippi Valley State University and merge it with Delta State University, and it appeared that the most expedient way to end the case would be for the state to funnel money to its Black colleges for programs, salaries, and facilities. Concerns over this solution lingered as some, including Chambliss, questioned the wisdom of focusing on settlement money in a desegregation case.

"Lawyers who had the case would move on, and we had to pick up other counsel," Thompson said. "There were just a few of us still left, so we decided to see if there was an opportunity to craft a settlement." Thompson became the lead plaintiff; then he was elected to Congress. By 2001, the parties had reached a tentative settlement. It was better to get something than keep fighting and run the risk of coming up empty. It had been nearly thirty years since the case began. The agreement called for $500 million split among the Black colleges over the course of seventeen years, including $246 million in funding over seventeen years for academic programs at the three public Black colleges in the state, $75 million over five years for capital investments, a $70 million public endowment, and a private endowment worth up to $35 million. The settlement became a landmark for how other states would seek to settle disputes over inequity and segregation in higher education.

In his final judgment, Neal Biggers, the district court judge, thought the state was going further than it needed to, and he said it raised "the question of how policymakers of the State choose to allocate state resources." But he deferred to the parties' agreement. As a result of the settlement, Biggers wrote, "there are no continuing state policies or practices or remnants traceable to de jure segregation, with present discriminatory effects, which can be eliminated, altered or repealed with educationally sound, feasible, and practical alternatives or remedial measures." The agreement, he continued, "accomplishes a full, complete and final resolution of this controversy."

But the result of the *Ayers* case was not too dissimilar from the win in *Bakke*. It was a major victory for the Black colleges in Mississippi and across the nation, but it sent the wrong message. The University of Mississippi could make $500 million in private donations in five years. To think that $500 million was enough to bring parity to Black colleges, in hindsight, was woefully inadequate. The state slipped away without being forced to account deeply for its legacy.

Black colleges are no longer alone in educating Black students, but even now, despite composing just 3 percent of America's four-year nonprofit institutions, they produce an outsize number of Black professionals. Their students make up 25 percent of Black undergraduates who earn degrees in science, technology, engineering, and mathematics. But they are struggling financially. The average HBCU endowment hovers around $12 million, whereas the median endowment for *all* US colleges is roughly $65.1 million. Black colleges are doing more with less for those who have always had less.

If Biggers thought the state was going too far, several plaintiffs did not think the settlement went far enough. For Chambliss, who had departed as the lawyer for the plaintiffs, it did not even begin to scratch the surface of what was necessary. "I could not spend 25 years of my life to take that settlement," he said. "It was blood money."

CHAPTER 9

What Hath We Wrought

John Fee built his college on a prayer that Paul delivered from the Hill of Ares, the prayer contained within Acts 17:26—"And He has made of one blood all peoples of the earth." Fee's vision ended at that verse, but the chapter of Acts does not stop with that admission. It continues by examining the divine nature. It is not "like gold or silver or stone, something shaped by art and man's devising," verse 30 says. Things shaped by man are imperfect; things shaped by man must be refined.

America is home to more prestigious colleges and universities than anywhere else in the world. And there is a pervasive, flawed assumption that America's colleges are open to all. It is true, in some respects, that any student can attend any institution, but it is false in others. The United States has not yet addressed the ills embedded in its ivory towers. The effect of more than a century of racial caste in higher education has been felt as a wave rather than just a gut punch. It ripples into the present. Black people were shackled at the beginning, and once loosed, were expected to make up stolen ground on their own; Black colleges were, too.

As laws that explicitly segregated the nation's colleges fell, Black students enrolled at universities across the country—both histori-cally Black and predominantly white. At Berea College, as elsewhere, the trickle happened slowly. There were six or seven Black students in the 1950s, a couple more in the 1960s, and by 1970, Black stu-dents made up a full 6 percent of the college's student body. As of 2020, Black students made up 25 percent of the college's enrollment; 14 percent of the college's students were Latino, and another 11 per-cent was made up of international students. It is the kind of diversity one might expect from an institution that was founded on the com-mitment to interracial education.

When Paul traveled to the city of Berea, he found people hun-gry for knowledge. When I traveled to Berea College in 2018, the students walking around campus betrayed the diversity of the sta-tistics. The college tucked away in Kentucky's mountains is Fee's dream, an institution with students living, working, and learning together. Forty years of government intervention may have blocked the college's original goal, but it could not kill it.

As I spoke with administrators, faculty, staff, and students, they acknowledged that the college's diversity was good, but it was not yet enough; it could be doing more. Berea's enrollment is small—necessarily so, since the university, with a billion-dollar endowment, offers free tuition to every student who enrolls—and there are only about 1,600 students on campus at any given time. But the university was a 50/50 school at one time; 50 percent of its students were white, 50 percent of its students were Black. The university will never return there and it likely would not want to, as those figures are not reflec-tive of what the country looks like today. But the college is inching back toward 50 percent minority enrollment, and it is desirous to get there.

Berea is doing better than other similarly situated liberal arts campuses, and even some public colleges. It was able to fend off the government's attempt to tear apart its original mission, but perhaps it was successful only because of that original mission. God made of one blood all people of the earth. The majority of higher-education institutions did not begin with that purpose; they had to learn it. And at every step, the government made that learning process as difficult in every way as it could.

National political leaders established colleges that locked Black people out. The Supreme Court argued that separate could be equal. State governments segregated schools. Both public and private white colleges in the North and West failed at meaningfully integrating their colleges. Then the court tried to walk back its mistake and argued that states could not segregate schools or public spaces, but the damage had already been done. States fought, with blood, against integration. Institutions tried to make up for a legacy of discrimination and then were blocked from doing so by the Supreme Court. And federal officials never meaningfully enforced the law to keep states honest in their desegregation efforts.

All told, there are a string of motifs that reveal a damning picture. Black students and colleges are trying to catch up, but they have been held back for so long.

The night before I arrived in Itta Bena, Mississippi, on February 27, 2018, a winter rain had pounded the silty clay of the Mississippi delta town. The sun was out the next day, but the campus of Mississippi Valley State University was soaked through, and the green spaces were muddied. It was odd to me. I had spent the last two weeks combing through every detail of the *Ayers* settlement. One million dollars had been set aside in the deal to address this specific issue. The drainage on campus had been busted for years, and administrators had hoped the money would fix it. To add insult to injury, the state of the campus looked nothing like the one I had just come from: Delta State University, the predominantly white college less than forty miles away, which Kenneth Starr had argued was most dissimilar from Valley in the 1990s. There, the streets dried quickly; the green spaces were made lush by the rain instead of brown.

As I walked around the campus, I saw very few white faces at Mississippi Valley. That seemed like it could present a problem for the college. There was money in the *Ayers* settlement tied to the enrollment of non-Black students. At Delta State, I was in a sea of them—99 percent of white undergraduates hoping to get a degree from one of Mississippi's public four-year colleges do so at one of the five predominantly white universities. As I bounced around different buildings on Valley's campus, it at turns felt like there had been revolutionary change there, and no change at all. There were high-tech science labs and molded-out vacant buildings; there were new construction sites and broken roads.

I had come to the Mississippi delta because the data were telling a story that did not seem to make sense. The three Black colleges in the state were being collectively funded at levels lower than in 2011, and at the third-lowest level they had been funded at in the sixteen years that had followed the *Ayers* settlement. The state had been cutting all university budgets in the wake of the Great Recession, but it was affecting the colleges unevenly. Jackson State University, after experiencing budget cuts, had laid off dozens of employees and consolidated some of its programs. Delta State closed its golf course.

If the *Ayers* settlement was supposed to make the colleges equal, it had clearly not performed its mission.

Then there were the declining enrollments. The percentage of Black students at the University of Mississippi had declined every year since 2012. And even as the university had experienced an overall growth in enrollment, the Black student population there had decreased every year outside of 2014. The percentages at the state's other premier, predominantly white colleges—Mississippi State University and the University of Southern Mississippi—were worse. At those colleges, the percentage of Black students had fallen in all but one year since 2011.

Perhaps I should not have been shocked by those numbers. Most state flagship universities have fewer than 10 percent Black enrollment. But more than 50 percent of the students who graduated from high school in Mississippi in 2016 were Black, and fewer than 12 percent of the students enrolled at the University of Mississippi were. Of course, racial composition will not be a 1:1 match at every flagship university, but there are only seven states—West Virginia, New Mexico, Montana, Idaho, Wyoming, Oregon, and South Dakota—where the percentages even come close. Less than 5 percent of the total population in each of those states is Black.

Auburn University, in Alabama, which received funding under the Morrill Act, was labeled the most segregated campus in the state in 1985, when a federal judge ordered Alabama to desegregate its colleges. Just over 2 percent of the students at the university that year were Black. The judge's ruling was issued the same day that Auburn's Bo Jackson won the Heisman Trophy as the best college football player in the country. The university was profiting from its Black students, but not serving them well. In 2020, 5 percent of the student body at Auburn was Black, and the Black student population has been declining as an overall share of the college's enrollment, and in actual people, nearly every year since 2007.

Poor Black enrollment is not only limited to the South, though. It also extends to the North and West, to states that have banned affirmative action, and those that have not. After Michigan banned the use of race in admissions in 2006, the Black population at the University of Michigan—which Lloyd Gaines attended while he sought admission to the University of Missouri—declined from 10 percent to 4 percent in 2020. "Underrepresented minorities" at the college account for just 12.8 percent of the overall student body.

The federal government is not investigating Michigan for its poor enrollment of Black students. But for a state like Mississippi, with such a long history of discriminating against Black students and the colleges they went to, what I was seeing in both the numbers and with my eyes added up to systemic failures. These were the type of things that the federal government should be monitoring, I thought.

After the Supreme Court handed down its ruling in the *Ayers* case, the Department of Education sent a memo to states and colleges outlining what they had to do to eliminate the vestiges of segregation in their higher-education systems, but it seemed quite clear that there were still some lingering problems down in Mississippi. I fired off an e-mail to the Department of Education: "Is the Office for Civil Rights monitoring compliance with desegregation laws at Mississippi's colleges?" They were not sure, and a spokesperson told me that he had to get back to me.

The department used to publish a full list of the states that it was monitoring that had not yet proved they had desegregated their higher-education systems, but department officials had become gradually less transparent about it, beginning in 2015. A few days later, a spokesman, on background, offered me a list of the states the department was monitoring and nothing else: "Florida, Maryland, Ohio, Oklahoma, Pennsylvania, and Texas."

The list was unsettling for a couple of reasons.

First, the states on the list were unexpected. Pennsylvania? Ohio? It turned out that both states had been targeted for investigation for the way they had treated their Black colleges. Pennsylvania is home to two of the oldest HBCUs in the nation: the Institute for Colored Youth, which became Cheyney University of Pennsylvania, and the Ashmun Institute, which became Lincoln University. Both are state supported. Both are struggling financially. Ohio's Central State University was in the same predicament. Then there was Oklahoma. The state was the home of the *Sipuel* and *McLaurin* cases. How could it still not have figured this out? The answer was its treatment of Langston University, which enrolls more Black students among its 1,900 students than the University of Oklahoma does in its student body of more than 22,000.

Second, Mississippi was not on the list. Nor were a handful of states that I knew to be experiencing lingering effects of segregation in their higher-education systems such as Alabama. But as

I quickly found out, there are two ways that a state can prove to the federal government that it has desegregated its colleges: the US Justice Department can join plaintiffs hoping to sue their way into settlements, or the Department of Education can threaten to withhold federal funds until a state comes into compliance. By signing the *Ayers* agreement, Mississippi had nominally addressed its legacy of discrimination. Several states—Alabama, Georgia, North Carolina, Louisiana—have made similar settlements.

That means Mississippi's Black colleges, and, indeed, other Black colleges throughout the South, must hang their hats on the *Ayers* funding or the funding they received under their respective settlement. In Mississippi, the money runs dry in 2022. At that point, its Black colleges will be left on their own to deal with the vestiges of slavery and segregation that remain—those in the student body, those in budget lines, and those in the green spaces that will not drain.

Like millions of millennials, I began college in the heart of a recession. States had to run balanced budgets as tax revenues declined, so they began tightening their fiscal belts. Student debt began to explode into a crisis. The two themes were not unrelated. When states look for areas in their budgets to make cuts, they often turn to higher education first. Despite the Founders' belief that colleges are the best way to teach people to be good citizens, higher education is seen as a private good. That belief makes it easy for lawmakers to say that students should support more of their own education.

But for many students, *supporting more of their own education* meant turning to student loans. As the cost of tuition rose, so did the amount of debt students took on. The student debt crisis is unevenly distributed, though—Black students are more likely to take out student loans than white students, are more likely to take on *more* student debt than white students, and are four times more likely to default on that debt after they finish college than white students.

These issues are not higher education's alone. Black students are often relegated to under-resourced K–12 schools due to decades of racist housing policy that intentionally segregated Black and white families. However, state disinvestment in public colleges has only exacerbated what were already systemic barriers.

When state lawmakers cut budgets, the reductions are not felt as acutely at flagship institutions and those that were buoyed by the initial Morrill Act: colleges such as the University of Florida, Ohio State University, Cornell University, and the University of California. Those institutions have had a head start; they have been able to build donor bases and amass large endowments, and they have benefited from the cycle that reputation breeds. More money means a better reputation; a better reputation means more money.

When states slash budgets, the effect is felt most at the colleges that enroll the highest proportion of Black students each year, whether they be the public regional colleges with piecemeal endowments, community colleges, or historically Black colleges. According to a report from the Center for American Progress, "public colleges spend approximately $5 billion less educating students of color in one year than they do educating white students"; that evens out to roughly $1,000 less per year, per student. There are a couple of factors that create that disparity.

Black students are more likely to attend colleges that cannot afford to spend as much on them: nonselective public four-year colleges and public two-year colleges. In Texas, 57 percent of Black students enrolled in higher education attended the state's community colleges, as opposed to 48 percent of white students. And in 2015, more than 75 percent of Black students who attended public colleges went to two-year schools.

Several states have switched to funding models based on the success of institutions: More-selective colleges, such as state flagships, generally pull from a crop of students who are often better prepared for the rigors of college. And, even if they are not, such institutions have the money to provide supplementary support for them in the form of counselors, tutoring, and other academic services. In these states, the more students an institution graduates, the more money it is awarded the next year; the more research it produces, the more money it receives. Predominantly white institutions have had more than a century to build up credit for these systems, even as they have had paltry Black enrollments. Meanwhile, the institutions that are access oriented, providing Black students a path to future success, are shut out of the added financial boost. The colleges are usually smaller, do a little less research, and do a lot more for minority students.

Even to this day, both state and federal lawmakers are failing to equally support Black colleges—including Morrill institutions. One of the stipulations of the 1890 Morrill Act, to which states were required to agree to if they accepted the funding, was for states to match the federal government's level of support to the schools. Every state in the country has held up its end of that bargain for the 1862 Morrill schools, which are the predominantly white colleges, but most states do not come close to matching the funding at their historically Black colleges. In fact, some states require their Black colleges to apply for a waiver of the funding or forfeit it altogether. The result is a growing gulf in funding. Between 2010 and 2012, 1890 land-grant colleges—which land-grant HBCUs are also known as—failed to receive more than $56,627,199 of the state support that was owed to them.

Federal officials, as ever, have been slow to penalize states for the disparity. It is not an unfamiliar posture. Just as the old Department of Health, Education, and Welfare failed to adequately police states operating segregated higher-education systems, the Departments of Education, Agriculture, and other agencies running matching programs with Black colleges fail to monitor states shirking their fiduciary duties.

One decade after my first semester at Alabama A&M, America

found itself in the throes of another crisis, and on the verge of another recession. A novel coronavirus, COVID-19, caused most states to close nonessential business in March 2020. Colleges, which are built for close contact among people, began shutting down their dormitories and sending students home. They moved classes online. They canceled graduation ceremonies. They took a short-term financial hit after refunding housing fees and closing dining halls; and they lost revenue from moneymakers like athletic programs. And then, colleges started to consider: What is going to happen to us next? Most public institutions are facing potential budget cuts, and many private colleges are expecting a decline in enrollment.

There are a couple of indicators that can predict when a college might close: it has fewer than one thousand students; it has a small endowment; it is in a rural area; it has difficulty raising money. Dozens of the one hundred HBCUs still operating fall into some if not all of these buckets, including some of those that receive state funds. Black colleges are resilient; they have made their way through more than 150 years of oppression. But they are not invincible.

Each year, there seems to be a new Black college that must prove its viability. In early 2019, that baton fell to a small college in North Carolina.

There are two historically Black women's colleges in the United States, Spelman College in Atlanta and Bennett College in Greensboro, North Carolina. In 2016, the Southern Association of Colleges and Schools (SACS) placed Bennett on probation because it did not have enough money. The technical term for the association's complaint was a lack of "financial stability"—SACS wanted to make sure that the college had enough money to continue supporting students and its own operation. The private college, which is heavily tuition dependent, had run budget deficits for seven of the prior eleven years, and it was down to a little more than four hundred students from a peak enrollment of nearly eight hundred students in 2009.

The college started making changes. It appointed Phyllis Worthy Dawkins as its interim president. It launched a fundraising campaign, and it began looking for ways to increase its student body size.

Bennett remained on probation for two years until, in 2018, SACS decided that it had seen enough. There was nothing the college could do, in its estimation, to right the ship. On December 11, leaders for the association informed Dawkins that they would be revoking the college's accreditation. The university was caught flat-footed. It had raised $4.2 million in the 2017–2018 school year and had increased its enrollment by 26 percent to just under five hundred students. It thought it was well on the way to financial stability. "There's no one way to demonstrate fiscal stability which is why we thought we were demonstrating fiscal stability," Dawkins told a local news station.

A loss of accreditation is typically a forecast of closure for a college. After that stamp of approval is lost, an institution is no longer eligible for federal and state financial aid programs. At schools such as HBCUs, where 61 percent of students are eligible for the federal Pell grant for low-income students, that federal funding is paramount. President Dawkins had a plan, though. The school appealed the decision and organized an aggressive fundraising effort. SACS set the appeal date for February 18, and if money was what they wanted, the college would raise money. In the fifty days before the hearing, they planned to raise $5 million.

Bennett launched the #StandWithBennett campaign in December, and it quickly began trending on social media. The historically important institution needed everyone to chip in, Dawkins said. "Since 1873, Bennett College has created a place for black women's voices and brilliance to be developed and cultivated," she argued. As the flash fundraising campaign became national news, donations both big and small began pouring in. Ten dollars here, a hundred dollars there, $10,000 from a local credit union, $500,000 from the

Papa John's Foundation. Students at Erwin Montessori elementary school scraped together dollars and cents to donate $77.25. Still, with two days left before its February 1 deadline, the school remained about $2 million short of its goal. The clock was ticking, and last-minute donations started coming in. Another North Carolina college ponied up and donated $1 million dollars. With one hour to go, Bennett College was $250,000 away from its goal. As January 31 turned into February 1, the money was still being counted, so the college extended its deadline to do the final math.

Three days later, on February 4, Bennett announced that it had reached the goal, and surpassed it: it had raised $8.2 million in a little more than fifty days. The college prepared to head into the appeals hearing proud, with lined coffers and proof of its vitality.

But the heroic effort obscured another fact: there were more than a dozen donations to universities of at least $5 million in the first month of 2019. None of those donations went to Bennett College, or any other historically Black college, for that matter.

Private money will not save Black colleges, but, perhaps, money from predominantly white institutions can—and there is an argument that it might be those colleges' responsibility to provide that aid.

Two months before SACS sent its letter to Bennett, the Universities Studying Slavery consortium held a symposium in Jackson, Mississippi. For the past two decades, colleges in the United States had been examining their legacies of slavery and discrimination. The movement began with institutions like Brown University, where then-president Ruth Simmons, the first Black person to lead an Ivy League institution, appointed a commission to explore the college's relationship with the slave trade. "Other institutions are not tied as closely to transparency," Simmons told me in 2018. "To hold on to the trust of the public, and sometimes to even earn it or reclaim it, universities have to be associated with this kind of disclosure." The commission examined the long history of the institution from slavery through Jim Crow. When Brown's committee issued its report, it found that roughly thirty members of the university's governing board in its early years owned people or captained slave ships. Donors to the university offered the labor of enslaved people to help with construction. And though the college itself did not own or trade people, the Brown family engaged in the slave trade.

After Brown learned of its history, the question became what should be done about it. Was it enough to build memorials remembering the violence of the trade, and the institution's role in it?

Georgetown University, which sold 272 people in 1838 to keep the institution alive, did a similar study. Does a subtle gesture make amends for its presence?

The University of Virginia rented enslaved people from local slaveholders to save money. It was cheaper to rent the labor than to buy the people outright. Before abolition, there were between 125 and 200 enslaved people on campus at any given time. Should the university atone for that?

Universities quickly developed a rhythm for answering those questions. They would apologize. They would build a memorial. They would remove the names of those who held people in bondage from their buildings. But there are descendants of those people who were used and abused by those institutions alive today. Their lives were indelibly changed by the fact that their ancestors were held in slavery. Don't they deserve more? Repair for that harm?

When the Universities Studying Slavery consortium met that October, these were exactly the questions its members had on their minds. One answer looked to the institutions that the descendants of those people turned to in the years that predominantly white colleges were shutting them out: historically Black colleges.

The leaders who had gathered discussed partnering with Black colleges, helping Black college professors with research proposals to secure federal grants and contracts, and other opportunities for collaboration. But true repair for that history likely looks a lot less like partnership and a lot more like reparations. Perhaps those institutions could redistribute some of their endowment funds—the unrestricted bequests, at least—to Black colleges or Black students themselves.

At Georgetown, students moved to tax themselves—in the form of a $27.20 fee, in honor of the 272 people who were sold—so that they could create a fund to support descendants of slavery. (A significant percentage of the 272's descendants live in Maringouin, Louisiana, a poor, rural area where most residents live below the poverty line.)

When Bennett College raised $8 million in fifty days, it was trying to save its accreditation, to keep its doors open to the hundreds of Black students that called it home each year. On February 22, SACS announced that it would not renew Bennett's accreditation. It was too little, too late. The university filed a lawsuit to prevent any immediate disruption to its ability to receive federal financial aid funds and sought accreditation with the Transnational Association of Christian Colleges and Schools. The college, which had been founded to educate those newly emancipated from slavery, was struggling to stay alive because it had no money. The colleges that had benefited from slavery were flush with it.

But such institutions could not have benefited from slavery in a vacuum; and repair for centuries of discrimination will not be fixed by one-off proposals by individual colleges or their students. After all, without a government that supported slavery, or, at least, did not blink at it, the history of the colleges would be radically different. The nation built its house on the backs of enslaved Black people, and higher education established its wings under the roof. There is a universal need for repair—not one limited to the colleges themselves.

In his seminal opinion in the *Bakke* **case, Justice Powell took pains to** make an observation. "It is far too late to argue that the guarantee of equal protection to all persons permits the recognition of special wards entitled to a degree of protection greater than that accorded to others." His argument has been repeated time and again by those who would argue that the burden for reparations should not fall upon the living because its debt is due the dead.

But those who are now dead fought for reparations then. Callie House, a Black woman born in Tennessee as slavery wound to a close, was supporting her family as a washerwoman in the late nineteenth century when she got the idea to start a movement. She launched the National Ex-Slave Mutual Relief, Bounty, and Pension Association. House had gone to one of the schools that were set up by the Freedmen's Bureau during Reconstruction and learned about the Constitution, about the inalienable rights that she supposedly had. But as surely as she lived, those rights had been taken away from millions of Black people. So, she began inspiring former enslaved people to demand payment for their work.

These people had been worked without pay; they had been barred from voting; they had been banned from receiving an education or reading books; they were not allowed to argue for their rights in court or to marry. They needed to be compensated for these years of discrimination, House argued.

Alongside members of the association, House pushed for Congress to provide reparations to previously enslaved people and their descendants. White people argued that House was "running the Negros wild" with her movement. They demanded that the Bureau of Pensions, which House had petitioned, stop the organization. Black people were never going to be paid what they were owed, people argued. The bureau agreed and sent agents to uncover if the group was planning a nefarious uprising. When bureau agents arrived at one of the meetings, they found nothing but groups of Black people filling out information sheets including the names of the plantations where they had been born and how old they were—at least, how old they thought they were. According to government records, House's organization had roughly 300,000 dues-paying members.

The argument that it is past time for reparations because the calls have come too late is blunted when one considers people like House, people who had been arguing for recompense from the beginning. In Powell's case, the question must be asked: How soon would have been soon enough? *Plessy*? *Berea*? *Gaines*? *Sipuel*? *McLaurin*? *Sweatt*?

All eyes were trained on Maryland, where the Black colleges, and the people fighting for them, had seen the struggles of the past. In 2006, the Coalition for Equity and Excellence in Maryland Higher Education, a group not unlike the Black Mississippians, filed a lawsuit against the state arguing that its Black colleges had been underfunded, and, as a result, the Black students in the state were being underserved.

The Department of Education's Office for Civil Rights had been lightly monitoring the state as one that had not yet desegregated its colleges. But states no longer believed that such monitoring had any teeth.

In January 2013, Catherine C. Blake, a US district court judge, ruled in the coalition's favor. The state of Maryland had not done enough to eliminate the unnecessary duplication of programs, to address funding disparities, and to address the racial identifiability of its state institutions. Each of these had "segregative effects" she wrote, and the state had maintained a "dual and segregated education system" under the precedent the *Ayers* case had set.

Blake ordered the case back to mediation. The Black colleges and the state would have to strike a deal to address the issues. If they could not, she would have to step back in. The two parties went back and forth: the Black colleges asked for $200 million, the state offered $100 million. The coalition asked for more, and the state would barely budge.

A presidential election cycle passed, and another one began. Then, in March 2020, the state legislature made a peace offering: $577 million to the state's four Black colleges spread across a decade.

It was well short of the $2.73 billion an expert witness suggested they would need to begin to achieve parity, and does not even match the inflation-adjusted settlement of the *Ayers* case. Maryland governor Larry Hogan vetoed the legislation, but a year later the legislature passed an identical bill with a veto-proof majority. Hogan signed it into law. The settlement is only a piece of what the colleges are owed. It is not reparations.

It is uncertain what repair for higher education's legacy could look like. It might be targeted debt cancellation and tuition-free college; it could look like cash transfers to students or the redistribution of endowments at a state level. States could base their funding formulas so that institutions that enroll more minority students receive a greater share of the pie.

What is clear, however, is that the US government has never atoned for what it has done to hamper the forward progress of Black people; nor has it adequately aided the historically Black colleges where those students learned and grew. The state has provided time and again for white students. Now it must do the same for those whom it has held back.

Acknowledgments

This book would not have been possible without my community. For me, that begins with my parents, who have always allowed me to dream. Even when my dreams may have annoyed, worried, or frightened them, I have been keenly aware that they were in my corner cheering me on. If I stumbled, they were there to sweep me up in their embrace. They embody patience, wisdom, and grace. I am forever grateful, Mom and Dad—love you. To my siblings, Audrey, Ashley, and Marcus, you always gave me something to look up to, and I am so proud to be your little brother.

When I set out to write this book, I had a narrow proposal. The idea of writing anything bigger than what was on my beat—a mix of federal higher-education policy, HBCUs, and a host of higher-education issues—seemed daunting; writing books already seemed like the province of others. But Alia Hanna Habib gave me the confidence and courage to push through the doubt. She believed in me from the beginning and her faith has sustained me. Thank you to Alia, Sarah Bolling, Anna Worrall, and everyone at Gernert.

I am honestly still in shock that I was lucky enough to work with as brilliant an editor as Denise Oswald. You have always stressed the urgency of this book and made my writing more precise. Thank you to everyone at Ecco who has supported my work and made this dream a reality: Daniel Halpern, Miriam Parker, Sara Birmingham, Norma Barksdale, Caitlin Mulrooney-Lyski, Paula Russell Szafranski, Helen Atsma, and so many others.

The copy room in Drake Hall, an unassuming symmetrical building near the top of the hill at Alabama A&M University, is behind the door in the back left. It doubles as storage. Old books that no longer fit on the shelves of professors in the Department of Social Sciences and advance copies that have outlived their *advance* label are piled high in boxes. I stumbled upon the treasure trove in 2011 while working as a student assistant in the department. It is where I fell in love with history. And, in a lot of ways, I owe this book to that department and all the professors there who challenged me while nourishing my hunger to learn more: Diane Wilkinson, Douglas Turner, Stephanie Allen, Dr. Emmanuel Obuah, Dr. Ronald Slaughter, and so many more.

I did not know I wanted to be a journalist when I left college; I only knew that I could write. I was blissfully naive about the difficulty of freelancing. I started pitching. Months later, the lines I had cast from my old Yahoo e-mail account had not yielded fruit. But then Jamilah Lemieux gave me a shot to write for *Ebony*, and Kate Dailey took a chance on letting me write for BBC. After two years of freelancing, Amanda Zamora hired me for my first professional newsroom position at ProPublica. Without these three, I would not be writing this right now. Thank you.

A great fortune in my life has been meeting a group of people who gave me the language to speak to what I had seen on campus and became my intellectual village. Thank you to all of my old colleagues from *The Chronicle of Higher Education*: Steve Kolowich, who has always paid such close attention to the building blocks of language, thank you for helping me love the craft of writing; Brock Read, thank you for taking a shot on a young guy who had not yet held a full-time reporting position; Sara Hebel, thank you for all the times I walked over to your desk and you didn't shoo me away but offered guidance and a hearty laugh; Jack Stripling, Audrey June, Goldie Blumenstyk, Nell Gluckman, Eric Hoover, Scott Smallwood, Eric Kelderman, Sara Lipka, Nick Desantis, Andrew Mytelka, Don Troop, Vimal Patel, Sarah Brown, and so many others, you all mean so much to me and I'm grateful for you. And finally, Andy Thomason, Fernanda Zamudio-Suarez, and Chris Quintana: long live the breaking-news team.

Thank you to Jeffrey Goldberg, Adrienne LaFrance, and everyone at *The Atlantic* for your support of this book—and for providing a home for my work more generally. To my colleagues past and present, Rebecca Rosen, Alia Wong, Joe Pinsker, Adrienne Green, Saahil Desai, Julie Beck, Gillian White, Swati Sharma, Ashley Fetters, Hannah Giorgis, Elaine Godfrey, Ed Yong, Natalie Escobar, Nora Kelly, Marina Koren, Emma Green, Isaac Dovere, Olga Khazan, Adam Serwer, Amal Ahmed, Steven Johnson, Vann Newkirk II, Clint Smith III, Isabel Fattal, John Hendrickson, Kit Rachlis, Nick Baumann, Caitlin Dickerson, and everyone who I've been fortunate enough to work with, you all amaze me every single day.

Thank you to my dear friend Astead Herndon, for dreaming out loud with me.

I am grateful to New America for its generous support of my work and for inviting me to be a part of such a dynamic group of fellows; special thanks to Awista Ayub and Sarah Baline. I would also like to thank the archivists at Berea College and the Library of Congress. No work of history is possible without the records of the archivists, journalists, historians, and others who chronicled what they observed; this book is no different. I am forever in debt to those who are committed to cataloging the truth.

Thank you to every single person who is reading this; you could have been doing anything else right now, but you've chosen to spend time with my words and there's no way I can thank you enough.

And, most important, I would not have been able to do this without my wife. Tisa, on the late nights and weekends when I would hunch over the computer writing, you were always there with a word of support or a cup of coffee. I am so lucky to be able to spend my life with you.

Finally, to my daughters: Dream.

Notes

INTRODUCTION

3 Section 256: Valerie Strauss, "FYI, Alabama's Constitution Still Calls for 'Separate Schools for White and Colored Children,'" *Washington Post*, March 10, 2017, https://www.washingtonpost.com/news/answer-sheet/wp/2017/03/10/fyi-alabamas-constitution-still-calls-for-separate-schools-for-white-and-colored-children/.

3 banned educating Black people: David Freedman, "African-American Schooling in the South Prior to 1861," *The Journal of Negro History* 84, no. 1 (Winter 1999): 1–47, https://doi.org/10.2307/2649081.

6 roughly 3 percent: Thurgood Marshall College Fund, "About HBCUs," accessed February 1, 2021, https://www.tmcf.org/about-us/member-schools/about-hbcus/.

CHAPTER 1: THE ROOTS

9 Fee walked a fine line: John G. Fee to Cassius Marcellus Clay, April 4, 1844, Papers of John G. Fee, RG 01, Berea College Archives.

9 To him, it was a law: For more on Clay's early life and experience at Yale, see Cassius Marcellus Clay, *The Life of Cassius Marcellus Clay: Memoirs, Writings, and Speeches, Showing His Conduct in the Overthrow of American Slavery, the Salvation of the Union, and the Restoration of the Autonomy of the States*, 2 vols. (Cincinnati: J. Fletcher Brennan, 1886).

9 The ivy-strewn institution: James Brewer Stewart, "The New Haven Negro College and the Meanings of Race in New England, 1776–1870," *The New England Quarterly* 76, no. 3 (September 2003): 323–55, https://doi.org/10.2307/1559806.

10 "In plain, logical": Clay, *Life of Cassius Marcellus Clay*, 56.

10 "Sir I am a stranger": Fee to Clay, 1.

11 "They feel that God": Fee to Clay, 2–4.

11 By his son's recollection: For more on the life of John G. Fee, see John G. Fee, *Autobiography of John G. Fee* (Chicago: National Christian Association, 1891), and Victor B. Howard, *The Evangelical War against Slavery and Caste: The Life and Times of John G. Fee* (Selinsgrove, PA: Susquehanna University Press, 1996).

11 of his father: Fee, *Autobiography*, 8.

11 The elder Fee: Fee, 9–10.

12 "By false teaching": Fee, 11.

12 conviction turned into action: Howard, *The Evangelical War*, 20.

12 fewer than three hundred permanent colleges: Thomas D. Snyder, *120 Years of American Education: A Statistical Portrait* (Washington, DC: US Department of Education, Office of Educational Research and Improvement, National Center for Education Statistics, 1993), 63–74.

12 "there is nothing": George Washington, First Annual Address to Congress, January 8, 1790, available online at the American Presidency Project, www .presidency.ucsb.edu/node/203158, accessed February 1, 2021. For more on the Founding Fathers' vision for American colleges, see Adam Harris, "George Washington's Broken Dream of a National University," *The Atlantic*, September 21, 2018, www.theatlantic.com/education/archive/2018/09 /founders-national-university/571003.

13 housekeeping and sewing: Benjamin Rush, *Thoughts upon Female Education, Accommodated to the Present State of Society, Manners and Government, in the United States of America* (Boston: 1791), available online from the Albert M. Greenfield Digital Center for the History of Women's Education, http://greenfield.brynmawr.edu/items/show/2828.

13 "irrespective of color": Frederick Alphonso McGinnis, *The Education of Negroes in Ohio* (Wilberforce, OH, 1962).

13 told the trustees: J. J. Shipherd pastoral letter, January 27, 1835, available online from Oberlin University, https://www2.oberlin.edu/external/EOG /History268/shipherd.html.

14 "Thou shalt love": Fee, *Autobiography*, 13.

14 "Bundle up your books": Fee, 18.

15 first known Black student: Princeton Historical Audit Committee, *Princeton Seminary and Slavery* (Princeton, NJ: Princeton Seminary, 2019), 28, https:// slavery.ptsem.edu/wp-content/uploads/2019/10/Princeton-Seminary-and -Slavery-Report-rev10-19.pdf.

15 "let the subject of slavery alone": Howard, *The Evangelical War*, 24.

15 she ardently supported: Daniela Pirela-Manares, "Matilda Hamilton Fee," *Berea College Magazine*, Spring 2019, 12–13, https://magazine.berea.edu /spring-2019/matilda-hamilton-fee/.

15 This was clearly a call: Fee, *Autobiography*, 46.

16 "The day will come": "John G. Fee," *The Examiner* (Louisville, KY), March 4, 1848, p. 2.

16 "testimony of God's word": Fee, *Autobiography*, 48.

17 obliged their invitation: Fee, 88.

17 Fee thought: Fee, 89.

17 "is due to Fee's own leadership": Clay, *Life of Cassius Marcellus Clay*, 212.

18 he later recalled: Fee, *Autobiography*, 95.

19 burned to the ground: For more on the history of the racist burning of Black meeting places, see Sarah Kaplan and Justin Wm. Moyer, "Why Rac-

ists Target Black Churches," *Washington Post*, July 1, 2015, https://www
.washingtonpost.com/news/morning-mix/wp/2015/07/01/why-racists
-burn-black-churches/.

19 "concubinage in Turkey: Fee, *Autobiography,* 102.

19 Clay hoped only: Clay routinely delivered speeches that were more conservative about the speed of abolition—and who was responsible for it—than his
listeners expected. One correspondent for the *Wheeling Daily Intelligencer*
wrote that Clay "made a much more conservative and argumentative address
that [*sic*] I would expect him to do on the Western Reserve, for you know
that the people here have got such a pass of frenzy upon that subject that
it takes generally something peculiarly ultra to elicit much attention." See
"Correspondence of the Intelligencer," *Wheeling Daily Intelligencer* (Wheeling, WV), September 30, 1856. For more on Fee's rendering of the disagreement between himself and Clay that day, see Fee, *Autobiography*, 102.

19 he publicly replied: Fee, 102.

20 "A law confessedly": Fee, 103.

20 "revolutionary, insurrectionary": Fee, 104.

20 Theirs was a disagreement: Fee, 104. There are few reports on the convention's proceedings that note much outside of the fact that Clay was named a
senatorial elector and that both Clay and Fee delivered "eloquent speeches."
See "The Fremont Electoral Ticket in Kentucky," *Belmont Chronicle* (Saint
Clairsville, OH), July 24, 1856.

20 "Cassius M. Clay, of this state": "Kentucky News," *The Louisville Daily Courier*, August 4, 1856.

20 "He has always been": Clay, *Life of Cassius Marcellus Clay*, 571.

21 "The immediate cause": J. Cummins, "Correspondence of the Cincinnati
Gazette," *The Courier-Journal* (Louisville, KY), July 22, 1857.

21 "pernicious": Abolitionists in Eastern Kentucky—Public Meeting to Secure
Their Removal," *The Louisville Daily Courier*, January 30, 1860.

21 passed a resolution: "*The Louisville Daily Courier*, January 30, 1860.

21 captured by a proslavery mob: "Missionaries in Trouble," *Anti-Slavery Bugle*
(New-Lisbon, OH), January 28, 1860.

22 more than 50 percent: Associated Press, "Farm Population Lowest Since
1850s," *New York Times*, July 20, 1988, www.nytimes.come/1988/07/20/us
/farm-population-lowest-since-1850-s.html.

22 Fewer than sixty thousand: The federal Office of Education began collect-
ing data on college enrollments in 1869, at which point 63,000 students were
attending America's higher-education institutions—or about 1 percent of
the eighteen- to twenty-four-year-old population. See Snyder, *120 Years of
American Education*, 64.

22 Jonathan Baldwin Turner, a professor: For more on Jonathan Baldwin Turner,
and his involvement with the Granville meeting, see Mary Turner Carriel,
The Life of Jonathan Baldwin Turner (Urbana: University of Illinois Press,
1961 [1911]).

23 "to take steps": Dean M. Inman, "Professor Jonathan Baldwin Turner and

the Granville Convention," *Journal of the Illinois Historical State Historical Society (1908–1984)* 17, no. 1/2 (April–July 1924): 144–50.

23 "Society has become": Turner's remarks were later memorialized in the conference proceedings. See Jonathan Baldwin Turner, *Proceedings of the Twenty-Sixth Annual Meeting of the Society for the Promotion of Agricultural Sciences*, vol. 24, (Philadelphia, 1905), 55–72.

24 "Others may feel a little alarm": Carriel, *Life of Jonathan Baldwin Turner*, 94.

25 agricultural education free of tuition: For an examination of how land grants rose to prominence, see Roger L. Williams, *The Origins of Federal Support for Higher Education: George W. Atherton and the Land-Grant College Movement* (University Park: Penn State University Press, 1991). Also, see Burt E. Powell, *The Movement for Industrial Education and the Establishment of the University, 1840–1870* (Urbana: University of Illinois, 1918).

25 "The science of agriculture": "A State Agricultural College," *Louisville Daily Journal*, March 27, 1855.

25 "I think it not unlikely": Powell, *The Movement*, 93

26 He had been born: For the most complete examination of Morrill's early years, see Coy F. Cross II, *Justin Smith Morrill: Father of the Land-Grant Colleges* (East Lansing: Michigan State University Press, 1999).

26 though sometimes "attractive": Morrill quoted in Cross, 15.

27 "I saved this darkee": Cross, 21.

27 the party's singular voice: William Belmont Parker, *The Life and Public Services of Justin Smith Morrill* (Boston: Houghton Mifflin, 1924).

28 roughly 2,500 votes: Morrill won 8,380 votes compared with his nearest competitor, J. W. D. Parker, who won 5,848, but he was elected with only a hair over 50 percent of the popular vote. Free-Soilers split from the party, "unconvinced" by Morrill's statements about the spread of slavery, and selected O. L. Shafter as their candidate. For more, see Cross, *Justin Smith Morrill*, 34–35.

29 "one or more": Cross, 84.

29 "of no use": Cross, 85.

29 Quietly, behind the scenes: Edmund J. James, *The Origin of the Land Grant Act of 1862 (the So-Called Morrill Act) and Some Account of Its Author, Jonathan B. Turner*, University Studies 4, no. 1 (Urbana-Champaign: University of Illinois Press, November 1910).

29 "Does not our general": Justin S. Morrill, "Speech on the Bill Granting Lands for Agricultural Colleges," April 20, 1858 (Washington, DC: Congressional Globe Office).

30 "We have schools": Morrill, 8.

30 "We, the Republican party": Lyman Trumbull, "Extract from the Speech of Hon. Lyman Trumbull, of Illinois," in F. P. Blair Jr., *Remarks of F. P. Blair Jr. in the House of Representatives of Missouri on the Repeal of the "Jackson Resolutions"* (Washington, DC: Buell & Blanchard), 97–98.

30 "any Central American state": Trumbull, 97.

31 "one of the most extraordinary": C. Wendell, "Agricultural Colleges," *Washington Union*, February 2, 1859, p. 2.

31 "one of the most monstrous": Senator Clement Clay of Alabama quoted in Wendell, 2.

31 Buchanan vetoed the bill: James Buchanan, "Veto Message Regarding Land Grant Colleges," February 24, 1859, available online from the Miller Center at the University of Virginia, https://millercenter.org/the-presidency/presidential-speeches/february-24-1859-veto-message-regarding-land-grant-colleges.

32 the bill urgent: Williams, *Origins of Federal Support*, 38–39, which suggests that the recent loss at Bull Run in Virginia was the battle that put the bill over the top.

32 "The notorious John G. Fee": Dispatch, *Maysville Weekly Bulletin*, September 1, 1864,p. 2.

CHAPTER 2: A COMPROMISE

33 "few sympathizing families": John G. Fee, *Autobiography of John G. Fee* (Chicago: National Christian Association, 1891), 173.

33 "the principal camp": For an examination of Fee's time at Camp Nelson, and the experience of Black troops there, see Richard D. Sears, *Camp Nelson, Kentucky: A Civil War History* (Lexington: University Press of Kentucky, 2002). Also, see Richard Sears, "John G. Fee, Camp Nelson, and Kentucky Blacks, 1864–1865," *The Register of the Kentucky Historical Society* 85, no. 1 (Winter 1987), 29–45.

34 "I have talked": John Fee to Simeon Jocelyn, June 6, 1864, quoted in Sears, *Camp Nelson*, 65.

34 another letter, and another: Sears, 66, 88.

35 "I have written you": John Fee to Simeon Jocelyn, July 12, 1864, quoted in Sears, 97.

35 "but we want teaching": Captain Theron E. Hall, the quartermaster, quoted in Amy Murrell Taylor, *Embattled Freedom: Journeys through the Civil War's Slave Refugee Camps* (Chapel Hill: University of North Carolina Press, 2018), 193.

35 Nat Turner's rebellion: For more on Nat Turner, see Patrick H. Breen, *The Land Shall Be Deluged in Blood: A New History of the Nat Turner Revolt* (New York: Oxford University Press, 2015).

36 so did their wives and children: Sears, "John G. Fee, Camp Nelson, and Kentucky Blacks," 34.

36 Fee began teaching: John G. Fee, *Autobiography of John G. Fee* (Chicago: National Christian Association, 1891), 179.

36 "Perhaps Berea is the place": John Fee to Simeon Jocelyn, August 1, 1864, quoted in Richard D. Sears, *A Utopian Experiment in Kentucky: Integration and Social Equality at Berea, 1866–1904* (Westport: Greenwood Press, 1996), 7.

36 "with such a people": John Fee to Simeon Jocelyn, August 8, 1864, quoted in Sears, *Camp Nelson*, 109.

37 The school grew: Richard Day et al. "Berea College—Coeducationally and Racially Integrated: An Unlikely Contingency in the 1850s," *Journal of Negro Education* 82, no. 1 (Winter 2013): 35–46, https://doi.org/10.7709/jnegroeducation.82.1.0035.

37 "Men are known": "Hon. Alvin Duvall of Scott County for Clerk of Court of Appeals," *Louisville Daily Courier*, August 1, 1866, p. 1.

37 "Our farmer's college": John Mahin, "Agricultural College Land Grant," *Muscatine Weekly Journal*, July 11, 1862, p. 1.

38 Slavery had been outlawed: *Lost in History: Alexander Clark* (Johnston: Iowa Public Television, Communication Research Institute of William Penn University, 2012), 27 min., http://www.iowapbs.org/video/story/4902/lost-history-alexander-clark.

38 in Massachusetts, five towns: Roger L. Williams, *The Origins of Federal Support for Higher Education: George W. Atherton and the Land-Grant College Movement* (University Park: Penn State University Press, 1991), 44.

39 moved up the list: In letters to the editors of various Illinois newspapers, cited in Mary Turner Carriel, *The Life of Jonathan Baldwin Turner* (Urbana: University of Illinois Press, 1961 [1911]), 234–37, Turner describes how aggressive the Champaign contingent was in pushing for the campus to be in town.

39 When the dust had: For an in-depth examination of how Indigenous land was stolen to serve as the foundation for these institutions, see Robert Lee et al., "Morrill Act of 1862 Indigenous Land Parcels Database," *High Country News*, March 2020, https://www.landgrabu.org/.

40 In March 1865: Christi M. Smith, *Reparation and Reconciliation: The Rise and Fall of Integrated Higher Education* (Chapel Hill: University of North Carolina Press, 2016).

40 "the first institution anywhere": Bobby L. Lovett, *America's Historically Black Colleges and Universities: A Narrative History from the Nineteenth Century into the Twenty-First Century* (Macon, GA: Mercer University Press, 2011), 12.

40 "for buildings for schools": "An Act making appropriations for the Support of the Army for the Year ending June thirtieth, eighteen hundred and sixty-eight, and for other purposes," 39th Cong. (1867), available from the Library of Congress at www.loc.gov/law/help/statutes-at-large/39th-congress/session-2/c39s2ch170.pdf.

41 it was being underfunded: Lovett, *America's Historically Black Colleges*, 23.

41 $7,545,405 was generated: Williams, *Origins of Federal Support*, 46.

41 Rhode Island sold: Williams, 46.

42 many families worried: J. L. Power and Harris Barksdale, "The Attempt of the Radical Authorities to Mongrelize the State University," *Semi-Weekly Clarion* (Jackson, MS), September 16, 1870, p. 2.

42 *"should the applicant"*: "Correspondence Between Hon. R. S. Hudson and the Faculty of the University," *Weekly Mississippi Pilot*, October 15, 1870, p. 2.

42 "As an evidence": For Lynch's complete recollections on Reconstruction in Mississippi, see John Roy Lynch, *The Facts of Reconstruction* (New York: Neale Publishing Company, 1913). Also see John Roy Lynch, *Reminiscences of an Active Life: The Autobiography of John Roy Lynch* (Chicago: University of Chicago Press, 1970).

43 "As a sense": "The Agricultural Colleges," *Nashville Union and American*, February 24, 1872, p. 5. For the full conference proceedings, including Morrill's full remarks, see *Proceedings of the National Agricultural Convention, Held at Washington, DC, February 15, 16, and 17, 1872* (Washington, DC: US Government Printing Office, 1872).

44 only 1.3 percent: Thomas D. Snyder, *120 Years of American Education: A Statistical Portrait* (Washington, DC: US Department of Education, Office of Educational Research and Improvement, National Center for Education Statistics, 1993), 64.

44 "by a committee": Alfred Charles True, *A History of Agricultural Education in the United States, 1785–1925* (Washington, DC: US Government Printing Office, 1929).

44 He took to the Senate: Justin S. Morrill, *National Colleges* (Washington, DC: Congressional Globe Office, December 5, 1872).

45 "a palpable discrimination": John Sherman quoted in Alfred Charles True, "Brief History of the Morrill Land-Grant College Act of 1890," *Proceedings of the Thirty-Seventh Annual Convention of the Association of Land-Grant Colleges* (Burlington, VT: Free Press Printing Company, 1924), 90.

45 The government had encouraged: Williams, *Origins of Federal Support*, 65.

45 "full of strangers": "Proceedings of the National Education Association," *Democrat and Chronicle* (Rochester, NY), August 7, 1873, p. 1.

46 many days and nights: Williams, *Origins of Federal Support*, 60.

46 In less than ten years: Williams, 68–69.

46 "The nation as a nation": George Atherton speech at the National Educational Association, *The Addresses and Journal of Proceedings of the National Educational Association*, (Peoria: The Association, 1873), 68.

47 "the breach nobly": Williams, 73–74.

47 op-eds in *The Nation*: There were several rebuttals to Atherton's speech. In a scathing article, *The Nation* opined that "the addresses of Dr. McCosh and Prof. Atherton at Elmira demonstrate the stupendous ignorance of Congress in matters of education, but show that in the last reckless attempt to fling 90,000,000 acres to a few agricultural colleges, 'so-called and miscalled,' the members really could not have known what they were themselves doing." "American Colleges and Legislators," *The Nation*, August 28, 1873, 140–41.

47 "which I drafted": Williams, *Origins of Federal Support*, 139.

47 He was even recruited: "A Scholar in Politics," *Monmouth Inquirer*, November 2, 1876, p. 5.

48 The money that the Republicans: James D. Anderson, "Philanthropy, the State and the Development of Historically Black Public Colleges: The Case of Mississippi," *Minerva* 35, no. 3 (Autumn 1997): 295–309.

49 "It would be vain": Justin S. Morrill, "On the Educational Bill" (Washington, DC: U.S. Government Printing Office, December 15, 1880).

49 Berea was their best option: Jacqueline G. Burnside, "Suspicion versus Faith: Negro Criticisms of Berea College in the Nineteenth Century," *Register of the Kentucky Historical Society* 83, no. 3 (Summer 1985): 237–66.

49 "How soon will": E. Henry Fairchild, *Inauguration of Rev. E. H. Fairchild, President of Berea College, Kentucky, Wednesday, July 7, 1869* (Cincinnati: Elm Street Printing Company, 1870), available from the Albert M. Greenfield Digital Center for the History of Women's Education, Bryn Mawr College, accessed February 1, 2021.

50 The discord at Oberlin: The sketch of the undoing of racial harmony at Oberlin that follows relies on newspaper accounts from the *Oberlin News* as well as the work of Cally Lyn Waite. See Waite, "The Segregation of Black Students at Oberlin College after Reconstruction," *History of Education Quarterly* 41, no. 3 (Autumn 2001): 344–64. See also Waite, *Permission to Remain Among Us: Education for Blacks in Oberlin, Ohio, 1880–1914* (Westport, CT: Praeger, 2002).

51 50 students out of 1,357: Waite, "Segregation of Black Students," 356.

51 177 were Black, 157 were white: Paul David Nelson, "Experiment in Interracial Education at Berea College, 1858–1908," *Journal of Negro History* 59, no. 1 (January 1974): 13–27, https://doi.org/10.2307/2717137.

52 "please advise me": Williams, *Origins of Federal Support*, 141.

52 "The Morrill Bill is dead": Williams, 142.

52 "on a basis": Williams, 144.

52 The bill requested: "Substitute for the Educational Bill," *Evening Star* (Washington, DC), May 1, 1890, p. 6.

52 "no American will long dwell": Justin S. Morrill, "Colleges for the Benefit of Agriculture and the Mechanic Arts" (Washington, DC: U.S. Government Printing Office, June 14, 1890).

52 "Let me urge": Morrill, 8.

53 Instead, the debate revolved around: For an excellent examination of the congressional debate around the Second Morrill Act, see Katherine Wheatle, "Neither Just nor Equitable: Race in the Congressional Debate of the Second Morrill Act of 1890," *American Educational History Journal* 46, no. 2 (2019): 1–20.

54 "I will simply say": 21 Cong. Rec., 6372 (June 23, 1890).

CHAPTER 3: THE FALL OF INTEGRATED EDUCATION

57 He made that food: For more on Carver's life, see Christina Vella, *George Washington Carver: A Life* (Baton Rouge: Louisiana State University Press, 2015). See also Gary R. Kremer, *George Washington Carver: A Biography* (Santa Barbara, CA: Greenwood, 2011). Kremer also compiled the most complete volume of Carver's autobiographical material: George Washington Carver, *George Washington Carver: In His Own Words*, ed. Gary R. Kremer, 2nd ed. (Columbia: University of Missouri Press, 2017).

57 He had been born: As noted in Vella, *A Life*, 1–10, Carver and his mother were kidnapped by white marauders near the end of the Civil War. His mother was never seen again, but George—then an orphan—was returned to Moses Carver, who moved George and his brother into the "big house." As Vella puts it, "the two boys seemed to occupy a special position, somewhere between sons and slaves," 8.

58 a student such as him: Carver, *In His Own Words*, 5.

58 more than forty degree-granting colleges: Vella, *A Life*, 36.

58 the school could not accept: Vella, 38.

58 "I shudder to think": Vella, 47.

59 he accepted: Vella, 53–58

60 Instead, he took his meals: Vella, 63.

61 "peculiar opportunity": William Goodell Frost to the Brethren of Berea, July 16, 1892, Special Collections and Archives, Hutchins Library, Berea College.

61 the school enrolled 350 students: *Catalogue of the Officers and Students of Berea College, Berea, Madison County, KY, 1891–1892*, Special Collections and Archives, Hutchins Library, Berea College.

61 white ancestors: Jacqueline G. Burnside, "Suspicion versus Faith: Negro Criticisms of Berea College in the Nineteenth Century," *Register of the Kentucky Historical Society* 83, no. 3 (Summer 1985): 245.

62 Black alumni began to sound: Though the criticisms of the racial policies at Berea grew loudest during the period after Hathaway's departure, Black alumni had formerly worried that the school was not living up to the guiding principles as Fee had expressed them. As Burnside notes, Berea's most outspoken critic, John T. Robinson, wrote in an 1893 article that concerns "date all the way back over twenty years, under this same *calm surface*" Frost had cheered ("Suspicion versus Faith," 246). His criticisms included the cautions around interracial dating and the growing idea Black students "owe their presence in the school to the forbearance of the whites."

62 "No darkie has nerve": Paul David Nelson, "Experiment in Interracial Education at Berea College, 1858–1908," *Journal of Negro History* 59, no. 1 (January 1974): 22, https://doi.org/10.2307/2717137.

62 The school began to segregate: Nelson, 22.

62 "We have tried": Burnside, "Suspicion versus Faith," 259.

63 an unassuming headline: "A Conviction under the Separate Car Act," *The Times-Picayune*, February 14, 1891, p. 8.

64 In the five years: Blair Murphy Kelley, *Right to Ride: Streetcar Boycotts and African American Citizenship in the Era of* Plessy v. Ferguson (Chapel Hill: University of North Carolina Press, 2010), 35.

64 "there is a dark cloud": *Arkansas Democrat*, August 1, 1891, p. 2.

64 The law had not established: Steve Luxenberg, *Separate: The Story of* Plessy v. Ferguson *and America's Journey from Slavery to Segregation* (New York: W. W. Norton, 2019), 411.

65 A private detective: Luxenberg, 432.

65 Tourgée presented twenty-three: Albion W. Tourgée, "Brief for Plaintiff in

Error," October term, 1895, no. 210, *Plessy v. Ferguson*, in Philip B. Kurland and Gerhard Casper, eds., *Landmark Briefs and Arguments of the Supreme Court of the United States: Constitutional Law*, vol. 13 (Washington, DC: University Publications of America, 1975), 27–63.

66 "enforced separation of the two races": Plessy v. Ferguson, 163 U.S. 537, 16 S. Ct. 1138 (1896).

66 "The object of the amendment": *Plessy v. Ferguson.*

67 "The judgment this day": *Plessy v. Ferguson.*

68 in December 1866: "The Legislative Charter for the Colored Manual Labor School," *Nashville American* May 2, 1867, p. 1.

68 "The thousands of colored orphans": Samuel Lowery et al., "To the Friends of Education and Human Improvement," *Nashville Union and American*, November 2, 1867, p. 3.

68 without the same resources: Bobby L. Lovett, *America's Historically Black Colleges and Universities: A Narrative History from the Nineteenth Century into the Twenty-First Century* (Macon, GA: Mercer University Press, 2011), 44.

69 Manual Labor University ceased operations: In July 1880, the Reverend Peter Lowery, the president of Tennessee Manual Labor University, went to New York in hopes of soliciting donations to pay off the university's debts. A year prior, in 1879, the institution suspended instruction after it was unable to make a payment on its property. Lowery told would-be donors that $5,000 could have saved the college. See "Tennessee Manual Labor School," *Memphis Daily Appeal*, July 25, 1880, p. 2.

69 When the college opened: Lovett, *America's Historically Black Colleges*, 48.

69 "The Negro isn't permitted": James D. Anderson, "Philanthropy, the State and the Development of Historically Black Public Colleges: The Case of Mississippi," *Minerva* 35, no. 3 (Autumn 1997): 297.

69 "Education is the preparation": Mifflin Wistar Gibbs, *Shadow and Light: An Autobiography, with Reminiscences of the Last and Present Century* (Lincoln: University of Nebraska Press, 1995 [1902]), 210–11.

70 "it is through the dairy farm": Booker T. Washington, "The Awakening of the Negro," *The Atlantic*, September 1896, https://www.theatlantic.com /magazine/archive/1896/09/the-awakening-of-the-negro/305449/.

70 Oklahoma was not yet a state: Leonard B. Cayton, "A History of Black Public Education in Oklahoma" (PhD diss., University of Oklahoma, 1977), 24, https://shareok.org/bitstream/handle/11244/4326/7732851.PDF.

70 "Let me say that": Nelson, "Experiment in Interracial Education," 23.

71 "No Contest over the Law": "No Contest over the Law Prohibiting Co-Education of the Races," *Nashville American*, April 30, 1901, p. 3.

71 Carter G. Woodson arrived: For a full-length treatment of Woodson's life, see Jacqueline Goggin, *Carter G. Woodson: A Life in Black History* (Baton Rouge: Louisiana State University Press, 1993), 11–12.

71 chosen by the Democrats: Staff, Breathitt County Man Nominated. *The Evening Bulletin,* May 20, 1903, p. 1.

71 "smooth and intellectual": The Louisville *Courier-Journal* gushed when describing Day, writing that he was "the very reverse from the common impression of the mountain man." "Against Mixing the Races," *The Courier-Journal* (Louisville, KY), January 11, 1904, p. 8.

72 "several important bills": "Several Important Bills Will Be Introduced by Representative Carl Day," *The Courier-Journal* (Louisville, KY), January 2, 1904, p. 8.

72 "An act to prohibit": Text of the bill as it appears in *The Courier-Journal*, "Against Mixing the Races."

73 It was clear that the bill: "Against Mixed Schools," *The Courier-Journal* (Louisville, KY), January 13, 1904, p. 1.

73 residents of Berea tell: Dr. Alicestyne Turley (former director of Carter G. Woodson Center at Berea College) in discussion with the author, September 2018.

74 "We have never claimed": "The True Story of the Efforts to Save Berea," *The Citizen* (Berea, KY), February 11, 1904, p. 1.

74 "I am humiliated": "True Story of the Efforts to Save Berea."

74 "it is likely": "Mixed Schools: Committee Reports in Favor of Measure Prohibiting Them," *Evening Bulletin* (Maysville, KY), February 2, 1904, p. 1.

75 a handful of amendments: For a full rundown of the amendments offered, see "Day Coeducation Bill Passes in the House," *Twice-A-Week Messenger* (Owensboro, NY), February 19, 1904, p. 1.

75 One day later: "The Sick," *Mount Sterling Advocate*, March 9, 1904, p. 7.

75 One month after: "Carl Day: Breathitt County's Representative Passes Away at Good Samaritan Hospital; Author of Anti Co-Racial Bill," *Lexington Leader*, April 12, 1904, p. 1.

76 "Have we become so inoculated": Berea College v. Kentucky, 211 U.S. 45 (1908).

CHAPTER 4: THE TRAGEDY OF LLOYD GAINES

79 Fifty-five years later: By 1940, only 7.7 percent of Black people over the age of twenty-five had completed high school. Twenty years later, while 43 percent of white Americans had completed high school, only 21.7 percent of Black people had. In 1960, 3 percent of Black Americans above the age of twenty-five had earned a bachelor's degree. See National Center for Education Statistics, *Rates of High School Completion and Bachelor's Degree Attainment among Persons Age 25 and Over, by Race/Ethnicity and Sex* (Washington, DC: US Department of Education, Institute of Education Sciences, 2020), https://nces.ed.gov/programs/digest/d19/tables/dt19_104.10.asp.

80 Tuskegee Institute: "May Plant Tree on Grounds of New Industrial and Normal School for Negroes," *Cincinnati Enquirer*, February 6, 1909, p. 8.

80 "While in some other affairs": Booker T. Washington, "The Case of the Negro," *The Atlantic*, November 1899, https://www.theatlantic.com/magazine/archive/1899/11/the-case-of-the-negro/476934/.

80 "bitter attacks": In an article published by *The Atlantic* in 1903, Booker

T. Washington recounts an incident in which a white friend—a Democrat running for Congress—spoke in one of Alabama's "white counties." As Washington wrote, "I speak of this man as my friend, because there was no personal favor in reason which he would have refused me. He was equally friendly to the race, and was generous in giving for its education, and in helping individuals to buy land. His campaign took him into one of the 'white' counties, where there were few colored people, and where the whites were unusually ignorant. I was surprised one morning to read in the daily papers of a bitter attack he had made on the Negro while speaking in this county." See Washington, "The Fruits of Industrial Training," *The Atlantic*, October 1903, https://www.theatlantic.com/magazine/archive/1903/10/the-fruits-of -industrial-training/531030/.

81 the Lincoln Institute: In a speech announcing the institution, Frost made clear his affinity for Washington's model at Tuskegee. "We are responsible to the great national givers that this school shall be organized on the general lines of Booker Washington's famous school in Alabama," he said. See "Great School," *The Courier-Journal* (Louisville, KY), February 8, 1909, p. 3.

81 "As the United States managed": "Great School."

81 Williams pulled no punches: "To Put Institution on Higher Plane State Negro Normal School to Be Improved," *The Courier-Journal* (Louisville, KY), March 31, 1909, p. 4.

82 The funds were often inequitably distributed: William E. Ellis, *A History of Education in Kentucky* (Lexington: University of Kentucky Press, 2011), 237.

82 Years later, a federal report: The Truman Commission cited an unpublished report from the president of Howard University, Mordecai Johnson, which found that the ratio of spending on colleges for white students in Kentucky compared with Black students was 42 to 1. See United States President's Commission on Higher Education, *Higher Education for American Democracy: A Report of the President's Commission on Higher Education* (Washington, DC: US Government Printing Office, 1947), 31.

82 Lloyd Lionel Gaines was born: Correspondence among Gaines, NAACP lawyers, and local attorneys—as well as NAACP correspondence in following chapters—come from the papers of the NAACP, reproduced from the collections of the Manuscript Division, Library of Congress. See Lloyd Lionel Gaines autobiographical letter to Charles Houston, University of Missouri, "Gaines Case," January–December 1935, 115 pp. Papers of the NAACP, Part 03: The Campaign for Educational Equality, Series A: Legal Department and Central Office Records, 1913–1940.

83 His one-room schoolhouse: Gaines autobiographical letter to Houston, undated, 2.

84 It had been established: Bobby L. Lovett, *America's Historically Black Colleges and Universities: A Narrative History from the Nineteenth Century into the Twenty-First Century* (Macon, GA: Mercer University Press, 2011), 21.

84 "long before finishing": Gaines autobiographical letter to Houston, undated, 5.

84 he wanted to practice: Gaines autobiographical letter to Houston, undated, 5.
85 wrote to his brother: Lloyd L. Gaines to George L. Gaines, February 13, 1935, available online at https://scholarship.law.missouri.edu/family_correspondence/3 (discusses Lloyd's financial situation and need for money for school at Lincoln University).
85 "neither the class of persons": Dred Scott v. Sandford, 60 U.S. (19 How.) 393 (1856).
85 For every 9,667 Black people: "Wide Opportunities for Negro Lawyers," *The Crisis*, December 1934, p. 371.
85 "The great cause": James W. Endersby and William T. Horner, *Lloyd Gaines and the Fight to End Segregation* (Columbia: University of Missouri Press, 2016), 16.
86 "the exclusion of Black students": Charles Houston to Sidney Redmond, July 15, 1935, in Papers of the NAACP, Part 3, Series A.
86 "I believe you will encounter": Redmond to Houston, July 18, 1935, Papers of the NAACP, Part 3, Series A.
86 "The president of the": Redmond to Houston, August 17, 1935, Papers of the NAACP, Part 3, Series A.
87 Zaid D. Lenoir: c, Papers of the NAACP, Part 3, Series A.
87 "I feel that we should": Redmond to Houston, September 24, 1935, Papers of the NAACP, Part 3, Series A.
87 "Please keep after Gaines": Houston to Redmond, September 26, 1935, Papers of the NAACP, Part 3, Series A.
87 The first lawsuit against: Jerry Gershenhorn, "*Hocutt v. Wilson* and Race Relations in Durham, North Carolina, During the 1930s," *North Carolina Historical Review* 78, no. 3 (July 2001): 275–308.
88 In Virginia, a young woman: "U. Va. Board of Visitors Directs That Negro Girl Be Refused Admittance," *The Staunton News-Leader*, September 20, 1935, p. 1.
88 The state of Missouri paid: "Negroes Receiving Tuition from the State During 1935," Papers of the NAACP, Part 3, Series A.
88 Kentucky, for example: Bennett Roach, "$23,344,026 State Budget Bill Is Ready," *The Courier-Journal* (Louisville, KY), March 18, 1936, pp. 1, 4.
88 Gaines's lawyers argued: State ex Rel. Gaines v. Canada, 342 Mo. 121, 113 S.W.2d 783 (Mo. 1938).
89 "It would be 'most unfortunate'": "Court Studying Plea of Negro to Enter Missouri U," *Saint Louis Post-Dispatch*, July 11 1936, p. 8.
89 "Japanese, Chinese, British Indian": "Court Studying Plea."
89 "I'll need that amount": Lloyd L. Gaines to George L. Gaines, October 27, 1936, available online at https://scholarship.law.missouri.edu/family_correspondence/6 (letter discusses financial needs).
90 "not of the least": Lloyd L. Gaines to Charles Houston, November 28, 1936, Papers of the NAACP, Part 3, Series A.
90 "island of prejudice": Gaines's counsel argument, Papers of the NAACP, Part 3, Series A,

90 "no constitutional prohibition": "Rules Negro Has No Right in White Schools of State," *Saint. Louis Post-Dispatch*, December 10, 1937, p. 8.

90 "decisive questions": "Negro, Denied Right to Enter University, Seeks Rehearing," *Saint Louis Post-Dispatch*, December 18, 1937, p. 11.

91 "strongly suggests that": "Supreme Court to Review Barring of Negro by M.U.," *Saint Louis Post-Dispatch*, October 10, 1938, p. 3.

91 "opportunity open to": Ibid.

91 "were permitted to speak": Richard L. Stokes, "Missouri U. Bar on Negro Argued in Supreme Court," *Saint Louis Post-Dispatch*, November 10, 1938, pp. 1, 10.

92 "How can you say": Stokes, p. 10

92 "Do you mean to suggest": Stokes, p. 10.

92 "undercurrent of emotion": Stokes, 1.

92 "save its own": Stokes, 10.

93 "We are of the opinion": Missouri ex Rel. Gaines v. Canada, 305 U.S. 337, 59 S. Ct. 232 (1938).

93 "will be compelled": Raymond P. Brandt, "Missouri U. Asks for Rehearing on Negro Law School; Challenges 'Equal Protection' Interpretation," *Saint Louis Post-Dispatch*, December 31, 1938, p. 2.

94 "It's just an attempt": "Negroes Oppose Lincoln U. Proposal at Senate Hearing," *Saint Louis Post-Dispatch*, April 11, 1939, p. 20.

94 "bill to raise": "Bill to Raise L.U. Standards Passes Senate," *Jefferson City Post-Tribune*, April 19, 1939, p. 1.

94 "iron out": "Bill to Raise L.U. Standards."

94 "without a staggering": "Bill to Raise L.U. Standards."

95 "I have come to Chicago": This and the quotations that follow are taken from Lloyd L. Gaines to Callie Gaines, March 3, 1939, available online at https://scholarship.law.missouri.edu/family_correspondence/13/. (This is the final letter Gaines is known to have sent to a family member before his disappearance.)

95 "choosing and achieving": Gaines to C. Gaines, March 3, 1939.

96 "subterfuge in violation": "Writ Asked to Open State U. to Negro," *Saint Louis Star-Times*, May 22, 1939, p. 3.

96 "because it in fact does": "Writ Asked to Open State U."

97 establish the law school: D. H. Davis, "Judge Reverses Decision in Bluford Case," *The Call*, February 11, 1939.

97 "An intensive drive": Sidney Redmond to Charles Houston, September 30, 1939, Papers of the NAACP, Part 3, Series A.

97 "stating that he was having": Houston to Redmond, January 30, 1940, Papers of the NAACP, Part 3, Series A.

98 "I cannot see for": Marshall to Houston, September 26, 1939, Papers of the NAACP, Part 3, Series A.

98 "Since we cannot find": Houston to Redmond, December 27, 1939, Papers of the NAACP, Part 3, Series A.

CHAPTER 5: A NEW GUINEA PIG

99 A white woman claimed: A reconstruction of Argo's murder relies on contemporaneous press accounts. See Robert W. Bagnall, "An Oklahoma Lynching," *The Crisis*, August 1930, p. 274. See also, Bill Bailey, "News Writer Sees Wounded Negro Stabbed by Husband," *Oklahoma News*, May 31, 1930, p. 3.

100 Then Skinner went back outside: Ada Lois Sipuel Fisher, *A Matter of Black and White: The Autobiography of Ada Lois Sipuel Fisher* (Norman: University of Oklahoma Press, 1996), 45–48.

101 "smart mouth": John Erling, *Ada Lois Sipuel Fisher: Her Son, Bruce, Tells the Story of His Pioneering Mother Who Became the First African-American to Attend OU's School of Law*, transcript of an oral history conducted October 22, 2015, by John Erling, p. 17. Available online at https://www.voices ofoklahoma.com/wp-content/uploads/2015/12/Fisher_Transcript.pdf.

101 "He was a forceful": Fisher, *Matter of Black and White*, 55.

101 "the most handsome, articulate": Fisher, 50.

102 "tragically separate": Fisher, 55.

102 Harvard itself admitted: Marcia G. Synnott, "The Changing 'Harvard Student': Ethnicity, Race, and Gender," in *Yards and Gates: Gender in Harvard and Radcliffe History*, ed. Laurel Ulrich (New York: Palgrave Macmillan, 2004), 300.

102 The town was founded: Zella J. Black Patterson, *Langston University: A History* (Norman: University of Oklahoma Press, 1979).

103 Sipuel's time at Langston: Fisher, *Matter of Black and White*, 71.

103 *second curriculum*: In Jelani Favors, *Shelter in a Time of Storm: How Black Colleges Fostered Student Activism* (Chapel Hill: University of North Carolina Press, 2019). Favors quotes James Weldon Johnson, who explained that HBCUs in the late nineteenth and early-to-mid-twentieth century held the second curriculum as central. "Students talked 'race.' It was the subject of essays, orations, and debates. Nearly all that was acquired, mental, and moral, was destined to be fitted into a particular system of which race was the center" (7).

104 "friend of the university": Fisher, *Matter of Black and White*, 74.

104 "I started praying": For a recounting of the senator's visit, see Fisher, 74–75.

104 she thought: Fisher, 75.

105 But that war had: Fisher, 78.

106 One case, *Hollins v. Oklahoma*: Hollins v. Oklahoma, 295 U.S. 394, 66 S. Ct. 784 (1935).

106 In the other case: Guinn & Beal v. United States, 238 U.S. 347 (1915).

106 "bustling with black businesses": Fisher, *Matter of Black and White*, 80.

106 "necessary courage and patience": Fisher, 80.

107 "Girlie, are you nervous?": Fisher, 81.

108 university letterhead: Fisher, 84. See also "Federal Court to Decide Equal Education Issue," *Oklahoma Daily*, January 15, 1946, p. 1.

109 "Delay developes [*sic*]": Roscoe Dunjee to Thurgood Marshall, March 13, 1946, Papers of the NAACP, Part 3, Series B.

109 "the Supreme Court takes": Thurgood Marshall to Roscoe Dunjee, March 19, 1946, Papers of the NAACP, Part 3, Series B.

109 Carter sent the petition: Robert Carter to Amos Hall, March 22, 1946, Papers of the NAACP, Part 3, Series B.

110 "We have appealed": Ray Parr, "Negro Student Denied Order to Enter OU," *Daily Oklahoman*, July 10, 1946, pp. 1–2.

110 "They haven't even": Parr, 2.

111 "legal fiction and judicial myth": "Brief Supports OU Entry Plea," *Daily Oklahoman*, December 10, 1946, p. 8.

111 "Plaintiff's position here": "Brief Supports OU Entry Plea."

112 "The only thing": "State Tribunal Defers Ruling in Sipuel Case," *Oklahoma Daily*, March 5, 1947, p. 1, 12.

112 "Perhaps it would be": "State Tribunal Defers Ruling," 12.

112 "does not necessarily": Sipuel v. Board of Regents of University of Oklahoma, 199 Okla. 36, 180 P.2d 135 (Okla. 1947).

112 "unquestioned duty": "OU Negro Ban Due Supreme Court Verdict," *Daily Oklahoman*, November 11, 1947, p. 1.

113 "had no trouble understanding": Ray Parr, "13 OU Students Visit Langston for Discussion," *Daily Oklahoman*, December 4, 1947, p. 32.

113 he use statistics and statements: Milton Konvitz to Thurgood Marshall, January 12, 1948, University of Oklahoma, Correspondence, January–May 1948, Papers of the NAACP, Part 3, Series B.

113 averaged 8.8 years: United States President's Commission on Higher Education, *Higher Education for Democracy: A Report of the President's Commission on Higher Education* (Washington, DC: US Government Printing Office, 1947), 30.

113 "Of these, approximately": Commission on Higher Education, 31.

114 "The ratio of expenditures": Commission on Higher Education, 31.

114 "Denial of professional": Commission on Higher Education, 33.

114 "United States Supreme Court": Cullen Johnson, "High Court Caustic on OU Negro Ban, Early Rule Hinted," *Daily Oklahoman*, January 9, 1948, p. 1.

114 "There is a way that a negro": For full exchange between the lawyers and the Supreme Court justices, see Johnson.

115 The state, the court said: Sipuel v. Board of Regents, 332 U.S. 631, 68 S. Ct. 299 (1948).

115 "The Sipuel decision": Fisher, *Matter of Black and White*, 124.

115 *Oklahoman* subheadline read: "Negro Law Student for OU in Prospect Under Court's Ruling," *Daily Oklahoman*, January 13, 1948, p. 1.

115 "The Monday decision": Roscoe Dunjee to Thurgood Marshall, January 14, 1948, University of Oklahoma, Correspondence, January–May 1948, Papers of the NAACP, Part 3, Series B.

116 Then, on January 24: Otis Sullivant, "Regents Name Trio for Negro School Faculty," *Daily Oklahoman*, January 25, 1948, p. 1.

116 "We are serious": Sullivant.

117 when Silas Hunt: "Negro Will Be Enrolled for Dixie School," *Bradenton Herald,* February 3, 1948. p. 5.

117 "For two and a half": Fisher, *Matter of Black and White,* 146–47.

CHAPTER 6: "SEGREGATED AS CONDITIONS ALLOW"

119 six Black students: The six students were George McLaurin, Mozeal Dillon, Helen Holmes, James Bond, Ivor Tatum, and Maurderie Hancock. See Ray Parr, "Six Negroes Apply At OU; Segregation Law Faces Showdown," *Daily Oklahoman,* January 29, 1948, p. 1.

119 "It must not be supposed": In United States President's Commission on Higher Education, *Higher Education for Democracy: A Report of the President's Commission on Higher Education* (Washington, DC: US Government Printing Office, 1947), 34–35, the commission discusses the quota systems employed by several northern universities—particularly for their graduate programs. "*Many colleges and universities, especially in their professional schools, maintain a selective quota system for admission, under which the chance to learn, and thereby to become more useful citizens, is denied to certain minorities, particularly to Negroes and Jews.*" (Italics present in original).

120 The board asked: Ray Parr, "Negro Question Is Tossed Back to Williamson," *Daily Oklahoman,* January 30, 1948, p. 1.

120 still the law: Interestingly, shortly after Williamson's declaration that the University of Oklahoma was not required to admit any of the six Black students on a technicality, Arkansas moved to ease its ban on admitting Black students to graduate and professional schools. The student, Clifford Davis, would be forced to sit in a separate classroom and take courses at different times from his white classmates, though. See "Arkansas Lets Its University Ease Race Ban," *Daily Oklahoman,* January 31, 1948, p. 1.

121 passed in 1968: "Negroes Pound OU, File Three New Suits against Segregation," *Daily Oklahoman,* June 18, 1948, p. 1. See also "George McLaurin, 81, First Negro to Attend University of Oklahoma, Dies in Los Angeles," *Sapulpa Daily Herald,* December 30, 1968, p. 7.

121 "no such weapon": "Negroes Pound OU."

122 "it seemed clear": George L. Cross, *Blacks in White Colleges: Oklahoma's Landmark Cases* (Norman: University of Oklahoma Press, 1975), 87.

122 state's graduate school: "Segregation Laws Are Attacked in New Court Action," *Lawton Constitution,* August 6, 1948, p. 5.

122 "To me that is": "State Faced with Allowing Negro Professor to Attend OU," *Miami Daily News-Record,* August 24, 1948, p. 2.

123 McLaurin again attempted: "OU Still Says No to Negro," *Daily Oklahoman,* September 17, 1948, p. 1.

123 "His application is": "OU Still Says No to Negro."

123 "In so far": "Jurists Uphold Negroes in OU," *Daily Oklahoman,* September 29, 1948, p. 1.

124 meet on Wednesday: "Regents Get Negro Case," *Oklahoma Daily*, October 6, 1948, p. 1.

125 a banner headline: The *Daily Oklahoman* ran two separate versions of the headline on October 7, 1948. One read in the text; the other was more explicitly focused on McLaurin: "Williamson Tells OU Admit Negro or Drop the Courses He Wants"; "Williamson Tells OU Admit Negro or Cancel Graduate Education Classes."

125 "basis of complete segregation": "Segregation School Study Asked by O.U.," *Ponca City News*, October 7, 1948, p. 1.

125 "faced with a similar": "Segregation for Negroes Plan at OU," *Miami News-Record*, October 8, 1948, p. 1.

126 "would not create": "Negro Files Suit; Regents Delay until November," *Daily Oklahoman*, October 9, 1948, p. 25.

126 Then, in a surprise: "Negro Will Enter OU Tomorrow on Segregated Basis," *Miami Daily News-Record*, October 12, 1948, p. 1.

126 "it was not": "Negro Will Enter OU Tomorrow."

126 "Equal education has": "Negro Will Enter OU Tomorrow."

126 "We want to welcome": "Class Moves to New Room So Negro Can Sit to One Side," *Daily Oklahoman*, October 15, 1948, p. 1.

127 A fifteen-by-eighteen-foot: "Negro Student Starts Work in OU Classes," *Stillwater Gazette*, October 15, 1948, p. 1.

127 the first floor: George Lynn Cross, *Blacks in White Colleges: Oklahoma's Landmark Cases* (Norman: University of Oklahoma Press, 1975), 95.

127 "Everything seems to be": "Negro Student Starts Work in OU Classes."

128 "That is not equal": "Negro Will Try to Break Down OU Segregation Ruling Today," *Daily Oklahoman*, October 25, 1948, p. 1.

128 "a strain and humiliating": "Segregation Rule Under New Fire," *Oklahoma Daily*, October 26, 1948, p. 1.

128 "obliterate social or racial": "Negro Seating Appeal Rushed," *Daily Oklahoman*, November 23, 1948, p. 1.

128 On December 11: Thurgood Marshall to Houston, December 2, 1948, Papers of the NAACP, Part 3, Series B.

129 in January 1949: "Officials at OU Waiting for Bid by City Negro," *Daily Oklahoman*, January 30, 1949, p. 1.

129 "both wise and expedient": "Board Recommends End to Segregation in Graduate Schools," *Daily Oklahoman*, January 30, 1949, p. 1.

129 "segregated as conditions allow": "Two Negro Women to Sit on Back Row in Classes at O.U.," *Ada Weekly News*, February 10, 1949, p. 1.

129 "news to me": "Two Negroes Will Try to Enroll at Stillwater Today," *Miami Daily News-Record*, February 22, 1949, p. 1.

130 "Ever since the first": "Legislator Told Negro Question's His Worry," *Miami Daily News-Record*, April 10, 1949, p. 1.

130 "I will spend": "Negro Woman Is Glad to Enter OU," *Galveston Daily News*, June 20, 1949, p. 3.

130 "I want no segregation": "Negro 'Thrilled' at O.U. Entry," *Sapulpa Daily Herald*, June 19, 1949, p. 1.

130 "We will prosecute": "Negro 'Thrilled.'"

131 "We want courses": "Negroes in All White Schools Group's Aim," *Stillwater Gazette*, November 11, 1949, p. 2.

131 "necessarily result in": "Negro's Appeal Is Attacked: Breakdown in Laws Seen by Official," *El Reno Daily Tribune*, March 22, 1950, p. 1.

131 "the brief pointed out": Associated Press, "State Defends Racial Policy," *Ardmore Democrat*, March 23, 1950, p. 1.

131 "humiliate and degrade": "State Defends Racial Policy." Hansen argued that the state was simply making an honest attempt to comport with its laws while not running afoul of the Fourteenth Amendment.

131 Yes, McLaurin was able: Jack Doherty, "School Racial Bans Debated in High Court," *Daily News* (New York), April 5, 1950, p. 27.

132 "the same treatment": "Segregation in Classrooms and Dining Cars Barred," *Saint Louis Post-Dispatch*, June 5, 1950, p. 1.

132 "There is a vast difference": McLaurin v. Oklahoma State Regents, 339 U.S. 637, 70 S. Ct. 851 (1950).

132 "Supreme Court Knocks Out": Cullen Johnson, "Supreme Court Knocks Out Graduate Segregation at OU," *Daily Oklahoman*, June 6, 1950, p. 1.

133 "separate educational facilities": Brown v. Board of Education, 347 U.S. 483, 74 S. Ct. 686 (1954).

CHAPTER 7: THIS WHOLE FACADE

137 a rugged-looking: "Weintraub and Burnley Battle on Floor of Kentucky's House; Sergeant at Arms Pulls Pistol," *The Courier-Journal* (Louisville, KY), March 17, 1950, p. 1.

137 On March 7: "Senate Passes Bill to Amend State Day Law," *Lexington Herald*, March 8, 1950, p. 1.

138 "Even if you don't": Vincent Crowdus, "House Votes Amendment to Day Law, 50 to 16," *The Courier-Journal* (Louisville, KY), March 17, 1950, p. 1.

138 "I don't see how": Crowdus, 1.

138 "I have never refused": Crowdus, 18.

139 "How does Kentucky's": Crowdus, 18.

139 "strictly a question": Crowdus, 18.

139 "I think it's time": Crowdus, 18.

140 "A fiery display": Hugh Morris, "Weintraub and Burnley Battle on Floor of Kentucky's House," p. 1.

140 "Governor Clement's puppet Senate": Astonished [pseud.], letter to the editor, *The Courier-Journal* (Louisville, KY), March 18, 1950, p. 4.

141 Many of the Black families: Dr. Alicestyne Turley (former director of Carter G. Woodson Center at Berea College) in discussion with the author, September 2018.

141 "We're too far": Crowdus, "House Votes Amendment to Day Law," 18.

141 James Meredith felt inspired: James Meredith has written several books on his fight to integrate the University of Mississippi. See his *Three Years in Mississippi* (Jackson: University Press of Mississippi, 2019 [1966]). For the most complete examination of the events as they unfolded in Mississippi, see William Doyle, *An American Insurrection: The Battle of Oxford, Mississippi, 1962* (New York: Doubleday, 2001), Kindle edition.

141 "The same revolutionary": John F. Kennedy, Inaugural Address, January 20, 1961, available online at the American Presidency Project, https://www.presidency.ucsb.edu/node/234470, accessed February 1, 2021.

142 "Please send me": Meredith, *Three Years*, 47.

142 "We are very pleased": Meredith, 47.

142 Down there, racial: Meredith, 51.

143 could use it: Hilary Herbold, "Never a Level Playing Field: Blacks and the GI Bill," *Journal of Blacks in Higher Education*, no. 6 (Winter 1994–1995): 104–8, https://doi.org/10.2307/2962479.

143 "I am very pleased": Meredith, *Three Years*, 51.

143 a sane plaintiff: Doyle, *An American Insurrection*, Kindle loc. 524 of 6930.

144 "The voice on the other": Meredith, *Three Years*, 51.

144 "I must give": Meredith, 51.

144 "This guy's gotta": Doyle, *An American Insurrection*, Kindle loc. 532 of 6930.

144 "The objective was": Philip A. Goduti Jr., *Robert F. Kennedy and the Shaping of Civil Rights, 1960–1964* (Jefferson, NC: McFarland, 2013), 122.

145 "All's Calm at Ole Miss": Edmond Noel, "All's Calm at Ole Miss," *The Clarion-Ledger* (Jackson, MS), February 8, 1961, p. 1.

146 "strengthen the employment": J. Chadwick, "Hiring Practices Due Kennedy Fire," *Fort Worth Star-Telegram*, March 2, 1961, p. 1.

146 In January, the US Commission: US Commission on Civil Rights, *Equal Protection of the Laws in Public Higher Education, 1960* (Washington, DC: US Government Printing Office, 1961).

146 "where the federal government": "JFK Says Economic Upturn Not Here Yet," *Knoxville News-Sentinel*, March 1, 1961, p. 2.

146 "take affirmative action": John F. Kennedy, Executive Order 10925—Establishing the President's Committee on Equal Employment Opportunity, March 6, 1961, The American Presidency Project https://www.presidency.ucsb.edu/node/237176, accessed February 17, 2021.

146 "both an announcement": "Kennedy Explains Stand on Job Discrimination," *The Times Record* (Brunswick, ME), April 11, 1961, p. 1.

147 served as the executive secretary: Oral history transcript, George L. P. Weaver, interview 1 (I), January 6, 1969, by Paige E. Mulhollan, LBJ Library Oral Histories, LBJ Presidential Library, p. 3, https://www.discoverlbj.org/item/oh-weaverg-19690106-1-74-50, accessed February 1, 2021.

147 Clennon King, a teacher: For more on King and Kennard, see Meredith, *Three Years*, 302–3.

148 "A Messiah complex": Doyle, *An American Insurrection*, loc. 538.

148 "I asked myself": Doyle, loc. 546.
148 In denying him: Meredith, *Three Years*, 72.
149 "We hold that": Meredith v. Fair, 298 F.2d 696 (5th Cir. 1962).
149 "Intermarriage in the South": Gene Roberts and Hank Klibanoff, *The Race Beat: The Press, The Civil Rights Struggle, and the Awakening of a Nation* (New York: Vintage Books, 2006), 271.
149 an amicus brief: "Action Asked on Meredith," *The Clarion-Ledger* (Jackson, MS), September 1, 1962, p. 1.
150 It was a sledgehammer: "Late Afternoon News Postscripts," *Huntsville Times*, September 10, 1962, p. 2.
150 "I have said in every": Ross Barnett, "Declaration to the People of Mississippi Broadcast via TV and Radio, September 13, 1962," part of *Integrating Ole Miss: A Civil Rights Milestone*, online exhibit at the John F. Kennedy Presidential Library and Museum, https://microsites.jfklibrary.org/olemiss /controversy/doc2.html.
150 "the good Lord": James Saggus, "Segregationist Is Mississippi Winner," *Shreveport Journal*, August 26, 1959, p. 2.
151 "We've got to know": Doyle, *An American Insurrection*, loc. 1179.
151 "Forget it, contempt": Doyle.
151 "You're fixin' to put": Doyle.
152 More than 150 reporters: Roberts and Klibanoff, *The Race Beat*, 279.
152 James Meredith wore: Dudley Morris, "Annotated Article by Dudley Morris to Birmingham, Time, Inc., 20 September 1962," The University of Mississippi Western Union Telegram Collection, 9.
152 The same day: "Move Bars Meredith," *The State Journal* (Frankfort, KY), September 20, 1962, p. 2.
152 "Nigger go home!": Morris, "Annotated Article."
152 unfurled a proclamation: Doyle, *An American Insurrection*, loc. 1230.
153 Both were true: The two stories ran under the top headline "U. of Mississippi Bows and Agrees to Accept Negro." See Claude Sitton, "Barnett Defiant," *New York Times*, September 25, 1962, p. 1. See also, Henrick Smith, "Court Is Obeyed," *New York Times*, September 25, 1962, p. 1.
153 "risked the open clash": Sitton, "Barnett Defiant," 1.
153 "I call on you": Claude Sitton, "Barnett Defies Court and Bars Negro from Enrolling in University of Mississippi," *New York Times*, September 26, 1962, pp. 1, 22.
154 "Yes sir": Sitton.
154 "We feel patriots": "Rights Party Chief Offers Volunteers," *The Clarion-Ledger* (Jackson, MS), September 27, 1962, p. 16.
154 "I'm going to": C. M. Hills, "Affairs of State," *The Clarion-Ledger* (Jackson, MS), November 23, 1963, p. 6.
154 "You people understand": Claude Sitton, "U.S. Court Defied by State 3d Time," *New York Times*, September 27, 1962, pp. 1, 28.
155 "It's all in": Sitton, 28.
155 "undoubtedly weaken their campaign": Sitton, 28.

155 A crowd of 2,500: Claude Sitton, "200 Policemen with Clubs Ring Campus to Bar Negro," *New York Times*, September 28, 1962, pp. 1, 22.

155 "I plead with you": Sitton, 1, 22.

156 "your action would": "Patterson Protests to President," September 27, 1962, *Alabama Journal*, p. 1.

156 He ordered a 110-man: Anthony Lewis, "110 Army Engineers Going to Memphis in Support Role," *New York Times*, September 28, 1962, pp. 1, 22.

156 "There was grave": Lewis, 1, 22.

156 "When the federal government": "Ike Says State Situation 'Absolutely Indefensible,'" *The Clarion-Ledger* (Jackson, MS), September 28, 1962, p. 12.

157 "The president was unable": John F. Kennedy, *Public Papers of the Presidents of the United States: John F. Kennedy; Containing the Public Messages, Speeches, and Statements of the President, January 1 to December 31, 1962* (Washington, DC: US Government Printing Office, 1963), 420.

157 "There's going to be": Doyle, *An American Insurrection*, loc. 1955.

158 "When Meredith presents": Doyle, loc. 1985.

158 "I think it is silly": "John F. Kennedy: The Mississippi Crisis," American Radio Works, American Public Media, 2018, http://americanradioworks .publicradio.org/features/prestapes/rfk_tw_bm_093062.html. Transcript of a September 30, 1962, telephone conversation among Attorney General Robert F. Kennedy, Governor Ross Barnett, Mississippi attorney Tom Watkins, and Burke Marshall.

158 "I have to be": Doyle, *An American Insurrection,* Kindle loc. 2002 of 6930.

158 "It may be": Doyle, loc. Kindle loc. 2079 of 6930.

158 along the runway: Doyle, Kindle loc. 2288 of 6930.

159 "That guy's a goddamn": Roberts and Klibanoff, *The Race Beat*, 290.

159 "We can't consider": For the discussion between Barnett and Kennedy, see Doyle, *An American Insurrection*, Kindle loc. 3233 of 6930.

160 "I will never yield": "Barnett Denies Peace Plea Was a Surrender," *Shreveport Journal*, October 1, 1962, p. 1.

160 The streetlights were shot: Members of the guard were forced to dig foxholes and shoot out streetlights for cover. Doyle, *An American Insurrection*, Kindle loc. 4126 of 6930.

161 the windows had been: Meredith, *Three Years*, 200.

161 "This is no": Meredith, 203.

CHAPTER 8: THIRTEEN YEARS A REMEDY, THIRTY YEARS A FIGHT, TWO CENTURIES A STRUGGLE

163 The only thing standing: Much of what follows regarding the Child Development Group of Mississippi and Ayers is with thanks to David Nevin, "Struggle That Changed Glen Allan," *Life*, September 1967, pp. 108–12. Details were also checked against contemporaneous newspaper reports, largely from the *Delta Democrat-Times* in Greenville, Mississippi.

163 register to vote in 1958: Nevin, "Struggle That Changed," 108.

164 "For so long as": Lyndon B. Johnson, Remarks upon Signing the Economic Opportunity Act, August 20, 1964, available online at the American Presidency Project, https://www.presidency.ucsb.edu/node/241884, accessed February 1, 2021.

164 its first director: For a history of Shriver's time as leader of the OEO, see Scott Stossel, *Sarge: The Life and Times of Sargent Shriver* (New York: Other Press, 2011 [2004]), 371

165 In 1963, he had convinced: Nevin, "Struggle That Changed," 108.

165 "You do not wipe": Lyndon B. Johnson, Commencement Address at Howard University: "To Fulfill These Rights," June 4, 1964, available online at the American Presidency Project https://www.presidency.ucsb.edu/node/241312, accessed February 1, 2021.

165 "Deborah entered the center": Child Development Group of Mississippi, *Histories of Children, Employees, Centers, Community Support* (Jackson, MS: HJK Publishing, 1966), available online from the Civil Rights Movement Archive, https://www.crmvet.org/docs/6609_cdgm.pdf, accessed February 1, 2021.

166 "I took her": Child Development Group of Mississippi, 7.

166 Teachers and staff: Nevin, "Struggle That Changed," 110.

166 "the children received": Nevin, 110.

166 It was reverse segregation: Nevin, 110.

167 The *New York Times*: John Herbers, "Rights Blocs Fear Easing of Enforcement by U.S.," *New York Times*, October 17, 1965, p. 1.

167 "[This bill] means": Lyndon B. Johnson, Remarks at Southwest Texas State College upon Signing the Higher Education Act of 1965, November 8, 1965, available online at the American Presidency Project, https://www.presidency.ucsb.edu/node/241092, accessed February 1, 2021.

168 On paper, students: Nevin, "Struggle That Changed," 110.

168 The Black school: *Civil Rights Act of 1984: Joint Hearing Before the Subcommittee on Education, Arts and Humanities and the Subcommittee on the Handicapped of the Committee on Labor and Human Resources*, United States Senate, 98th Cong. 68 (1984) (testimony of Jake Ayers).

168 "If we have gained": *Civil Rights Act of 1984.*

169 Then, Ayers was fired: Nevin, "Struggle That Changed," 110.

169 He was arrested: The *Delta Democrat-Times* chronicled the people who were sentenced in city court the same day as Jake Ayers was arrested. While Ayers was sentenced to pay $55 for speeding—and $30 for "failure to obey officer"—no other person sentenced that day was forced to pay more than $15 for speeding. See "News of Record," *Delta Democrat-Times* (Greenville, MS), August 16, 1965, p. 3.

169 "Mr. Shriver," he said: Nevin, "Struggle That Changed," 112.

169 By the next day: Nevin, 112.

169 Nearly every college: Some institutions—largely faith-based colleges—do

not accept federal grants or loans, such as Hillsdale College, Principia College, Christendom College, and others.

170 Between January 1969: For the facts of the compliance review, see Adams v. Richardson, 480 F.2d 1159 (D.C. Cir. 1973).

170 The department appealed: *Adams v. Richardson*, 1159.

170 Allan Bakke was thirty-one: The author is grateful to the work of the scholars Rebecca Stefoff and Howard Ball. See Stefoff, *The Bakke Case: Challenging Affirmative Action* (New York: Marshall Cavendish Benchmark, 2006); Ball, *The Bakke Case: Race, Education, and Affirmative Action* (Lawrence: University Press of Kansas, 2000).

171 "I have an excellent": Ball, *The Bakke Case*, 58.

171 "When an applicant is": Ball, 58.

171 In 1968, there were: James L. Curtis, *Affirmative Action in Medicine: Improving Health Care for Everyone* (Ann Arbor: University of Michigan Press, 2003), 21.

171 nearly 70 percent: Dennis B. Dove, "Minority Enrollment in U.S. Medical Schools, 1969–70 Compared to 1968–69," *Journal of Medical Education* 45, no. 3, (March 1970): 179–81, https://doi.org/10.1097/00001888-197003000-00010.

172 "enhance diversity in": Ball, *The Bakke Case*, 62.

172 In Davis's first year: Ball, 63.

172 The university decided: Ball, 63.

172 no white student: Ball, 63.

173 "a well-qualified": Ball, 69.

173 "I want to study": Robert Lindsey, "White/Caucasian—and Rejected," *New York Times Magazine*, April 3, 1977, https://www.nytimes.com/1977/04/03/archives/whitecaucasian-and-rejected.html, accessed February 17, 2021.

173 "I feel compelled": Lindsey.

174 "remarkably able and": Joel Dreyfuss and Charles Lawrence III, *The Bakke Case: The Politics of Inequality* (New York: Harcourt Brace Jovanovich, 1979), 21.

174 "pursue your research": Dreyfuss and Lawrence, 22.

174 A state trial court: For facts of the case, see DeFunis v. Odegaard, 82 Wn. 2d 11, 82 Wash. 2d 11, 507 P.2d 1169 (Wash. 1973).

175 "I appreciate your interest": Stefoff, *The Bakke Case*, 72.

175 "It seems to me": Stefoff, 72.

175 "The disturbing feature": Lindsey, "White/Caucasian."

176 "My own impression": Lindsey.

176 a third time: Lindsey.

176 "the victim of racial": Ball, *The Bakke Case*, 71.

176 In fact, there were: Lindsey, "White/Caucasian."

177 "Where the State": Lindsey.

177 Affirmative action had moved: As Dove, "Minority Enrollment," 179, notes, the number of Black students in medical schools increased dramatically between 1968 and 1969 and between 1969 and 1970. In the later academic year,

there were nearly 300 more Black students enrolled at the nation's medical schools—and the majority of the growth happened at predominantly white schools with affirmative action programs rather than Howard and Meharry.

177 Between 1965 and 1975: Louis W. Sullivan, "The Education of Black Health Professionals," *Phylon* (1960–) 38, no. 2 (2nd Qtr. 1977): 181–93, https://doi.org/10.2307/274681.

177 froze those numbers: In 2018–19, according to the Association of American Medical Colleges, 1,238 Black students graduated from medical school in the U.S. See, AAMC Data Warehouse: STUDENT and IND as of August 19, 2019. Accessed at https://www.aamc.org/data-reports/workforce/interactive-data/figure-13-percentage-us-medical-school-graduates-race/ethnicity-alone-academic-year-2018-2019.

178 Several of the predominantly: Thomas John Carey, "Desegregation of Public Colleges and Universities" in *The Mississippi Encyclopedia* (Center for Study of Southern Culture, 2018), https://mississippiencyclopedia.org/entries/desegregation-of-public-colleges-and-universities/.

178 On January 28: Brenda Boykin, "Suit Seeks Quality Education for Blacks," *The Clarion-Ledger* (Jackson, MS), January 29, 1975, p. 19.

178 The petition requested: Boykin, 19.

179 "the continued propagation": Carl C. Bringham and Robert M. Yerkes, *A Study of American Intelligence,* (Princeton: Princeton University Press, 1923), 210. https://www.theatlantic.com/technology/archive/2019/05/college-board-sat-adversity-score/589681/.

179 Nearly all Black students: Ayers v. Allain, 674 F. Supp. 1523 (1987).

179 "We believe that quality": Boykin, "Suit Seeks Quality."

179 Born in in Hinds County: Adam Harris, "They Wanted Desegregation. They Settled for Money, and It's About to Run Out," *Chronicle of Higher Education*, April 6, 2018, https://www.chronicle.com/article/they-wanted-desegregation-they-settled-for-money-and-its-about-to-run-out/.

180 "I was made aware": Harris.

180 nine groups filed: Ball, *The Bakke Case*, 73.

181 Colvin argued that: Ball, 73.

181 On September 16, 1976: Bakke v. Regents of University of California, 18 Cal. 3d 34 (1976).

181 The state supreme court went: W. Trombley, "State High Court Voids Preferential Admissions," *Los Angeles Times*, September 17, 1976, p. 1.

182 "Our society cannot": Quoted in John H. Bunzel, "Bakke vs. University of California," *Commentary*, March 1977, https://www.commentarymagazine.com/articles/commentary-bk/bakke-vs-university-of-california/.

182 "abundantly clear": Bunzel.

182 Appeals began to pour in: Ball, *The Bakke Case*, 78.

183 The *Bakke* case became: Ball, 103–4.

183 "Allan Bakke's position": For the high court back-and-forth that follows, see Regents of the University of California v. Bakke 438 U.S. 265 (1978).

184 "There is no perceived": *Regents of the University of California v. Bakke.*

185 "If the Equal Protection": Ball, *The Bakke Case*, 125.

185 "On the quota question": Ball.

185 "I can't join Thurgood": Ball.

186 "I repeat, for the next": Thurgood Marshall Memorandum to the Conference, April 13, 1978, Harry Blackmun papers, 1913–2001, box 261, 76–811, Library of Congress.

186 "This case is here": Thurgood Marshall Memorandum.

187 "On the assumption": Lewis Powell Memorandum to the Conference, June 21, 1978, Harry Blackmun papers, 1913–2001, box 261, 76–811, Library of Congress.

187 Powell said: Powell opinion announcement, *Regents of the University of California v. Bakke*.

187 "There is a measure": *Regents of the University of California v. Bakke*.

188 "Race if considered": *Regents of University of California Regents v. Bakke*.

188 "I suspect that": *Regents of University of California Regents v. Bakke*.

189 Each time the constitutionality: For more on affirmative action and the strength in its weakness, see Adam Harris, "The Supreme Court Justice Who Forever Changed Affirmative Action," *The Atlantic*, October 13, 2018, https://www.theatlantic.com/education/archive/2018/10/how-lewis-powell-changed-affirmative-action/572938/. See also Adam Harris, "Harvard Won This Round, but Affirmative Action Is Weak," *The Atlantic*, October 2, 2019, https://www.theatlantic.com/education/archive/2019/10/harvard-wins-affirmative-action-case-plaintiff-will-appeal/599281/.

190 Between 1976 and 1982: Susan T. Hill, *The Traditionally Black Institutions of Higher Education, 1860 to 1892* (Washington, DC: National Center for Education Statistics, 1984), 45.

190 However, nearly half: Hill.

190 How long is too long: Author interview with Bennie Thompson, US representative for the Second Congressional District of Mississippi, February 2018, Washington D.C.

190 "This is the case": Jerry Mitchell, "Suit Could Affect Future of Colleges," *The Clarion-Ledger* (Jackson, MS), April 27, 1987, p. 1.

191 "the gap between": Mitchell.

191 Southern Mississippi: Jerry Mitchell, "Universities' Courses Duplicated, Expert Says," *The Clarion-Ledger* (Jackson, MS), April 28, 1987, p. 1.

191 "The thrust of this": Mitchell, 10.

191 "never really gave": Jerry Mitchell, "Ayers Name May Become Famous in Civil Rights," *The Clarion-Ledger* (Jackson, MS), May 4, 1987, p. 1.

192 "racially motivated to bring": Ayers v. Allain, 674 F.Supp. 1523, 43 Ed. Law Rep. 972 (1987).

192 "A state violates": Ayers v. Allain, 914 F.2d 676, 62 Ed. Law Rep. 910 (1990).

192 On November 13: Harris, "They Wanted Desegregation."

193 "would be to establish": United States v. Fordice, 505 U.S. 717, 112 S. Ct. 2727 (1992).

193 "You will always see": *United States v. Fordice*.

193 "that has continued": *United States v. Fordice.*

194 "In today's world": *United States v. Fordice.*

194 "race neutral on their face": *United States v. Fordice.*

195 "It would be ironic": *United States v. Fordice.*

195 "What other kind": Reagan Walker, "Supreme Court's Order: Desegregate," *The Clarion-Ledger* (Jackson, MS), June 27, 1992, p. 1.

195 "This decision is": Scott Jaschik, "High-Court Ruling Transforms Battles over Desegregation at Colleges in 19 States," *Chronicle of Higher Education*, July 8, 1992, https://www.chronicle.com/article/high-court-ruling-transforms-battles-over-desegregation-at-colleges-in-19-states/.

195 "Lawyers who had": Harris, "They Wanted Desegregation."

195 The agreement called for: For a full copy of the settlement agreement and its details, see Ayers v. Musgrove, no. 4:75CV009-B-D (N.D. Miss., February 15, 2002), https://www.justice.gov/sites/default/files/crt/legacy/2010/12/14/ayersag.pdf.

196 "the question of how": Ibid.

196 The state slipped away: Harris, "Long March."

196 always had less: Adam Harris, "Why America Needs Its HBCUs," *The Atlantic*, May 16, 2109, https://www.theatlantic.com/education/archive/2019/05/howard-universitys-president-why-america-needs-hbcus/589582/.

196 "I could not spend": Harris, "Long March."

CHAPTER 9: WHAT HATH WE WROUGHT

198 international students: "Enrollment Highlights: During COVID-19 Pandemic," Office of Institutional Research, Berea College, Fall 2020. https://4efrxppj37l1sgsbr1ye6idr-wpengine.netdna-ssl.com/ira/wp-content/uploads/sites/27/2020/11/Fall2020EnrollmentHighlights.pdf, accessed on February 17, 2021.

199 instead of brown: Adam Harris, "The Long March to Equality," *Chronicle of Higher Education*, April 6, 2018, https://www.chronicle.com/article/they-wanted-desegregation-they-settled-for-money-and-its-about-to-run-out/.

200 99 percent: Harris. This figured had remained unchanged from when Ayers and other Black Mississippians challenged the segregated system in Ayers v. Allain, 674 F.Supp. 1523 (1987).

200 The state had been cutting: Harris. See also Michael Mitchell, Michael Leachman, and Kathleen Masterson, "A Lost Decade in Higher Education Funding: State Cuts Have Driven Up Tuition and Reduced Quality" (Washington, DC: Center on Budget and Policy Priorities, August 23, 2017), https://www.cbpp.org/sites/default/files/atoms/files/2017_higher_ed_8-22-17_final.pdf.

200 Jackson State University: Jimmie E. Gates, "Jackson State University Proposing to Slash Employees, Programs Due to Budget Woes," *The Clarion-Ledger* (Jackson, MS), May 31, 2017, https://www.clarionledger.com/story/news/2017/05/31/jackson-state-university-proposing-slash-employees-and-programs-due-budget-woes/354659001/.

200 Delta State closed: Harold Gater, "Budget Cuts Force Delta State to Close

Golf Course," *The Clarion-Ledger* (Jackson, MS), February 25, 2017, https://www.clarionledger.com/story/news/2017/02/24/delta-state-golf-course-closing/98352758/.

200 The percentage of Black: Author's analysis of enrollment data in Mississippi between Fall 2010-2018. US Department of Education, National Center for Education Statistics, Integrated Postsecondary Education Data System (IPEDS). https://nces.ed.gov/ipeds/, accessed on February 17, 2021.

200 At those colleges: Integrated Postsecondary Education Data System.

200 Most state flagship: "Disparities at State Flagships," *Hechinger Report*, January 29, 2018, http://web.archive.org/web/20190203045830/https://hechingerreport.org/disparities-state-flagships/.

201 But more than 50: "Disparities at State Flagships."

201 Auburn University, in Alabama: Associated Press, "Alabama Is Ordered to Desegregate Colleges," *New York Times*, December 9, 1985, https://www.nytimes.com/1985/12/09/us/alabama-is-ordered-to-desegregate-colleges.html.

201 In 2020, 5 percent: "Total Enrollment by Gender and Race/Ethnicity Selected Fall Terms, 1976–2020," Office of Institutional Research, Auburn University, September 25, 2020, https://auburn.edu/administration/ir/factbook/enrollment-demographics/historical-summaries/enrollment-gender-ethnicity.html.

201 percent in 2020: Adam Harris, "What Happens When a College's Affirmative-Action Policy Is Found Illegal," *The Atlantic*, October 26, 2018, https://www.theatlantic.com/education/archive/2018/10/when-college-cant-use-race-admissions/574126/.

201 "Underrepresented minorities": "Underrepresented minorities" include Black, Hawaiian, Hispanic, Native America, and two or more races. See "U-M Enrollment Growing as Campus Readies for Go Blue Guarantee Start," press release, University of Michigan, October 26, 2017, https://news.umich.edu/u-m-enrollment-growing-as-campus-readies-for-go-blue-guarantee-start/.

202 The answer was: Integrated Postsecondary Education Data System.

203 Despite the Founders' belief: Scott Carlson, "When College Was a Public Good," *Chronicle of Higher Education*, November 27, 2016, https://www.chronicle.com/article/when-college-was-a-public-good/.

203 The student debt crisis: Ben Miller, "The Continued Student Loan Crisis for Black Borrowers" (Washington, DC: Center for American Progress, December 2, 2019), https://cdn.americanprogress.org/content/uploads/2019/11/26071357/Student-Debt-BRIEF.pdf.

204 "public colleges spend": Sara Garcia, "Gaps in College Spending Shortchange Students of Color" (Washington, DC: Center for American Progress, April 5, 2018), https://cdn.americanprogress.org/content/uploads/2018/04/03090823/Gaps-in-College-Spending-brief.pdf.

204 And in 2015: Garcia.

204 Several states have switched: For an examination of the inequity embedded

in performance-based funding, see Kayla C. Elliott, "The Influence of State Performance-Based Funding on Public Historically Black Colleges and Universities: A Case Study of Race and Power" (PhD diss., Florida Atlantic University, 2019), https://fau.digital.flvc.org/islandora/object/fau:41923.

205 failed to receive: John Michael Lee Jr. and Samaad Wes Keys, "Land-Grant but Unequal: State One-to-One Match Funding for 1890 Land-Grant Universities" (Washington, DC: Association of Public and Land-Grant Universities, Report No. 3000-PB1, September 2013), https://www.aplu.org/library/land-grant-but-unequal-state-one-to-one-match-funding-for-1890-land-grant-universities/file.

206 There are a couple: Alvin J. Schexnider, "Governance and the Future of Black Colleges," *Inside Higher Ed*, December 20, 2017, https://www.insidehighered.com/views/2017/12/20/struggling-hbcus-must-consider-new-options-survival-opinion.

206 The private college: John Newsom, "'Our Fight Continues': Bennett College Loses Its Accreditation but Files Suit and Gets It Back," *News & Record* (Greensboro, NC), February 22, 2019, https://greensboro.com/news/education/our-fight-continues-bennett-college-loses-its-accreditation-but-files-suit-and-gets-it-back/article_635e4532-6940-5405-8bbc-091254304d37.html.

207 "There's no one way": Naomi Prioleau, "Bennett College Must Raise $5 Million by February," WUNC, December 13, 2018, https://www.wunc.org/post/bennett-college-must-raise-5-million-february.

207 61 percent of students: Committee on Education and Labor, "Investing in Economic Mobility: The Important Role of HBCUs, TCUs, and MSIs in Closing Racial and Wealth Gaps in Higher Education" (Washington, DC: Committee on Education and Labor, US House of Representatives, September 2019), 9, https://edlabor.house.gov/imo/media/doc/Ed_and_Labor_HBCU_TCU_and_MSI_Report_FINAL.pdf.

207 "developed and cultivated": Adam Harris, "Will Anyone Save Black Colleges?," *The Atlantic*, February 2, 2019, https://www.theatlantic.com/education/archive/2019/02/what-bennett-colleges-pledge-drive-foreshadows-for-black-colleges/581863/.

208 more than a dozen: "Big Charitable Gifts: Where Donors Have Given $1 Million or More," database, *Chronicle of Philanthropy*, October 12, 2020, https://www.philanthropy.com/factfile/gifts/.

208 "Other institutions are not": Adam Harris, "Career Advice from a Groundbreaking President," *Chronicle of Higher Education*, January 1, 2018, https://www.chronicle.com/article/Career-Advice-From-a/242131.

208 When Brown's committee: "Slavery and Justice" (Providence, RI: Brown University Steering Committee on Slavery and Justice, October 2006), https://www.brown.edu/Research/Slavery_Justice/documents/SlaveryAndJustice.pdf

209 Georgetown University, which sold: Rachel L. Swarns, "272 Slaves Were

Sold to Save Georgetown. What Does It Owe Their Descendants?," *New York Times*, April 16, 2016, https://www.nytimes.com/2016/04/17/us/george town-university-search-for-slave-descendants.html.

209 Before abolition, there were: "Report to President Teresa A. Sullivan" (Charlottesville, VA: President's Commission on Slavery and the University, University of Virginia, 2018), https://vpdiversity.virginia.edu/sites/vpdiversity .virginia.edu/files/PCSU%20Report%20FINAL_July%202018.pdf.

209 these were exactly: Marc Parry, "A 'Long Overdue Conversation': Do Universities That Benefited from Slavery Owe a Debt to Black Colleges?," *Chronicle of Higher Education*, November 28, 2018, https://www.chronicle.com /article/a-long-overdue-conversation-do-universities-that-benefited-from -slavery-owe-a-debt-to-black-colleges/.

210 At Georgetown, students moved: Saahil Desai, "The First Reparations Attempt at an American Colleges Comes from Its Students," *The Atlantic*, April 18, 2019, https://www.theatlantic.com/education/archive/2019/04 /why-are-georgetown-students-paying-reparations/587443/.

210 On February 22: Newsom, "'Our Fight Continues.'"

210 "It is far too late ": University of California Regents v. Bakke, 438 U.S. 265 (1978).

211 for their work: For a complete examination of House and her work, see Mary Frances Berry, *My Face Is Black Is True: Callie House and the Struggle for Ex-Slave Reparations* (New York: Alfred A. Knopf, 2005).

211 "running the Negroes wild": Adam Harris, "Everyone Wants to Talk about Reparations. But for How Long?," *The Atlantic*, June 19, 2019, https://www .theatlantic.com/politics/archive/2019/06/house-committee-explores-bill -study-reparations/592096/.

211 According to government: Harris.

212 "segregative effects": Dominique Maria Bonessi, "Maryland's Black Caucus Takes Fight for HBCU Funding to Legislature," WAMU, November 14, 2019, https://wamu.org/story/19/11/14/marylands-black-caucus-takes-fight -for-hbcu-funding-to-legislature/.

212 $577 million: Dominique Maria Bonessi, "Hogan Vetoed Millions for HBCU Settlement. Maryland Lawmakers Now Ponder Next Step," WAMU, May 15, 2020, https://wamu.org/story/20/05/15/hogan-vetoed-millions-for-hbcu -settlement-maryland-lawmakers-now-ponder-next-step/.

Index

Berea *Citizen*, 74
Berea College, 37, 49, 50, 60–63,
    67, 70–71, 79–82, 111, 133,
    139, 141, 198
  Day Law and, 72–76, 79
  Fairchild as president of, 49–50,
    61
  Fee's founding of, 16, 18–22,
    197, 198, 227n
  Frost as president of, 60–63, 70,
    74–76, 80–81, 227n, 230n
  Hathaway at, 61–63, 227n
  Lincoln Institute and, 81, 82,
    230n
  number of students at, 198
  racial makeup of students at,
    51, 61–63, 70, 198
  segregated spaces introduced
    at, 62
Berea Literary Institute, 37
Biggers, Neal B., Jr., 190–92,
    196
Bingham, Kinsley S., 25
Black, Hugo, 92, 150
Black Dispatch, 104
Black Mississippians Council on
    Higher Education/Ayers case,
    178–80, 189–96, 199, 200,
    202, 203, 213
Blackmun, Harry, 185, 188
Black people
  Freedmen's Bureau and, 40–42,
    211
  Great Migration of, 82
  middle class, 69, 103, 165
  soldiers, 33–36, 68, 84
Black people, education for, 3, 13,
    34, 35, 39–42, 69
  declining enrollment and,
    200–201, 205
  high school completion, 79,
    229n
  in K–12 schools, 204
  Truman Commission on,
    113–14, 119–20, 138, 230n
  underfunding of, 4, 6, 204–5
  see also historically Black

colleges and universities;
    integrated education
Black Wall Street, 101
Blake, Catherine C., 212
Bluford, Lucile, 97–98
Bond, James, 120
Brennan, William, 185
Brigham, Carl, 178–79
Brown, Henry Billings, 66–67
Brown, R. Jess, 148
Brown University, 208–9
Brown v. Board of Education, 133,
    140, 141, 145, 148, 177, 179,
    184, 186, 187, 195
Buchanan, James, 31
Budd, Etta, 59
Budd, Joseph, 59
Buel Institute, 22
Bullock, W. A. J., 101, 105–7
Bureau of Pensions, 211
Burnley, Charles W., 140
Bush, Jeb, 189
Buttram, Frank, 116

California, 189
Campbell, John Milton, 14
Camp Nelson, 33–37
Canada, Silas W., 87, 89
Candee, George, 18, 19, 21
Carter, Robert L., 109–11, 131
Carver, George Washington,
    57–60, 125, 227n
Center for American Progress, 204
Central State University, 202
Central University, 71–72
Chamber of Commerce, U.S., 183
Chambliss, Alvin O., 190–93, 195,
    196
Cheyney University of
    Pennsylvania, 202
Chicago Sun-Times, 157
Child Development Group in
    Mississippi (CDGM), 164,
    166, 168–69
Chronicle of Higher Education,
    195
Citizens' Committee to Test the